Reading for Thinking

Second Edition

Laraine E. Flemming

HOUGHTON MIFFLIN COMPANY
Boston   New York

Sponsoring Editor: Renée Deljon
Senior Associate Editor: Ellen Darion
Editorial Assistant: Kate O'Sullivan
Senior Project Editor: Charline Lake
Production/Design Coordinator: Jennifer Waddell
Senior Manufacturing Coordinator: Marie Barnes
Senior Marketing Manager: Nancy Lyman

Cover design: Judy Arisman, Arisman Design
Cover image: Julian Opie, *Incident in the Library 1*, 1993. Courtesy the artist
and Lisson Gallery, London

Photo credits: p. 314: © M. Siluk, The Image Works; p. 354: © Lawrence Pringle,
Photo Researchers; p. 433: Margaret Bourke-White, Life Magazine © Time Inc.

Printed in the U.S.A.

Library of Congress Catalog Card Number: 96-76902

Student Text ISBN: 0-395-78290-2
Instructor's Edition ISBN: 0-395-78291-0

456789-DH-00 99 98

CONTENTS

TO THE INSTRUCTOR

As in the previous edition, the second edition of *Reading for Thinking* offers a clear, step-by-step approach to improving comprehension and developing critical reading skills. Starting with paragraphs and ending with longer readings, *Reading for Thinking* shows students how to identify an author's key points and then evaluate those points in terms of their logic and evidence. As in the first edition, all terminology is clearly defined. Skills are also carefully modeled so that students know exactly what to do when left on their own to tackle reading assignments.

Like its predecessor, this edition of *Reading for Thinking* encourages students to abandon the notion that the goal of reading is to uncritically absorb the ideas of others. The exercises, critical reading questions, and writing assignments that appear in each chapter consistently suggest that the real goal of reading is to develop informed opinions and support them with sound logic and factual evidence. Students who use *Reading for Thinking* will become more confident, more effective, and more critical readers. They will also become more aware of how reading can expand and enrich their perspective on the world.

Organization and Content

Part 1: Understanding an Author's Meaning provides a review of basic comprehension skills such as identifying the main idea, evaluating supporting details, and recognizing organizational patterns. **Part 2: Becoming a Critical Reader** builds and expands on those comprehension skills by showing students how to evaluate what they read. Students learn how to distinguish fact from opinion and how to identify tone, purpose, and bias. They also learn how to analyze arguments and make judgments about a writer's evidence and logic. The additional readings in **Part 3: Putting It All Together** give students a chance to apply everything they have learned in the first two parts of the book. Here, longer reading selections and carefully composed questions and writing assignments lead students to create and express their own points of view on significant issues such as racism in the military, the connection between gender and speech, and the use of animals in medical research.

As with the first edition, the extended readings in Part 3 have been grouped into four thematically linked units so that students can absorb and analyze several different perspectives on the same issue or topic. By the time students finish a unit, they will be able to speak and write with the confidence that comes with being truly knowledgeable about a particular issue.

The chief benefit of this three-part approach is the way each reading skill builds on the previous one so that students are never on totally unfamiliar ground. Instead, they are always using what they've already learned to master new material. This integrated method of instruction guarantees a thorough understanding of what good comprehension and sound critical reading entail.

New to This Edition

End-of-Chapter Reviews

Each chapter now ends with a review section titled **Summing Up,** which provides a list of the key points in the chapter. Accompanying page references tell students where they can look to find explanations of any points they might not have fully understood. This method of review not only encourages students to take responsibility for what they've learned, it also provides an excellent means of preparing for the tests that conclude each chapter.

End-of-Chapter Tests

The second edition of *Reading for Thinking* includes review tests that teachers can use to determine students' level of mastery. Chapter by chapter, the tests cover all of the skills and concepts introduced in *Reading for Thinking.*

Chapter Objectives

Each chapter now begins with a list of key skills and concepts taught in the chapter.

Paraphrasing and Synthesizing

Because the ability to paraphrase and synthesize is essential to both comprehension and critical reading, this edition devotes a good deal of space to explaining and modeling those terms. In addition, questions and exercises accompanying the longer readings in Part 3 ask students to paraphrase and synthesize. Thus, students get numerous chances to practice those two very essential cognitive skills.

Annotating, Outlining, and Summarizing

This edition of *Reading for Thinking* offers students three methods of condensing and organizing information for review: annotating, outlining, and summarizing. Students learn what each method entails and how to decide—based on their purpose in reading and the kind of text involved—when one method is more appropriate than another. Because taking notes relies heavily on a student's ability to recognize main ideas and evaluate supporting details, the new Chapter 5 on note-taking provides an excellent review of all the comprehension skills introduced in Chapters 1 through 4.

Drawing Inferences

Because making sense out of an author's words depends so heavily on a reader's ability to infer information that's suggested but never stated, *Reading for Thinking* now includes an entire chapter on drawing inferences. Students learn not only how to draw an inference but also how to evaluate that inference in terms of textual evidence.

Abundant and Wide-ranging Exercises

This new edition of *Reading for Thinking* certainly contains more exercises. But in addition, there are now many different types of exercises. Along with circling the letter of the correct answer, students are asked to fill in unfinished outlines, write summaries, create paraphrases, and compose short answers to comprehension and critical reading questions.

More Excerpts from Textbooks

The increased number of textbook selections in this edition serves two purposes. First, the excerpts help familiarize students with textbook style, content and organization. Second, and equally important, the presence of these excerpts clearly implies that textbooks are not exempt from critical evaluation. Many students erroneously believe that textbooks consist of unadulterated fact devoid of any personal opinion or bias. *Reading for Thinking* challenges that assumption and encourages students to raise their critical antennae even when reading textbooks.

Vocabulary Coverage Integrated Throughout the Book

Instead of a single chapter on vocabulary, *Reading for Thinking* now concludes each chapter with a brief section titled **Working with Words.** The vocabulary exercises in this section give students a chance to review those words footnoted with an asterisk and defined within the chapter. This method of vocabulary instruction is grounded in current vocabulary research. That research stresses the need to introduce definitions in a context and provide additional practice before asking students to use the words on their own.

In addition to words footnoted with an asterisk, a number of words have been footnoted with a dagger. These footnotes define words, terms, or names that might be unfamiliar to students. Obviously those definitions are designed to aid comprehension. However, they are also intended to increase students' general background knowledge, thereby making it easier for them to grasp an author's cultural or historical allusions.

More Emphasis on Study Skills

A good deal of research suggests that skillful readers are likely to be in conscious possession of strategies that aid concentration and memory. For this reason, Chapter 1—which originally dealt only with previewing a textbook chapter—has been considerably expanded to include an explanation of *SQ3R*. Chapter 1 also includes pointers for improving both memory and concentration.

The Cornell Method of Note-taking

With its three-column format and emphasis on summarizing and synthesizing, the Cornell method of note-taking is an ideal addition to this version of *Reading for Thinking*. The Cornell method offers students a sound note-taking format. Equally important, the use of this format helps students sharpen their ability to summarize and synthesize.

More Cultural Diversity in the Readings

Even more than the first edition, this edition for *Reading for Thinking* acknowledges the cultural diversity of most college classrooms. Many of the reading selections have been selected because they highlight the history, customs, and traditions of different cultures or groups.

Revised Explanations and a Glossary of Key Terms

All explanations of the key terms introduced in Parts 1 and 2 of the text have been revised to make them as clear and succinct as they can possibly be. To make reviewing of key terms even easier, this edition provides a glossary of essential terminology so that students will never be at a loss to define any of the terms repeatedly referred to throughout the text.

Also Available

Reading for Thinking is the third text in a three-part series. *Reading for Success*, the first book in the series, introduces essential reading skills such as identifying main ideas and recognizing supporting details. As with all the books in the series, the emphasis in *Reading for Success* is on clear explanations, numerous exercises and a lively collection of readings drawn from textbooks, newspapers, and magazines. The second book in the series, *Reading for Results*, is written at a slightly higher level of instruction and includes more detailed explanations of the skills and concepts introduced in *Reading for Success*. In addition, *Reading for Results* lays the groundwork for the critical reading skills developed more extensively in *Reading for Thinking*. Although together the three books provide an effective sequence of instruction, they can also be used independently of one another.

Acknowledgments

As always, special thanks to Joan Hellman of Catonsville Community College, whose thoughtful commentary is a wonderful source of both guidance and inspiration. In addition, I would also like to thank the following reviewers: Lynn Anderson, Navarro College, TX; William J. Bean, Daytona Community College, FL; Dee Bostick, Midlands Technical College, SC; Barbara Bretcko, Raritan Valley Community College, NJ; Larry A. Cain, Chabot College, CA; Eloise Fredrickson, Minneapolis Community College, MN; Joan Hellman, Catonsville Community College, MD; Barbara Radigan, Community College of Allegheny County, PA; Louise Rice, Augusta College, GA; Lorraine Segal, Napa Valley College, CA; Dianne BeLitsky Shames, Delaware County Community College, PA; and Sylvia Ybarra, San Antonio College, TX.

And finally, many thanks to Ellen Darion, whose hard work helped keep this book on schedule. Thanks, too, to Renee Deljon whose thoughtful suggestions were an important contribution to this edition of *Reading for Thinking*.

questions like, "What do I know about this topic?" and "Do I agree with the author's point of view?" Questions like these will help you focus your attention while you read and help you maintain concentration.

Raising and answering questions will also strengthen your motivation. Each time you can answer one of your own questions, you'll feel a sense of accomplishment. The more successful you feel, the more likely you are to keep reading.

R-1: Read

As you might expect, the first *R* in *SQ3R* stands for *read*. But here again you need to be systematic. Don't just read a chapter straight through from beginning to end. Instead, read it in sections or in bites, going from chapter section to chapter section and pausing to review after each one.

Each time you begin a chapter section, raise questions based on the heading. Whenever possible, predict how you think the author's train of thought will develop. For example, if you see the heading *Differences Between Broadcast and Print Media*, mentally make a prediction and pose a question like the following: "The author will probably point out several differences between television journalists and newspaper journalists. What exactly could those differences be?"

Even if you have to revise your questions and predictions when you finish reading a chapter section, those questions and predictions will still serve their purpose. They will keep you focused on the material and alert you to differences between what you expected to read and what the author actually said.

R-2: Recite

Each time you finish a chapter section, your goal is to monitor, or check, your understanding of what you've read and to decide if you need to reread it. Try to answer the questions you posed about the heading, or simply ask yourself, "What were the key points in this reading?" Then see if you can recite some or all of those points. If you can't answer your own questions, you should reread the entire chapter section immediately or mark it for a later rereading with the letters *RR*.

If the reading assignment is particularly difficult or particularly important, it's a good idea to write out the answers to your questions. When you write your answers, you can't fool yourself into thinking you've understood material that is actually vague or unclear in your mind.

R-3: Review

When you finish your assignment, go back over the chapter and look at the headings. For each heading, try to mentally recite a few of the author's key points. Even better, ask a friend to quiz you on each of the headings.

Yes, using *SQ3R* will take extra time. Simply reading a chapter straight through without surveying or reciting, for example, is a quicker method of studying. Unfortunately, it's not particularly effective. Thus, it's very much worth your while to make *SQ3R*—or some similar method—a regular study habit.

■ EXERCISE 1

DIRECTIONS Test your understanding of what you've read by briefly naming and describing each step in *SQ3R* without looking back at the chapter. When you finish, compare what you've written with the actual chapter section to see how complete your answers are.

S. *Survey a chapter before you read it, Read only the title & the introduction and the last page.*

9. *Question, you ask yourself Why, what & Who, to Transform heading into a question*

◤▨ Chapter 1: Review Test

1. Name and describe each step in *SQ3R*.

S: Survey — Read only the title, the introduction, and the last page.

Q: Question — the reader may ask why, what, and how, to transform heading into Question

R: Read — section the chapter in bites pausing after each one to review.

R: ReCite — after reading a chapter you should know all the key points.

R: Review — try to mentally reciting a few of the author's key points.

2. Name and describe the four kinds of context clues described in Chapter 1.

a. Contrast clues — in Antonyms — word or phrases opposite in meaning

b. Restatement — say the same thing two different ways.

c. Example clues — illustration to help explain unfamiliar words.

d. General Knowledge clues — familiarity with the experience or situation described — in the text.

3. Write a sentence that illustrates each type of context clue.

a. Contrast: Jack was very quick to accept advice from Harry. However, he was reluctant to even listen to Joe.

b. Restatement: Let move on this proposition. We must push this matter forward.

c. *Example: Never have enough time to do important things is an example of procrastination.*

d. *General Knowledge: I've never taken any formal classes on the subject. I've learned primarily by reading and observing others*

4. Explain the effect of context on meaning.

The context of a word can provide clues as to its meaning within a sentence

5. What is specialized vocabulary?

Vocabulary unique to a particular subject, but must be understood in order for one to understand a particular passage.

6. Why is it important to consistently study at the same time and in the same place?

Becomming familiar with a particular place help one develop a successful pattern of studying and proformance.

7. Why is it a good idea to set time limits for each assignment?

Setting time limits make one more conscious of making the best use of available time.

8. Why should you annotate while you read?

An effective way to maintain concentration and pay of attention to the author's message.

9. Describe a *critical reader.*

One who critically evaluates the authors points of view.

10. Why should you vary your assignments?

Combat mental fatigue and to enhance concentration.

and the general public. They do so by emphasizing narrow legal compliance*—rather than taking a positive and broad view of ethical responsibility toward all company stockholders—and by focusing on conflicts of interest that will harm the company. (William C. Frederick, James E. Post, and Keith Davis, *Business and Society.* New York: McGraw-Hill, 1992, p. 94. Copyright © 1992. Reproduced with permission of the publisher, The McGraw-Hill Companies.)

Topic a. U.S. corporations

  b. ethics codes

  c. penalties for violations of ethics codes

 3. Matthew failed the first grade. His handwriting was messy. He did not know the alphabet and never attended very well to the lessons the teacher taught. Matthew is almost always in motion. He can't sit still for more than a few minutes at a time. His mother describes him as very fidgety. Matthew has attention-deficit* hyperactivity disorder. Attention-deficit disorder, as it is commonly called, is characterized by a short attention span, distractibility, and high levels of physical activity (Barkley, 1989; Berman, 1992; O'Connor, Crowell, and Sprafkin, 1993). In short, children with this disorder do not pay attention and have difficulty concentrating on what they are doing. Estimates of the number of children with attention-deficit hyperactivity disorder vary from less than 1 percent to 5 percent. While young children or even infants may show characteristics of this disorder, the vast majority of hyperactive children are identified in the first three grades of elementary school. This is the point at which teachers are likely to recognize that children have great difficulty paying attention, sitting still, and concentrating on their schoolwork. (Adapted from Santrock, *Life-Span Development,* p. 281.)

Topic a. learning disorders

  b. attention-deficit disorder

  c. the first three grades of elementary school

 4. From the 1960s to the 1980s, inflation was the single most critical issue facing the world's economies. A high level of inflation creates so much instability and social unrest that it restricts business's capacity to operate successfully and a society's ability to function. In some countries, the value of local money has been cut to one-hundredth or even one-thousandth of its value. What formerly cost

---

*compliance: obedience.
*deficit: lack, loss.

one unit of currency now costs 1,000 or more: in other words, an ice cream cone that originally cost 20 cents would now cost 20,000 cents, or $200! (Frederick et al., *Business and Society*, p. 196.)

Topic a. society's ability to function

      b. world economies

      c. inflation

5. Throughout the seventeenth and eighteenth centuries, the rulers of Russia allowed most Russians to live in miserable poverty. But in 1855 a new emperor, Alexander II, came to the throne and, unlike his predecessors, he was determined to improve the lot of the Russian people. Alexander II relaxed press censorship and permitted the Russians to travel abroad more freely. Under his rule, minorities in the empire were treated better, and the courts were reorganized so that criminals might have a trial by jury. Alexander's greatest achievement was his decision to free the serfs, the poor men and women who had been the slaves of the rich landowners.

Topic a. the suffering of the Russian people

      b. the achievements of Alexander II

      c. the rulers of Russia

From Topic to Main Idea

Once you know the topic of a paragraph, the next logical step is to determine the main idea. The **main idea** is the central point or message of the paragraph. The main idea is what unites, or ties together, all the sentences in the paragraph.

To discover the main idea of a paragraph, you need to ask two key questions: (1) What does the author want to say *about* the topic? and (2) What idea or thought is developed throughout most of the paragraph?

To illustrate how those two questions can help you determine the main idea, let's look once more at the paragraph on page 37. You already know the topic—Gothic novels—but you still have to figure out what about that topic the author wants to communicate to readers.

For a period of about seventy-five years (1765–1840), the Gothic novel, an early relative of the modern horror story, was popular throughout Europe. Many of the most popular novels, those written by Horace Walpole, Ann Radcliffe, and Monk Lewis, were sold by the thousands, quickly translated, and frequently plagiarized. The stories were the object of fascination because they described a world where mysterious happenings were a matter of course, and ghostly, hooded figures flitted through the night. Gothic novels were read and discussed by men and women of the upper classes, and publishers, ever alert to a ready market, made sure that copies of the books were available at bargain prices. Thus, even the poorest members of the working class could afford to pay a penny to enter the Gothic world of terror, and they paid their pennies in astonishing numbers.

In this example, the opening sentence announces that the Gothic novel enjoyed great popularity for almost a century. The remaining sentences either give specific examples of how popular the novels were or explain the source of their popularity. Because the author repeatedly returns to the idea that the Gothic novel was very popular, we can say that this is the main idea of the paragraph.

Now, try to determine the main idea in an unfamiliar paragraph. As you read the following example, look for the topic—the subject repeatedly mentioned or referred to—and keep asking yourself, "What does the author want to say about that topic?" and "What one idea is developed throughout most of the paragraph?"

Well before the middle of the next century, the world faces an energy shortage of extraordinary proportions. By the year 2040, the total population on earth is expected to double to about 10 billion people. With the continued industrialization of Asia, Africa, and the Americas, world energy consumption is expected to triple. At that rate of consumption, the world's known oil supply will be depleted in about sixty years. The supply of gas will be depleted in about 100 years. If we are to maintain an acceptable quality of life, we must find new sources of energy that will make up for the shortages that are bound to occur in the coming decades.

The topic of this paragraph is "the energy shortage." That's the subject repeatedly mentioned or referred to. However, we still need to figure out what the author wants to say about that topic. We need to discover the one idea that is developed, not just in a single sentence, but throughout the paragraph.

If you go through the paragraph sentence by sentence, you'll see that each one further develops the point made in the first sentence: We're facing an energy shortage that's likely to arrive very soon. This is the main idea that's developed not just in the opening sentence but throughout the entire paragraph.

EXERCISE 2

DIRECTIONS Read each paragraph. Then circle the appropriate letter to identify the topic and the main idea.

EXAMPLE Impatient for victory as World War II dragged on, American leaders began to plan a fall invasion of the Japanese islands, an expedition that was sure to incur high casualties. But the successful development of an atomic bomb by American scientists provided another route to victory in World War II. The secret atomic program, known as the Manhattan Project, began in August 1942 and cost $2 billion. The first bomb was exploded in the desert near Alamogordo, New Mexico, on July 16, 1945. Only three weeks later, on August 6, the Japanese city of Hiroshima was destroyed by a bomb dropped from an American B-29 airplane called the *Enola Gay.* A flash of dazzling light shot across the sky; then, a huge purplish mushroom cloud boiled 40,000 feet into the atmosphere. Dense smoke, swirling fires, and suffocating dust soon engulfed the ground for miles. Much of the city was leveled almost instantly. Approximately 130,000 people were killed; tens of thousands more suffered severe burns and nuclear poisoning. On August 9th, another atomic bomb flattened the city of Nagasaki, killing at least 60,000 people. Four days later, the Japanese, who had been sending out peace feelers since June, surrendered. Formal surrender ceremonies were held September 2 on the battleship *Missouri.* (Norton et al., *A People and a Nation,* p. 827.)

Topic a. the invasion of Japan
     (b.) the atomic bomb
     c. World War II

Main Idea a. Desperate for a victory, American leaders planned an invasion of the Japanese islands.
     (b.) The atomic bomb gave the American forces another way to bring World War II to an end.

EXPLANATION Most of the sentences in the sample paragraph explain how the atomic bomb helped end World War II. That makes *b* the best answer for both the topic and the main idea.

1. Increased numbers of women are now going to college and graduating with degrees in law and medicine. More women than ever before are pursuing careers and earning as much as men. Many career women who are married have also achieved economic equality with

their husbands. The number of women in elected office has also increased, and a large majority of Americans are now willing to vote for a qualified woman for president. A growing number of women are entering the military, with the United States now having more female soldiers than any other country. These are all signs that the feminist movement has made significant headway toward gender equality. (Adapted from Alex Thio, *Sociology*. New York: HarperCollins, 1992, p. 289.)

Topic a. progress made by the feminist movement

b. gender equality in the workplace

c. women in the military

Main Idea a. Many married women make as much money as their husbands do.

b. The feminist movement has helped to advance equality between the sexes.

2. *Fiber* is generally defined as that part of plants (cell wall material) that is essentially indigestible. Though not a direct source of nutrition, dietary fiber serves at least two vital functions in the body. It speeds the passage of food waste through the colon, allowing less time for absorption of dietary cholesterol and less tissue exposure to potential cancer-producing substances in the feces. In addition, some high fiber foods (especially vegetables such as cabbage, cauliflower, and broccoli) may stimulate the production of cancer-fighting enzymes in the intestinal tract. (Robert L. Williams and James D. Long, *Manage Your Life*. Boston: Houghton Mifflin, 1991, p. 70.)

Topic a. nutrition

b. cancer-producing substances

c. fiber

Main Idea a. Fiber is the indigestible portion of plants.

b. Fiber serves the body in two important ways.

3. The U.S. government has a real interest in knowing what types of products U.S. businesses are exporting to the rest of the world. The federal government is understandably concerned that products that say "Made in America" are of good quality. U.S. companies have sometimes exported products to other nations that were banned from sale at home because of safety concerns. In addition, the government is concerned that U.S. companies not sell military technology to unfriendly nations. In the 1980s, a number of cases arose in which U.S. and West German businesses illegally sold sophisticated technology with potential military applications to Libya, Iran, and Iraq. These transactions violated U.S. laws that restrict the sale of classified military technology to only those customers approved by the Department of Defense. (Adapted from Frederick et al., *Business and Society*, p. 252.)

Topic a. federal regulations

        b. the export of American products

        c. the weapons industry

Main Idea a. The U.S. government needs to be sure that U.S. companies are not selling weapons to unfriendly governments.

        b. The U.S. government needs to be informed about the products that U.S. businesses export to other countries.

4. One important line of thinking about stress focuses on the differences between Type A and Type B personalities. Type A individuals are extremely competitive, are very devoted to work, and have a strong sense of time urgency. They are likely to be aggressive, impatient, and very work-oriented. They have a lot of drive and want to accomplish as much as possible as quickly as possible. Type B individuals are less competitive, less devoted to work, and have a weaker sense of time urgency. Such individuals are less likely to experience conflict with other people and more likely to have a balanced, relaxed approach to life. They are able to work at a constant pace without time urgency. Type B people are not necessarily more or less successful than are Type A people. But they are less likely to experience stress. (David Van Fleet and Tim Peterson, *Contemporary Management*. Boston: Houghton Mifflin, 1994, p. 349.)

Topic a. stress reduction for Type A individuals

        b. the differences between Type A and Type B people

        c. the personality traits of Type B individuals

Main Idea a. Type A people are likely to experience a high degree of stress.

        b. One theory about stress divides people into two different kinds of personalities, Type A and Type B.

5. The Love Canal is a mile-long trench, fifteen yards across, located near Niagara Falls, New York. The canal was dug in the late 1800s by William T. Love to transport goods. In the 1940s, the Hooker Chemicals and Plastics Corporation used Love Canal to bury some 20,000 tons of toxic wastes, and that's when canal residents began to notice some disturbing things. At night, the dump site seemed to glow, and thick sludge oozed into basements and clogged sewers. Residents complained of headaches, while children swimming in a pond near the canal developed ugly rashes. Most disturbing of all was the increase in miscarriages, birth defects, and cancer. Citizen complaints led to an investigation by the Environmental Protection Agency, and, in 1978, Love Canal was officially declared a disaster area.

Topic a. the Environmental Protection Agency

b. toxic waste

c. the Love Canal

Main Idea a. The Love Canal was dug in the late 1800s; its purpose was to transport goods along the eastern coast.

b. When the Hooker Chemicals and Plastics Corporation used Love Canal to bury toxic wastes, residents began to notice a number of disturbing side effects.

 # Recognizing Topic Sentences

Look back at the sample paragraphs on pages 40 and 41, and you'll see that the main idea of each one appears in the first sentence. This fact is worthy of your attention because both of those first sentences are **topic sentences**. Topic sentences are general sentences that express in writing the main idea of a paragraph. In effect, they put the author's main idea into words.

Although not all paragraphs include a topic sentence, a good many do. In fact, textbook authors are particularly fond of topic sentences. They use them because topic sentences are a quick and efficient way to communicate key points.

As a reader of textbooks, it's in your interest to recognize topic sentences. You need to be alert to the presence of general sentences that are explained in more specific detail throughout the paragraph. Be forewarned, however, that the topic sentence isn't always the first sentence in a paragraph. Topic sentences can and do appear just about anywhere. The following examples illustrate several different locations for the topic sentence.

Topic Sentence in Second Position

It's very common for the first sentence in a paragraph to be the topic sentence. However, it's not unusual for an author to begin a paragraph with one or two introductory sentences and then follow with a topic sentence. Here's an example:

Topic Sentence The Industrial Workers of the World (IWW), an international labor organization founded in 1905, did not have many successes; public distrust and a lack of organization combined to destroy the fledgling* labor movement. <u>One victory, however, stands out in the pages of IWW history: the 1912 textile workers' strike in Lawrence, Massachusetts.</u> The strike began when employers decided to enforce a cut in wages. The workers reacted with rage, and the IWW quickly moved in to help organize a strike. IWW leaders William Haywood and Elizabeth Gurley Flynn arrived in Lawrence, and their fiery rhetoric* combined with a particularly brutal offensive launched by the employers helped unite the striking workers. Meanwhile, the IWW soup kitchens helped keep the workers from starving during the two months it took to win the strike.

In this paragraph, the first sentence is an **introductory sentence** that sets forth the topic but isn't developed in the rest of the paragraph. The real point of the paragraph comes in the second sentence, which tells us that the IWW had one huge success. Like the topic sentence in first position, topic sentences in second position are very common.

Topic Sentence in the Middle

Sometimes authors don't introduce the topic sentence until the middle of the paragraph. Look, for example, at where the topic sentence appears in the following paragraph:

In general, bats have a varied diet. Flowers, insects, and fish are among their favorite foods. Some bats, however, really are like the

---

*fledgling: young, inexperienced.
*rhetoric: method of speaking, style of language.

essential and nonessential details. In short, you need to ask yourself questions like the following:

> 1. **Does this detail help explain, clarify, or prove the main idea of the paragraph?**
> 2. **If this detail had been left out, would the main idea be less clear or less convincing?**
> 3. **Does this detail simply repeat or emphasize a point that's already been made?**

If you can answer "yes" to the first two questions and "no" to the last one, you can be sure that the detail is essential.

■ EXERCISE 4

DIRECTIONS Read each paragraph, looking carefully at the underlined topic sentence. Then answer the questions that follow.

EXAMPLE

[1]Strong emotions are accompanied by physiological changes (Thompson, 1988). [2]When we are extremely fearful or angry, for example, our heartbeat speeds up, our pulse races, and our breathing rate tends to increase. [3]The body's metabolism accelerates, burning up sugar in the bloodstream and fats in the tissues at a faster rate. [4]The salivary glands become less active, making the mouth feel dry. [5]The sweat glands may overreact, producing a dripping forehead, clammy hands, and "cold sweat." [6]Finally, the pupils may enlarge, producing the wide-eyed look that is characteristic of both terror and rage. (Rubin et al., *Psychology*, p. 370.)

1. What question or questions about the topic sentence do the supporting details help to answer?

   What physiological changes accompany strong emotions?

   _____

2. According to the supporting details, what happens to your heartbeat when you feel strong emotions?

   It speeds up. _____

3. What happens to your pulse?

It races.

4. Circle the letter of the correct statement.

(a.) Sentences 2 and 3 are both essential details.

b. Sentence 2 is an essential detail and sentence 3 is a nonessential detail.

c. Sentences 2 and 3 are both nonessential details.

EXPLANATION Because the topic sentence announces that strong emotions produce physiological changes, the natural question is, "What are those changes?" To answer that question, the supporting details tell us, among other things, that, under the influence of strong emotions, the heartbeat speeds up and the pulse races. Because sentences 2 and 3 both help to answer the question raised by the topic sentence, both are essential details.

1. ¹The orchestra conductor Arturo Toscanini was born with a phenomenal memory, and throughout his career it served him well. ²He could, for example, remember every note of every musical score he had ever studied. ³Once when he couldn't find a musical score he needed for a performance, he simply wrote it down from memory. ⁴When the score was finally discovered, it was clear that Toscanini had not made one single error. ⁵When late in life his eyesight failed him, Toscanini conducted all of his concerts from memory. ⁶Audiences agree that blindness did not in any way hinder the conductor's performance.

1. What question or questions about the topic sentence do the supporting details help to answer?

   that how his phenomenal memory served his carrea

2. What three examples does the author use to prove to readers that Toscanini had a phenomenal memory?

   a. *he simple wrote down from memory*

   b. *Remembe every score*

c. _____

_____

3. Circle the letter of the correct statement.

a. Sentences 3 and 4 are both essential details.

b. Sentence 3 is an essential detail and sentence 4 is a nonessential detail.

c. Sentences 3 and 4 are both nonessential details.

4. Circle the letter of the correct statement.

a. Sentence 6 is an essential detail.

b. Sentence 6 is a nonessential detail.

2. ¹What makes an effective leader? ²To be sure, no one characteristic or trait defines an effective leader. ³However, it is true that most effective leaders consistently hold group members to high standards of performance. ⁴Setting such standards increases productivity, as people tend to live up to the expectations set for them by superiors. ⁵This is called the *Pygmalion effect*, and it works in a subtle, almost unconscious way. ⁶When a managerial leader believes that a group member will succeed, the manager communicates this belief without realizing that he or she is doing so. ⁷Conversely, when a leader expects a group member to fail, that person will not disappoint the manager. ⁸The manager's expectation of success or failure becomes a self-fulfilling prophecy. ⁹The manager's perceptions contribute to the success or failure. (Andrew DuBrin, *Leadership.* Boston, Houghton Mifflin, 1995, p. 85.)

1. What question or questions about the topic sentence do the supporting details help to answer?

It help to explain how leaders hold their group member to high Standards

2. What is the Pygmalion effect?

people tend to live up to expectation of their Leader

3. What negative result of the Pygmalion effect is described in the supporting details?

The managers expectator of success or failure become a self fulfilling prophecy

4. Circle the letter of the correct statement.

   a. Sentences 8 and 9 are both essential details.

   b. Sentences 8 and 9 are both nonessential details.

   c. Sentence 8 is an essential detail and sentence 9 is a nonessential detail.

Because 8 & 9 repeat what is already restated.

3. [1]Despite its rapid spread, Islam is not a religion for those who are casual about regulations; adhering to its rules takes effort and discipline. [2]One must rise before dawn to observe the first of five prayers required daily, none of which can take place without first ritually cleansing oneself. [3]Sleep, work, and recreational activities take second place to prayer. [4]Fasting for the month of Ramadan,† undertaking the pilgrimage to Mecca at least once in a lifetime, paying tax for relief of the Muslim poor, and accepting Islam's creed require a serious and energetic commitment. [5]And the vast majority of Muslims worldwide do observe those tenets.* (Adapted from Jan Goodwin, *Price of Honor.* New York: Penguin Books, 1994, p. 29.)

1. What question or questions about the topic sentence do the supporting details help to answer?

   Islam is not a religion for those who are casual about regulation

2. According to the supporting details, believers in Islam must rise *before dawn* to begin *cleansing oneself*.

3. In the religion of Islam, *prayer* comes before work, sleep, and recreational activities.

4. Circle the letter of the correct statement.

   a. Sentences 2 and 3 are both essential details.

   b. Sentence 2 is an essential detail and sentence 3 is a nonessential detail.

   c. Sentences 2 and 3 are both nonessential details.

---

†Ramadan: Muslim holy month.
*tenets: rules, principles.

4. Circle the letter of the correct statement.

    a. Sentences 2 and 3 are both essential details.

    b. Sentence 2 is an essential detail and sentence 3 is a nonessential detail.

    c. Sentences 2 and 3 are both nonessential details.

5. Circle the letter of the correct statement.

    a. Sentence 5 is an essential detail.

    b. Sentence 5 is a nonessential detail.

10. [1]The rise of cities dramatically increased the effect of humans on the environment, often with serious consequences. [2]Food produced in the countryside was consumed in the city. [3]Thus, food wastes were no longer returned to the soil, and the soil became less productive. [4]Also, the concentration of population in the cities meant that human wastes were concentrated, sometimes in amounts too great for the local river or stream to decompose effectively. [5]The problems resulting from urbanization grew over the centuries. [6]The urban poor often lived in horrendous circumstances, suffering from the ill effects of crowding, poverty, and hunger. (Adapted from Donald G. Kaufman and Cecilia M. Franz, *Biosphere 2000*, p. 155. Copyright © 1996. Used with permission of Kendall/Hunt Publishing Company.)

1. What question or questions about the topic sentence do the supporting details help to answer?

    _____

    _____

2. According to the supporting details, what effect did the consumption of food in the city have on the soil?

    _____

    _____

3. What effect did the concentration of population in the cities have?

    _____

    _____

4. Circle the letter of the correct statement.

   a. Sentences 2 and 3 are both essential details.

   b. Sentence 2 is an essential detail and sentence 3 is a nonessential detail.

   c. Sentences 2 and 3 are both nonessential details.

5. Circle the letter of the correct statement.

   a. Sentences 5 and 6 are both essential details.

   b. Sentence 5 is an essential detail and sentence 6 is a nonessential detail.

   c. Sentences 5 and 6 are both nonessential details.

C H A P T E R 3

Moving Beyond Paragraphs: Reading Longer Selections

 In this chapter, you'll learn

- **how to identify main ideas in longer readings.**

- **how to recognize thesis statements.**

- **how to evaluate the supporting details.**

Now that you've learned how to get the most information out of a paragraph, you're ready to adapt what you've learned to longer reading selections. Like single paragraphs, longer readings have two essential elements: a main idea and supporting details. Even though there's more information to process, understanding longer readings does not require a whole new set of thinking skills. As Chapter 3 shows, everything you've learned so far can easily be applied to readings longer than a paragraph.

71

Main Ideas in Longer Readings

When working with readings that are longer than a paragraph, you still have to analyze each individual paragraph and determine (1) what main idea the author wants to communicate and (2) which supporting details are essential to your understanding of that main idea.

However, in addition to analyzing individual paragraphs, you also have to look for the *one* main idea that focuses or controls the entire reading. It helps to think of that main idea as the *controlling idea*, because it controls or directs the content of every paragraph.

To find the main idea of a multiparagraph reading, you should once again start with the topic. Fortunately, reading selections longer than a paragraph often include titles or headings that either identify the topic or give you a good clue to what it might be. If the title or heading doesn't identify the topic, then read the opening paragraphs and look for the word or phrase most often referred to or repeated.

After you establish the topic, ask yourself what point or thought *about* the topic the author develops *not just in a single paragraph but throughout the entire reading.* For an illustration, read the following selection. As you do, notice how the second sentence of the first paragraph is developed throughout the entire reading.

Studying Leadership

Main Idea of the Entire Reading

1 At the University of Michigan, researchers have been studying leadership behavior. The studies of the Michigan researchers suggest that in the context of business management, leadership behavior falls into two categories: job-centered behavior and employee-centered behavior.

Main Idea of Paragraph 2

2 Leaders who practice job-centered behavior closely supervise their employees in an effort to monitor and control their performance. They are primarily concerned with getting a job done and less concerned with the feelings or attitudes of their employees—unless those attitudes and feelings affect the task at hand. In general, they don't encourage employees to express their opinions on how best to accomplish a task.

Main Idea of Paragraph 3

3 In contrast, leaders who practice employee-centered behavior focus on reaching goals by building a sense of team spirit. An employee-centered leader is concerned with subordinates' job satisfaction and group cohesion. Employee-centered leaders are also willing to let employees have a voice in how they do their jobs.

Main Idea of 4
Paragraph 4

The Michigan researchers felt that job-centered and employee-centered behaviors represent a single continuum,* with one of the two basic behaviors at each end. That is, they believed that if leaders become more job centered, they simultaneously become less employee centered, and vice versa. They also felt that leaders who were employee centered would generally be more effective as managers than leaders who were primarily job centered. That is, their employees would perform at a higher level and also be more satisfied. (Adapted from Van Fleet and Peterson, *Contemporary Management*, p. 332.)

Read through the opening paragraph of the selection, and you're bound to raise a key question: "What's the difference between job-centered and employee-centered leaders?" Do you see how the remaining paragraphs answer that question and thereby clarify the second sentence in the first paragraph? If you do, then you've already grasped the relationship that binds together the main idea of the whole reading and the main ideas in the individual paragraphs. Here is a diagram of that relationship:

Main Idea

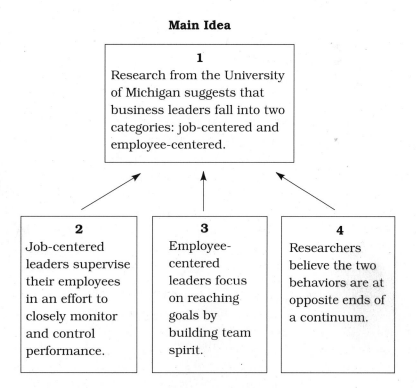

1
Research from the University of Michigan suggests that business leaders fall into two categories: job-centered and employee-centered.

2
Job-centered leaders supervise their employees in an effort to closely monitor and control performance.

3
Employee-centered leaders focus on reaching goals by building team spirit.

4
Researchers believe the two behaviors are at opposite ends of a continuum.

*continuum: a continuous series.

As the diagram shows, paragraphs 2, 3, and 4 tell more about job-centered and employee-centered behavior. Because paragraphs 2, 3, and 4 all help to clarify the second sentence in paragraph 1, we can say with certainty that we have found the main idea of the entire reading.

EXERCISE 1

DIRECTIONS Read each selection. Then circle the appropriate letter to identify the main idea of the entire reading.

EXAMPLE

Illusion of the Perfect Mate

1 The illusion that you have found the perfect partner—one who will be all things to you and vice versa—will carry you through courtship. But the reality is very different. You have not found the perfect mate—there isn't one. Anyone you marry will come with a minus quality, and the one quality that is lacking may become the only one you regard as important (Sammons, 1984).

2 Columnist Ann Landers (1977) asked her readers, "If you had it to do over again, would you marry the same person?" She received 50,000 responses. Fifty-two percent replied "no," and 48 percent said "yes." Marital happiness is hard to predict because the drug of the premarital period—love—alters your view of the partner; but this view is only an illusion.

3 Your illusion of the perfect mate is helped along by some deception on the part of your partner, who is showing you only his or her best side. At the same time, you are presenting only favorable aspects of yourself to the other person. Such deceptions are usually not deliberate but are an attempt to withhold undesirable aspects of one's self for fear that the partner may not like them.

4 For example, one male student said he knew he drank too much but that if his date found out, she would be disappointed and maybe drop him. He kept his drinking hidden throughout their courtship. They married and are now divorced. She said of him, "I never knew he drank whiskey until our honeymoon. He never drank like this before we were married." (Adapted from David Knox, *Choices in Relationships*. St. Paul: West Publishing, 1985, pp. 230, 234.)

a. If they had their lives to live over, most people would not marry the same mate.

b. The perfect mate simply doesn't exist.

EXPLANATION Sentence *b* is the correct answer because the title and every paragraph in the reading indicate that the perfect mate doesn't exist. This idea is developed throughout the reading in both general and specific terms; therefore, we can be sure it's the main idea of the entire selection.

1. Amish† Fashion

1 With the possible exception of their horse and buggy, the most striking feature of the Amish is their clothing. Men's hats—one of their hallmarks—have a low crown and wide brim, smaller models being worn by the youngsters. Coats have no collars, lapels, or pockets, and are usually worn with a vest. Belts and sweaters, however, are taboo. Trousers are plain, without crease, and are always worn with suspenders. Shirts are also plain and are worn without neckties, the latter being considered useless decorations.

2 Following a biblical injunction,* Amish women keep their heads covered at all times: indoors, by a small white lace cap; outdoors, by the familiar black bonnet. Perfume and makeup of any kind are prohibited. Dresses are of a solid color, with long skirts and aprons. In public, women also wear shawls and capes.

3 Amish clothes never go out of style, although this is not the reason for the Amish standardized mode of dress. Their attire is based on descriptions in biblical passages, plus the fact that throughout Amish history their clothing "has always been so." Also, "Amish patterns of dress form a strong basis of identity and exclusion. . . . Dress serves to keep the insider separate from the world and to identify the outsider."[1]

4 As might be expected, the Amish do not wear jewelry of any kind. In general, whatever is worn must have practical value. An ornamental exception might be the Amish man's beard, though in one sense this has recognition value. Prior to marriage, young men are clean-shaven, but married men are required to let their beards grow. (Mustaches are taboo at all times.) (Adapted from William M. Kephart and Davor Jedlicka, *The Family, Society, and the Individual.* New York: HarperCollins, 1991, pp. 107–108.)

---

†The Amish people are a religious group living primarily in Pennsylvania.
*injunction: law, order, command.
[1]John A. Hostetler, *Amish Society* (Baltimore: Johns Hopkins University Press, 1980), p. 237.

[Handwritten margin notes:]

① the most striking feature of the Amish is their clothing

② Tell how the Amish women dress

③ attire base on identity and exclusion keep the insider separation from the outside world.

the Amish men do not put value on jewelry, however the young men are clean shave, but the married men let beards grow.

(Handwritten margin notes:)
① A- only talk about the Amish woman head.
B- Stress more about the Amish men & woman and their distinctive clothing or life style.
Aids sufferers are often stigmatized

a. Whether they are indoors or outdoors, Amish women must keep their heads covered at all times.

b. Amish dress is one of the most distinctive features of the Amish people.

2. The Stigma of AIDS

1   When three Florida boys were diagnosed as having AIDS, their barber refused to cut their hair, their minister asked them to stop coming to church, and their house was burned down by neighbors (Robinson, 1987). These reactions may be extreme, but other AIDS sufferers have experienced job loss, eviction, cancellation of insurance, and even rejection by their families and friends (Tross and Hirsch, 1988). Social scientists use the term *stigma* to describe the discredit and shame that public hostility can impose on a group of people. In short, AIDS sufferers are often stigmatized.

2   Where do these stigmatizing attitudes come from? AIDS forces us to confront our own mortality in a particularly acute way, because most of its victims are young. Some people fend off feelings of vulnerability by convincing themselves that AIDS victims are not like them and deserve their fate. They define AIDS as something that can happen only to members of certain groups (Herek and Glunt, 1988). Because homosexuals are already a target of prejudice, people's intolerance becomes linked to victims of the disease.

3   The stigma of AIDS has created a dilemma for people who think they may be at risk. Should they have themselves tested for HIV—and risk discrimination if their test results are positive? Or should they avoid being tested? Many people take the latter course. Even when HIV testing is required by law, many people go to great lengths to avoid it. Between 1988 and 1989, when Illinois required couples to be tested for HIV prior to being married, the rate of marriages dropped in that state (McKillip, 1991). The tragic result is that many people who have the virus do not find out about it, do not receive treatment, and remain likely to spread the virus to others.

4   How can the stigma of AIDS be reduced? The knowledge that even our society's heroes are not immune to AIDS may help. Earvin (Magic) Johnson, one of America's most admired athletes, performed an important service when he called a press conference in November 1991 and bravely announced that he had tested positive for HIV. But whether the AIDS sufferer is a basketball star or

a plumber, homosexual or heterosexual, we should resist the impulse to blame the victim—to conclude that "he got what he deserved." Rather, we must recognize that AIDS sufferers—like the victims of other fatal diseases—are people of worth who deserve our help and sympathy. (Rubin et al., *Psychology*, p. 453.)

a. People who suffer from AIDS are often the victims of public hostility.

b. People at risk of AIDS are faced with a cruel dilemma.

■   **DIGGING** In "The Stigma of AIDS," the author poses a question: "How can the
       DEEPER stigma of AIDS be reduced?" What suggestions would you make in response to that question?

  ## Identifying Thesis Statements

In the exercise you just completed, both readings included a sentence that summed up the main idea of the entire reading. In reading 1, it was the first sentence of the first paragraph: "With the possible exception of their horse and buggy, the most striking feature of the Amish is their clothing." In reading 2, it was the last sentence of the first paragraph: "In short, AIDS sufferers are often stigmatized." Both of these sentences are good illustrations of **thesis statements.**

Like the topic sentence in a paragraph, the thesis statement in a reading sums up the entire reading. Like a topic sentence, a thesis statement is a written expression of an author's main idea. Unlike a topic sentence, however, a thesis statement can consist of more than one sentence. Here's a good example:

The Trail of Tears

Thesis 1 Throughout the nineteenth century, the Cherokee Indians proved
Statement themselves to be highly inventive and enterprising. They also showed a willingness to adapt and excel at whatever they learned from white settlers. Unfortunately, their success did not save them from being evicted from their tribal lands.

2   In 1820, the tribe established a system of government modeled

on that of the United States. It elected a principal chief, a senate, and a house of representatives.

3   In 1821, Sequoya, a Cherokee warrior who had been crippled in a hunting accident, produced a workable alphabet of Cherokee characters. The Cherokees studied the alphabet enthusiastically, and within months thousands could read and write the new alphabet. By 1828, the Cherokees were producing their own weekly newspaper, and the paper's readership was growing faster than the papers could be produced.

4   Unfortunately, in the same year, the Georgia legislature outlawed the Cherokee government. Gold had been discovered on tribal lands almost ten years before, and greedy land speculators* were determined to take control of those lands, even if it meant illegally evicting the Cherokee people. In 1832, the U.S. Supreme Court ruled in favor of the Cherokees' right to their lands. But that decision was ignored by federal authorities, and, in 1838, federal troops drove about 20,000 Cherokees west on a forced march for three hundred miles. During the march so many Cherokees died from hunger, disease, and exposure that the route they followed came to be called the "Trail of Tears."

In this reading, the thesis statement consists of three sentences rather than one. The thesis statement tells readers that the author intends to explore two related points: (1) The Cherokees were highly enterprising and inventive and (2) their achievements did not save them from being evicted from their tribal lands. Paragraphs 2, 3, and 4 then provide the supporting details that clarify both parts of this thesis statement.

Looking for the Thesis Statement

Don't be fooled by the previous example, which shows the thesis statement appearing in the first paragraph. Although the first paragraph is a very likely location for the thesis statement—particularly in textbooks—it's not the only place you should look. Authors often begin longer readings with an introduction that (1) provides background or (2) stimulates interest. In the following reading, for example, the thesis statement appears in the second paragraph rather than the first.

---

*speculators: people who engage in risky business ventures in order to earn high profits.

Looking Back at the Death Penalty

Introduction 1 Today the penalty of death is reserved for "serious" crimes such as murder, treason, espionage,* and rape. And when it is actually carried out (as it is in only one of every thirty death sentencings in the United States), the means of execution in Western countries are by firing squad, hanging, gas chamber, electric chair, and lethal injection—all relatively fast ways to go.

Thesis
Statement 2 <u>In ancient and medieval times, however, death was handed out for many more offenses, some trivial by modern standards.</u> In India, you could have been sentenced to death for spreading falsehoods, killing a cow, or stealing a royal elephant. In Egypt, during the peak of feline worship, death was the punishment for injuring a cat (even if it recovered). Judeans imposed the death penalty for cursing; the Babylonians for selling bad beer; the Assyrians for giving a bad haircut, since stylish coiffures were signs of class.

3 In parts of the Middle East, perjurers were executed by being intravenously embalmed while still alive. The embalming solution replaced the victim's blood and quickly caused cardiac arrest, and in that regard the mode of execution was a forerunner of the modern lethal injection.

4 The oldest reference to a death sentence dates back to 1500 B.C. The criminal was a teenage male, and his crime was recorded simply as "magic." The mode of death was left to his choosing (poisoning or stabbing), and the executioner was to be himself.

5 In Rome during the same period, a citizen could be executed for many serious offenses, but also for trivial matters, as prescribed by law: for "publishing lies," for singing "insulting songs" about high-ranking officials, for "cheating by a patron of his client," and for "making disturbances in the city at night." (Adapted from Charles Panati, *Extraordinary Endings*. New York: Harper & Row, 1989, pp. 136–137.)

In this example, the thesis statement appears in the second paragraph. The first paragraph is an introductory paragraph that paves the way for the second one by telling readers how the death penalty is currently viewed. The thesis statement then announces that the death penalty was once applied to even very trivial offenses. The supporting details develop that point by providing specific examples of trivial offenses that resulted in the death penalty.

In textbooks, the first paragraph after the heading is the most likely place to look for the thesis statement. However, even in text-

---

*espionage: spying.

books, writers can and do introduce the thesis statement in other locations, so be prepared to look beyond the opening paragraph.

■ **WRITING SUGGESTION** Write a paper of four to five paragraphs explaining why you do or do not support the death penalty.

■ **EXERCISE 2**

DIRECTIONS Underline the thesis statement in each of the following readings.

EXAMPLE

Creativity

1 Most of us would like to be both gifted and creative. Why was Thomas Edison able to invent so many things? Was he simply more intelligent than most people? Did he spend long hours toiling away in private? Surprisingly, when Edison was a young boy, his teacher told him he was too dumb to learn anything. Other famous people whose creative genius went unnoticed when they were young include Walt Disney, who was fired from a newspaper job because he did not have any good ideas; Enrico Caruso,† whose music teacher told him that his voice was terrible; and Winston Churchill,† who failed one year of secondary school.

2 Disney, Edison, Caruso, and Churchill were intelligent and creative men; however, experts on creativity believe that intelligence is not the same as creativity. Creativity is the ability to think about something in new and unusual ways, and to come up with unique solutions to problems. When creative people, such as artists and scientists, are asked what enables them to solve problems in new ways, they say that the ability to find affinities* between seemingly unrelated elements plays a key role. They also say that they have the time and independence in an enjoyable setting to entertain a wide range of possible solutions to a problem.

3 How strongly is creativity related to intelligence? Although most creative people are quite intelligent, the reverse is not necessarily true. Many highly intelligent people (as measured by IQ tests) are not very creative.

4 Some experts remain skeptical that we will ever fully understand the creative process. Others believe that a psychology of cre-

---

†Enrico Caruso: a famous opera singer.
†Winston Churchill: the Prime Minister of England during World War II.
*affinities: similarities.

ativity is within reach. Most experts agree, however, that the concept of creativity as spontaneously bubbling up from a magical well is a myth. Momentary flashes of insight, accompanied by images, make up only a small part of the creative process. At the heart of the creative process are ability and experience that shape an individual's effort, often over the course of a lifetime (Baer, 1993). (Adapted from Santrock, *Life-Span Development*, pp. 298–299.)

EXPLANATION In this reading, the thesis statement opens the second paragraph. The thesis statement consists of two sentences. Those sentences indicate that the author will define creativity and distinguish it from intelligence.

1. Altering Consciousness

1   People throughout history have sought ways to alter consciousness. A dramatic example is the sweat lodge ritual of the Sioux Indians. During the ritual, several men sit in total darkness inside a small chamber heated by a bed of coals. Cedar smoke, bursts of steam, and the aroma of sage fill the air. The men chant rhythmically. The heat builds. At last, they can stand it no more. The door is thrown open. Cooling night breezes rush in. And then? The cycle begins again—often to be repeated four or five times more. Among the Sioux, this ritual is viewed as a cleansing of mind and body. When the experience becomes especially intense, it brings altered awareness and personal revelation.*

2   Some altered states of consciousness are sought primarily for pleasure, as is often true of drug intoxication. Yet, as the Sioux example illustrates, many cultures regard changes in consciousness as pathways to enlightenment. Almost every known religion has accepted at least some altered states as a source of mystical experience. Accepted avenues have ranged from fasting, meditation, prayer, isolation, sleep loss, whirling, and chanting, to self-inflicted pain and mind-altering substances.

3   In many cultures, the special powers attributed to medicine men, shamans, or healers are believed to come from an ability to enter a trance and communicate with spirits. Often, rituals that help form tribal bonds among community members are accentuated by altered states of consciousness.

4   In short, all cultures recognize and accept some alterations of consciousness. However, the meanings given various states vary greatly—from signs of "madness" and "possession" by spirits, to

---

*revelation: sudden insight or understanding.

life-enhancing breakthroughs. Thus, cultural conditioning greatly affects what altered states a person recognizes, seeks, considers normal, and attains (Ward, 1989). (Dennis Coon, *Essentials of Psychology.* St. Paul, Minn.: West Publishing, 1994, p. 222.)

2. Our Oldest Enemy: The Locust

1   On July 28, 1962, radar operators at the Indian National Physical Laboratory in Delhi sounded the alarm. They had spotted a gigantic airborne invasion in progress, and the enemy was already only sixty miles south of the city.

2   Specialized emergency teams were instantly alerted. India and her traditionally hostile neighbor, Pakistan, joined forces: Aircraft from both countries roared into action, flying only sixty-five feet above the ground in a skillful counterattack. The initial battle raged for a week; sporadic fighting continued until December, when the two countries declared themselves victorious. The enemy dead numbered more than one-hundred *billion.*

3   It had been no human invasion but a far more fearsome and rapacious* threat: locusts. Using chemicals sprayed from aircraft, humans wreaked havoc on these prodigiously* destructive pests. Nevertheless, throughout most of history, the reverse has been true. When a plague of locusts arrives, it has been people who have suffered more than the locusts.

4   The earliest written record of a locust plague is probably in the Book of Exodus, which describes an attack that took place in Egypt in about 3500 B.C.: "They covered the face of the whole earth, so that the land was darkened . . . and there remained not any green in the trees, or in the herbs of the field, through all the land of Egypt." Another biblical account, in the Book of Job, describes trees "made white" as locusts even stripped the bark from the branches.

5   Locusts have always spelled disaster. In 125 B.C., they destroyed the grain crop in northern Africa; 80,000 people died of starvation. In A.D. 591, a plague of locusts in Italy caused the deaths of more than a million people and animals. In 1613, disaster struck the French region of La Camargue when locusts ate enough grass in a single day to feed 4,000 cattle for a year. The Nile Valley suffered in 1889 when locusts so thoroughly destroyed crops that even the mice starved in their wake. Between 1949 and 1963 locust swarms in Africa caused an estimated $100 million worth of damage annually. In 1958, the Ethiopian cereal crop

---

*rapacious: greedy.
*prodigiously: enormously.

was laid waste, leaving a million people without food. (Simon Adams and Lesley Riley, eds., "The Ravenous Millions," *Facts and Fallacies.* Pleasantville, N.Y.: *Readers Digest*, p. 50.)

 # The Function of Supporting Details

Once you've discovered the main idea of a reading, you need to follow the same sequence that you used for paragraphs: You need to look for and evaluate the supporting details. Like topic sentences, thesis statements cover a lot of ground and are, therefore, subject to misunderstanding. To avoid confusion, writers—good ones at least—provide examples, reasons, definitions, exceptions, studies, statistics, and other facts designed to ensure communication between reader and writer. As the reader, it's your job to decide which of those details are essential and which ones are not. For example, the thesis statement in the following reading claims that love is made up of three elements: intimacy, passion, and commitment. As you read the selection, ask yourself two questions: "What supporting details does the author use to make the thesis statement convincing?" and "Which of those details are essential to my understanding of the main idea?"

Defining Love

1   What is love? No one knows for sure. However, researcher R. J. Sternberg has a theory. *According to Sternberg, love consists of three separate ingredients, and each one is crucial either to falling in love or to staying in love.*

Thesis Statement

2   Passion is a feeling of heightened sexual arousal, and it's usually accompanied by a strong, romantic attraction. In a fit of passion, each lover feels that life is barely worth living when the other is not present. Unfortunately, passionate feelings almost always diminish over time, particularly if two people see one another every day. However, when there's a strong sense of intimacy between the partners, the loss or decrease of passion can be tolerated, and the love maintained.

3   Intimacy—feelings of closeness, sharing, and affection—is essential to staying in love. Both partners need to feel that they view the world in similar ways and can turn to one another in times of great sadness or joy. If the one you love is not the one

you feel particularly close to, you may find that, over time, love doesn't last. Typically in a relationship, intimacy grows steadily at first and then levels off.

4   Commitment refers to the decision to stay with a person both in good times and in bad. Like intimacy, a conscious sense of commitment is essential to staying in love over time. But unlike intimacy, commitment frequently requires some hard work and a conscious effort. It doesn't always come naturally.

While reading the thesis statement in this selection, you probably wondered what the three ingredients were that the author had in mind. As you can see, the author anticipated that question and described each ingredient in some detail. Your job as a skillful reader is to decide which of the supporting details are essential and which are not.

The three ingredients and their general definitions are certainly essential to understanding the thesis statement. But what about this sentence in paragraph 3? Do you think it's essential? "Both partners need to feel that they view the world in similar ways and can turn to one another in times of great sadness or joy." Most readers would say that this statement is not essential. It's not essential because the author has already defined intimacy, and this statement just adds more specific detail to the original definition.

A more essential detail is the author's claim that without intimacy love does not last. This detail is essential because it helps explain a key part of the thesis statement—that the three ingredients are crucial "either to falling in love or to staying in love." Given that portion of the thesis statement, we need to know which of Sternberg's ingredients help us fall in love and which ones help us remain in love.

When you're completing your reading assignments for school, always distinguish between essential and nonessential details. After all, you can't possibly remember every supporting detail. Nor, for that matter, can you record every single detail in your notes. Instead, look at each supporting detail and ask yourself questions like these:

1. **Does this detail help explain or prove the main idea of the entire reading?**

2. **If this detail had been left out of the reading, would the main idea be less clear or less convincing?**

3. **Does the detail merely add emphasis or create interest?**

Whenever you answer "yes" to the first two questions and "no" to the third, you're looking at an essential detail.

■ **DIGGING DEEPER** Do you agree or disagree with Sternberg about the ingredients essential to falling and remaining in love? Why or why not?

■ **WRITING SUGGESTION** Write a paper explaining what you think makes love last. What are the characteristics of a relationship that you think help love to survive over time?

◄ EXERCISE 3

DIRECTIONS Read each selection and answer the questions that follow by filling in the blanks or circling the correct answer.

EXAMPLE

Striving for Superiority

Thesis Statement

1 Psychologist Alfred Adler suggested that the primary goal of the psyche* was superiority. Although initially he believed that individuals struggled to achieve superiority over others, Adler eventually developed a more complex definition of the drive for superiority.

2   Adler's concept of striving for superiority does not refer to the everyday meaning of the word *superiority.* He did not mean that we innately seek to surpass one another in rank or position, nor did he mean that we seek to maintain an attitude of exaggerated importance over our peers. Rather, Adler's drive for superiority involves the desire to be competent and effective, complete and thorough, in whatever one strives to do.

3   Striving for superiority occasionally takes the form of an exaggerated lust for power. An individual may seek to play god and exercise control over objects and people. The goal may introduce a hostile tendency into our lives, in which we play games of "dog eat dog." But such expressions of the desire for superiority do not reflect its more positive, constructive* nature.

4   According to Adler, striving for superiority is innate and is part of the struggle for survival that human beings share with other species in the process of evolution. From this perspective, life is not motivated by the need to reduce tension or restore

---

*psyche: mind, spirit.
*constructive: useful.

equilibrium,* as Sigmund Freud tended to think; instead, life is encouraged by the desire to move from below to above, from minus to plus, from inferior to superior. The particular ways in which individuals undertake their quest for superiority are determined by their culture, their unique history, and their style of life. (Adapted from Barbara Engler, *Personality Theories.* Boston: Houghton Mifflin, 1995, p. 101.)

a. According to the reading, Adler's drive for superiority involves the *desire to be competent and effective in whatever one strives to do*.

Do you consider this detail to be (essential)/nonessential?

b. According to the reading, striving for superiority may take the form of *a lust for power*.

Do you consider this detail to be (essential)/nonessential?

c. According to the reading, the quest for superiority is shaped by the individual's *culture*, *unique history*, *style of life*.

Do you consider this detail to be (essential)/nonessential?

EXPLANATION All of the details are essential because they clarify the theory of superiority introduced in the thesis statement.

1. Circus, First Century B.C., Rome

Thesis Statement 1 The first circus, like its twentieth-century counterpart, boasted several death-defying acts. The only difference was that those early circus events were designed not so much to defy death as to guarantee it. The circus then offered thrills and spills, with the latter often involving the spilling of animal as well as human blood.

2 The Circus Maximus of Rome was where it began. Originating in the first century B.C. during the reign of Julius Caesar, its entertainment ran from brutal man-fights-beast-to-the-death encounters to spectacular horse racing and charioteering, which also were likely to end in the death of a horse or rider. The arena, as was true of later Roman circuses, was modeled on the Greek

---

*equilibrium: balance.

hippodromes,† in which chariot races and athletic games were staged.

3   Charioteers often were slaves racing to win their freedom. Understandably, they drove their horses, which ran in teams of two, four, or up to eight animals, unmercifully hard, each man obsessed with victory. Serious accidents were common, and the drivers, who wore helmets and wrapped lengths of reins around their bodies for stability, carried knives to cut themselves free if a spill occurred.

4   The circus event that was in vogue depended on who was emperor at the time. Julius Caesar favored aggressive horse racing; his successor, Augustus, liked to watch giant muscular men slay beasts. During Augustus's reign, from 27 B.C. to A.D. 14, more than 3,500 lions, tigers, and other jungle cats perished in the arena, taking with them hundreds of gladiators. Under Nero, in the first century A.D., the most popular circus event became the notorious lion-versus-Christian spectacle. The savage practice, using Christians and, later, slaves, finally was outlawed in A.D. 326 by Constantine.

5   Although the Christian torture was staged at the Circus Neronis, most of the Romans' taste for bizarre spectacles was satisfied in amphitheaters, of which the largest was the Colosseum. The capacity of this great stadium, completed in A.D. 79, was between 45,000 and 50,000, all paying customers who came to view various forms of gladiatorial combat. In one season, 2,000 gladiators and 230 wild animals were killed. Gladiatorial combat and the killing of jungle animals continued in the Colosseum until A.D. 523. (Adapted from Charles Panati, *Browser's Book of Beginnings*. Boston: Houghton Mifflin, 1984, pp. 262–264.)

a. The arena in which the Circus Maximus was held was modeled on the <u>Greek hippodromes</u>

Do you consider this detail to be essential/nonessential?

b. Charioteers in the Roman circus were often <u>Slaves</u> <u>Serious</u>, and accidents were <u>Common</u>.

Do you consider these two details to be essential/nonessential?

----

†hippodromes: open-air stadiums.

c. During the reign of Augustus, more than ___3500___ ~~lion, Tiger, and other jungle cats~~ perished in the arena, taking with them ~~hundred of gladiators~~

Do you consider this detail to be essential/nonessential?

d. Julius Caesar is said to have favored ___aggressive horse racing___.

Do you consider this detail to be essential/nonessential?

2. A New First Lady

1   In the nineteenth and early twentieth centuries, presidents' wives did not engage in political activity. Even if they were privately active, as in the case of President Warren G. Harding's wife, publicly they played the role of the dutiful wife whose opinions perfectly matched those of her husband.

Thesis 2   With the election of Franklin D. Roosevelt to office in 1933,
Statement   however, the image of the First Lady underwent a dramatic change. The first truly active First Lady, Eleanor Roosevelt embraced the idea of a caring government committed to helping the poor, minorities, and women, and she made no secret of her desire for social changes.

why these are thesis statement

3   Throughout her husband's presidency, Eleanor Roosevelt did everything she could to make herself the voice of people in need. She crisscrossed the country meeting, listening to, and talking with coal miners, waitresses, farmers, housewives—a cross section of American society. Those who missed her personal visits could read her daily newspaper column, "My Day," or write to her. And thousands did write, generally describing their hardships and asking for help. It was not uncommon for her to receive as much personal mail as the president. Rarely able to provide any direct assistance, Eleanor Roosevelt's replies emphasized hope and explained changes being made by the New Deal.† Within the White House, she was a constant goad* to her husband and New Dealers not to neglect the poor, women, and minorities.

4   Eleanor Roosevelt took the lead in supporting women. She worked publicly and privately to reduce discrimination in the government and throughout the country. In 1933, she helped to convene a special White House conference on the needs of women,

---

†New Deal: programs designed to promote economic recovery.
*goad: agent of change.

and, with the help of other women in the administration, she labored to ensure that women received more than just token consideration from New Deal agencies and the Democratic party.

5   Eleanor Roosevelt was just as determined to affirm the equality and the significant contributions of African-Americans. Working with black educators and administrators like Mary Bethune of the National Youth Administration, she sought to generate new opportunities for blacks. In 1939, she graphically demonstrated her commitment to racial equality when the Daughters of the American Revolution refused to allow renowned black opera singer Marian Anderson to sing at their concert hall in Washington, D.C. In a highly visible protest, Eleanor Roosevelt resigned her membership in the DAR and helped arrange a larger, public concert on the steps of the Lincoln Memorial. Marian Anderson's performance before Lincoln's statue attracted more than 75,000 people. (Carol Berkin, Christopher L. Miller, Robert W. Cherny, and James Gormly, *Making America*. Boston: Houghton Mifflin, 1995, pp. 785–786.)

a. Eleanor Roosevelt crisscrossed the country in order to *meeting listening to and talking with Coal miners, waitress farmers, house wife*

Do you consider this detail to be essential or nonessential?

b. Eleanor Roosevelt worked publicly and privately to reduce *discrimination in the government and throughout the country.*

In 1933, she helped convene *a special white house Conference on the needs of women.*

Do you consider these two details to be essential or nonessential?

c. In addition to helping women, Roosevelt was just as determined to *affirm the equality and the significant Contribution of African-Americans.*

Do you consider this detail to be essential or nonessential?

d. In 1939, the Daughters of the American Revolution refused to let *renowned black opera singer Marian Anderson to sing at their concert hall in Washington, D.C.*

As an act of public protest, Roosevelt _resigned her Membership in the DAR and help arrange larger public concert_.

Do you consider these two details to be essential or nonessential?

⊿ Summing Up

Listed below are the most important points in Chapter 3. Put a check mark in the box if you think the point is clear in your mind. Leave the box blank if you need to review the material one more time. The page numbers in parentheses tell you where to look in order to review each point on the list.

☐ 1. When reading passages longer than a paragraph, you still have to analyze each individual paragraph. However, you also have to look for the one main idea that ties together all the paragraphs in the reading. (pp. 72–74)

☐ 2. Similar to topic sentences in individual paragraphs, thesis statements sum up the main idea of the entire reading. Unlike topic sentences, however, thesis statements can consist of more than one sentence. (pp. 77–80)

☐ 3. Once you've discovered the main idea of a reading, you need to look for and evaluate the supporting details. As you did with paragraphs, you need to decide which details are essential to your understanding the main idea. (pp. 83–84)

study these words 3/

 Working with Words

Here are some of the words defined in Chapter 3. Use the following exercises to gain practice with these words and to learn more about their history and meaning.

EXERCISE 4

DIRECTIONS Use the following words to fill in the blanks.

continuum: a continuous series

injunction: law, rule

speculators: people who engage in risky business ventures hoping to make a profit

espionage: spying

revelation: sudden insight or understanding

rapacious: greedy

prodigious: huge ✓

psyche: mind, spirit

constructive: useful

equilibrium: balance

1. Maintaining one's _equilibrium_ while walking a tightrope is not easy.

2. Her body was in perfect physical shape; unfortunately, her _psyche_ was not so finely tuned.

3. The plague of _rapacious_ mealy bugs had destroyed most of her garden.

4. The little boy piled a _prodigious_ mound of mashed potatoes onto his plate.

5. _Constructive_ criticism is helpful, but his brand of endless nitpicking doesn't do anyone any good.

6. The war-torn city was overrun with _speculators_ expecting to buy low and sell high after the war was over.

7. In literary criticism, there's no right or wrong interpretation; instead, there's a _continum_ of possible interpretations with some being better than others.

8. In a moment of ___revelation___ she suddenly knew the course her life would take.

9. In the 1950s, Julius and Ethel Rosenberg were found guilty of ___espionage___ and condemned to death.

10. Most Muslims take seriously the ___injunction___ against eating pork.

EXERCISE 5

DIRECTIONS To answer the following questions, you'll need a hardbound dictionary.

1. In the reading on page 88, the word *goad* is used as a noun. However, it can also be used as ___a verb___, meaning ___goaded agent of change___.

2. In the reading on page 80, the word *affinities* means similarities. However, in the context of biology, an *affinity* is a ___relationship or resemblance in structure between species that suggest a common origin___.

3. In the reading on page 82, *rapacious* means "greedy." However, the word has two other meanings. They are ___taking by force, plundering___ and ___Subsisting on live prey___.

4. The word *espionage* comes from the Old French word ___espionnage___, meaning ___to spy___.

5. In the context of the law, the word *injunction* refers to ___a court order prohibiting a party from a specific course of action___.

▶◣ Chapter 3: Review Test

DIRECTIONS Answer the questions that follow each reading.

1. Protecting the Nation's Water Resources

1 Legislation, or the lack of it, determines how water is managed in the United States. The Safe Drinking Water Act and the Federal Water Resources Protection Act are two major pieces of legislation specifically designed to protect the nation's water resources.

2 **Safe Drinking Water Act.** The Safe Drinking Water Act of 1974 set national drinking water standards to protect against pollutants, or harmful agents, that might adversely affect human health; three years later, in 1977, the first standards went into effect. The Act established standards to protect groundwater from hazardous wastes being injected into the soil, once a common waste disposal practice. Over 200 pollutants have been identified in groundwater alone.

3 **Federal Water Pollution Control Act.** In 1972, Congress enacted the Federal Water Pollution Control Act, commonly known as the Clean Water Act. Amended in 1977, the act divides pollutants into three classes: toxic, conventional, and unconventional. It stipulated that industries must use the best available technology (BAT) to treat toxic wastes before releasing them into waters. Conventional pollutants, such as municipal wastes, must be treated using the best conventional technology (BCT). All other pollutants, classified as unconventional, must meet BAT standards, though waivers can be granted for pollutants in this class.

4 The Safe Drinking Water Act and the Federal Water Pollution Control Act have done enormous good, but some environmentalists fear that attempts to place restrictions on either of these acts may undo the good that's been done. For example, in 1995, the House of Representatives voted to bar the Environmental Protection Agency from imposing fines on states that violated the Clean Water Act. If Congress continues to make it harder for the EPA to monitor and control water pollution, the water we drink and the fish we eat may no longer be safe. (Adapted from Kaufman and Franz, *Biosphere 2000*, pp. 305–306.)

1. Which statement correctly paraphrases the thesis statement?
   a. The Safe Water Drinking Act set national standards for the

water we drink; it also set standards designed to help protect
groundwater.

b. The Safe Water Drinking Act and the Federal Water Pollution
Control Act are two pieces of legislation created to help protect
the nation's water supply.

2. The Safe Drinking Water Act of 1974 set _National drinking
water standard protect against Po_. In addition, the Act _harmful agent)
established standard to protect groundwater from
hazardous waste being injected into the soil._

With which of the following statements do you agree?

a. This supporting detail is essential.

b. This supporting detail is nonessential.

3. The Clean Water Act divides pollutants into three classes:
___Toxic___, ___Conventional___, and
___Unconventional___.

With which of these statements do you agree?

a. This detail is essential.

b. This detail is nonessential.

4. What do the letters BAT stand for?

_____

5. With which of these statements do you agree?

a. This detail is essential.

b. This detail is nonessential.

2. Karen Horney's View of American Culture

1 Karen Danielson Horney (pronounced "horn-eye") was born in
1885 near Hamburg, Germany. Her father was of Norwegian descent, and her mother was Dutch. Horney received her degree in
medicine from the University of Berlin and then became associated with the Berlin Psychoanalytic Institute. Although she was
heavily influenced by the theories of Sigmund Freud, Horney eventually broke with Freud to develop her own theory of the psyche
and its distresses.

2   After moving to the United States in 1934, Karen Horney began to think seriously about the nature of American culture, and she argued that one of its primary characteristics is hypercompetitiveness, a sweeping desire to compete and win in order to keep or heighten the belief that one is worthy. Trying to avoid defeat at any price, individuals are willing to cheat, manipulate, speak out against, abuse, and behave aggressively toward other people. Horney insisted that this stance has a negative effect on the growth and development of children and adults.

3   "Our modern culture," she wrote, "is based on the principle of individual competition. . . . The . . . individual has to fight with other individuals of the same group, has to surpass them, and frequently, thrust them aside." Horney believed that the consequence of this "is a hostile tension between individuals" that "pervades all human relationships. Competitive stimuli are active from the cradle to the grave . . . [making] a fertile ground for the development of neurosis."

4   According to Horney, people who are hypercompetitive view others as evil and feel that the best way to survive is not to trust other people until it can be confirmed that the people are trustworthy. In their sexual relations, they have a need to dominate and embarrass their partners. They have a neurotic need to prove that they are superior. (Adapted from Engler, *Personality Theories*, pp. 118–119.)

1. Which statement correctly paraphrases the thesis statement?

   a. Karen Horney was influenced by Sigmund Freud, but she eventually moved away from his view of the mind and its workings.

   b. Karen Horney argued that American society was dominated by a desperate desire to compete against and win over others.

2. Karen Horney was born near _Hamburg, Germany_.

   With which of the following statements do you agree?

   a. This detail is essential.

   b. This detail is nonessential.

3. Karen Horney claimed that modern culture was based on _the Principle of individuals Competition_.

   With which of the following statements do you agree?

a. This detail is essential.

b. This detail is nonessential.

4. Horney thought that people who are hypercompetitive view ___ other as evil and feel that to survive is not to trust other people until confirmed that people are trustworthy

With which of the following statements do you agree?

a. This detail is essential.

b. This detail is nonessential.

5. According to the supporting details, in their sexual relations people who are hypercompetitive need to dominate and embarrass their partner .

With which of the following statements do you agree?

a. This detail is essential.

b. This detail is nonessential.

CHAPTER 4

Reading Between the Lines: The Art of Drawing Inferences

 In this chapter, you'll learn

- how to infer the main idea of a paragraph.
- how to infer the main idea of a longer reading.
- how to evaluate your inferences.
- how to infer supporting details.

Until now, you've been reading selections in which the main ideas were stated rather than implied, or suggested. However, don't be fooled. Authors don't always supply topic sentences or thesis statements. Nor for that matter do they always put every supporting detail into words.

Sometimes they rely on their readers to draw the appropriate inferences. Readers are expected to use what the author actually says in order to arrive at some conclusion that is strongly suggested but not explicitly, or directly, stated.

Inferring main ideas and supporting details is a crucial reading skill and, like any skill, it takes a little training and practice. Step by step, Chapter 4 shows you how to draw and evaluate inferences based on your reading.

Inferring Main Ideas in Paragraphs

Although many paragraphs contain topic sentences, not all of them do. Sometimes authors choose to imply, or suggest, the main idea. Instead of stating the point of the paragraph in a sentence, they offer specific statements designed to help their readers draw the appropriate inference, or conclusion. Here's an example:

> The philosopher Arthur Schopenhauer lived most of his life completely alone; separated from his family and distrustful of women, he had neither wife nor children. Irrationally afraid of thieves, he kept his belongings carefully locked away and was said to keep loaded pistols near him while he slept. His frequent companion was a poodle called *Atma* (a word that means "world soul"), but even Atma occasionally disturbed his peace of mind. Whenever she was bothersome or barked too much, her master would grow irritated and call her *mensch*, the German word for "human being."

In this paragraph the author makes several specific statements about Schopenhauer's character and behavior: (1) he lived most of his life alone, (2) he distrusted women, (3) he always thought he was going to be robbed, (4) his only companion was a dog, and (5) he would call his dog a "human being" if she irritated him. However, none of those statements sums up the point of the paragraph. That's because the paragraph lacks a topic sentence.

Nevertheless, the paragraph does imply, or suggest, a main idea like the following: Schopenhauer did not care for his fellow human beings. This inference follows quite naturally from statements made in the paragraph. We can say, then, that it's an appropriate inference.

the main idea is
Schopenhauer did not
care for his fellow
human beings.

Distinguishing Between Appropriate and Inappropriate Inferences

Experienced readers know that authors do not always state their main ideas in a sentence. Thus, if readers can't find a sentence that sums up the paragraph, they read between the lines and infer one. However, they are always careful to draw an **appropriate inference,** an inference solidly based on statements made in the paragraph.

To recognize the difference between an appropriate and an inappropriate inference, imagine that we had drawn this inference from the sample paragraph about Schopenhauer:

> Schopenhauer's miserable childhood made it impossible for him to have a healthy relationship with other people.

Although the sample paragraph offers plenty of evidence that Schopenhauer did not have a healthy relationship with people, it does not discuss his childhood.

Because our second inference is not based on information drawn from the paragraph, we have to dismiss the inference as inappropriate. Although personal experience and general knowledge do suggest that an adult who has problems may have had a troubled childhood, we cannot rely solely on personal experience or knowledge to draw inferences. To be useful, *inferences in reading must combine what the reader already knows with what the author explicitly says.* Inferences that do not combine the two can produce misreadings that distort the author's intended meaning.

To judge your ability to distinguish, or see the difference, between appropriate and inappropriate inferences, read the following paragraph. When you finish, look over the two inferences that follow and decide which one is appropriate and which one is not.

> In the West, the Middle Eastern country of Kuwait has a reputation for being more liberal than other Middle Eastern countries where women's rights are concerned. Yet the majority of female students are not permitted to study abroad, no matter how good their grades. Similarly, female students almost never receive funding for international athletic competitions. Although the Kuwaiti government promised to give women the right to vote once the Gulf War was over, the women of Kuwait are still not allowed to participate in elections. Kuwaiti feminists, however, still hope that the government will one day keep its promise.

Based on this paragraph, which of the following inferences do you think is appropriate?

1. The government of Kuwait will never honor its promise to let women vote.

2. Despite Kuwait's liberal reputation, in many key areas women are not treated as the equals of men.

If you chose inference 2, you've grasped the difference between appropriate and inappropriate inferences. Inference 2 is solidly backed by statements in the paragraph, statements that support the idea that women lack equality in key areas. In addition, inference 2 is not contradicted by any statements in the paragraph.

The same cannot be said, however, for inference 1, which is contradicted by the last sentence in the paragraph. If Kuwaiti feminists still have hope, there's no reason to infer that the Kuwaiti government will *never* honor its promise to give women the vote.

Another problem with inference 1 is that the paragraph does not focus solely on voting rights. The paragraph also addresses funding for female athletes and travel privileges for female students. None of the statements addressing these issues can be used as the basis for inference 1, making it clear that the inference is inappropriate.

Appropriate inferences are solidly based on—or follow from—statements made in the paragraph, and they are not contradicted by any statements in the paragraph.

Inappropriate inferences do not follow from statements made in the paragraph, and they are likely to be contradicted by the author's actual words. Overall, they tend to rely too heavily on the reader's personal experience or general knowledge rather than on the author's statements.

EXERCISE 1

DIRECTIONS After reading each paragraph, circle the letter of the appropriate inference or implied main idea.

EXAMPLE In the past twenty years, countless numbers of men and women have paid large sums of money for a treatment commonly known as *cell therapy*. Their reason was simple: They believed that the injection of cells taken from baby sheep could help them maintain their youth. They either did not know or did not choose to believe what any doctor would tell them. Animal cells when injected into the body of a human being are treated like any other foreign substance. The body gathers its defenses to reject the cells, and within three or four days they are destroyed.

Implied Main Idea (a.) Cell therapy is both expensive and useless.

b. Cell therapy should be available for everyone, not just for the rich.

> **EXPLANATION** Nothing in the paragraph suggests that cell therapy should be made available to everyone. On the contrary, most of the statements in the paragraph suggest that cell therapy is useless against aging, making inference *a* the better choice for an implied main idea.

1. Meet Rebecca. She's three years old, and both her parents have full-time jobs. Every evening, Rebecca's father makes dinner for the family—Rebecca's mother rarely cooks. But when it's dinnertime in Rebecca's dollhouse, she invariably chooses the mommy doll and puts her to work in the kitchen. Now meet George. He's four, and his parents are still loyal to the values of the sixties. He was never taught the word "gun," much less given a war toy of any sort. On his own, however, he picked up the word "shoot." Thereafter he would grab a stick from the park, brandish* it about and call it his "shooter." (Adapted from Laura Shapiro, "Guns and Dolls," *Newsweek*, May 28, 1990, p. 56.)

Implied Main Idea (a.) Despite parental example or training, many children still embrace traditional roles for girls and boys.

b. Girls are born with an instinct to mother while boys are born with an instinct for aggression.

2. In World War II while America was at war with Japan, more than 100,000 Japanese-Americans living on the Pacific Coast were rounded up and put into special camps. During this same period, many Japanese-Americans were forced to give up their jobs because fellow employees were convinced that anyone of Japanese origin must be on the side of the Axis powers.† Families were forced out of their homes because constant threats made life unbearable. For some Japanese men and women, it was not even safe to be seen on the street because the color of their skin was liable to arouse hostile feelings.

---

*brandish: display, wave.
†Axis powers: the union of Italy, Germany, and Japan during World War II.

Implied Main Idea a. Many Japanese-Americans were mistreated because of the hostile feelings aroused by World War II.

b. Many of the Japanese-Americans who lived through World War II have found it hard to forgive or forget the way they were mistreated.

3. On the one hand (if you can forgive the pun*), left-handers have often demonstrated special talents. Left-handers have been great painters (Leonardo da Vinci, Picasso), outstanding performers (Marilyn Monroe, Jimi Hendrix), and even presidents (Ronald Reagan, George Bush). (As these examples suggest, left-handedness is considerably more common among males than among females.) And left-handedness has been reported to be twice as common among children who are mathematical prodigies* as it is in the overall population (Benbow, 1988). On the other hand, left-handers have often been viewed as clumsy and accident-prone. They "flounder about like seals out of water," wrote one British psychologist (Burt, 1937, p. 287). The very word for "left-handed" in French—*gauche*—also means "clumsy." Because of such negative attitudes toward left-handedness, in previous decades parents and teachers often encouraged children who showed signs of being left-handed to write with their right hands. (Rubin et al., *Psychology*, p. 59.)

Implied Main Idea a. Left-handed people tend to be more creative than right-handed people; nevertheless, the world has been organized to suit right-handers rather than left-handers.

b. Although some very gifted people have been left-handers, left-handed people have a reputation for being clumsy or awkward.

4. The topaz, a yellow gemstone, is the birthstone of those born in November. It is said to be under the influence of the planets Saturn and Mars. In the twelfth century, the stone was used as a charm against evil spirits, and it was claimed that a person could drive off evil powers by hanging a topaz over his or her left arm. According to Hindu tradition, the stone is bitter and cold. If worn above the heart, it is said to keep away thirst. Christian tradition viewed the topaz as a symbol of honor, while the fifteenth-century Romans thought the stone could calm the winds and destroy evil spirits.

Implied Main Idea a. There are many superstitions associated with the topaz.

---

*pun: play on words.
*prodigies: people with exceptional talents or powers.

the paragraph did not stated that b. The superstitions surrounding the topaz are yet another example of human stupidity.

5. For the record, no mushroom has ever attacked a person, even when provoked. Touching mushrooms does not produce poisoning, rashes, or warts. And of the thousands of North American mushroom species, only six are known to be deadly. Many dozens are edible, and many thousands are strikingly beautiful. All are ecologically* important, giving back nutrients to the earth and enhancing the lives of trees, herbs, and flowers. (Montgomery, *Nature's Everyday Mysteries*, pp. 81–82.)

Implied Main Idea (a.) For the most part, mushrooms are both beautiful and beneficial.

b. Most people are afraid of eating wild mushrooms, but they shouldn't be.

■ Exercise 2

DIRECTIONS Read each paragraph. On the blank lines that follow, write the implied main idea of the paragraph.

EXAMPLE The plant known as kudzu was introduced to the South in the 1920s. At the time, it promised to be a boon† to farmers who needed a cheap and abundant food crop for pigs, goats, and cattle. However, within half a century, kudzu had overrun seven million acres of land, and many patches of the plant had developed root systems weighing up to three hundred pounds. Currently, no one really knows how to keep kudzu under control, and it's creating problems for everyone from boaters to farmers.

Implied Main Idea *Intended to help farmers, kudzu has proven to be more harmful than beneficial.*

EXPLANATION At the beginning of the paragraph, the author tells readers that in the 1920s kudzu was viewed as a help to farmers. However, by the end of the paragraph, the author tells us what a pest the plant has become. Thus, it makes sense that the implied main idea unites these two different perspectives on kudzu.

---

*ecologically: having to do with the relationship between organisms and their environment.
†boon: benefit, favor.

1. For football and baseball players, the mid-twenties are usually the years of peak performance. Professional bowlers, however, are in their prime in their mid-thirties. Writers tend to do their best work in their forties and fifties, while philosophers and politicians seem to reach their peak even later, after their early sixties. (Adapted from Coon, *Essentials of Psychology*, p. 138.)

Implied Main Idea *the age at which a person reaches peack performance tends to depend on their professional.*

2. The webs of some spiders contain drops of glue that hold the spiders' prey fast. Other webs contain a kind of natural velcro that tangles and grabs the legs of insects. Then, too, spiderwebs don't always function simply as traps. Some webs also act as lures. Garden spiders use a special silk that makes their intricate decorations stand out, and experiments have shown that the decorated parts attract more insects. Other kinds of spiders, like the spitting spider, use their webs as weapons. The web is pulled taut to snap shut when a fly enters.

Implied Main Idea *Spider webs are used for a variety of purposes. Some are traps & lures and as weapon.*

3. The day you learned of your acceptance to college was probably filled with great excitement. No doubt you shared the good news and your future plans with family and friends. Your thoughts may have turned to being on your own, making new friends, and developing new skills. Indeed, most people view college as a major pathway to fulfilling their highest aspirations. However, getting accepted may have caused you to wonder: What will I study? How will I decide on a major? Will I do the amount of studying that college requires? Will I be able to earn acceptable grades? (Adapted from Williams and Long, *Manage Your Life*, p. 157.)

Implied Main Idea _____

_____

4. Every year the scene is so unchanging I could act it out in my sleep. In front of the Hayden Planetarium on a muggy Saturday morning, several dozen parents gather to wave goodbye to their boys as the bus ferries them off for eight weeks of camp. First-time campers are clutchy. Old-timers are cocky. My own sons fret at length about carsickness. Then the parents give the kids a final hug and shuffle sullenly back to their depopulated urban nests. But not this year. When the bus pushed out of the planetarium's circular driveway four Saturdays ago, at last removing the waving boys at the tinted windows completely from our view, one parent interrupted the usual hush by very tentatively* starting to clap. Then other parents joined in, first clapping and finally laughing uproariously. (Frank Rich, "Back to Camp," *New York Times*, July 22, 1995, p. 19.)

Implied Main Idea The parent are happy when the children went off to camp. However some of the children were sad & some were

5. In the nineteenth century, when white settlers moved into territory inhabited by Navaho and other tribal peoples, the settlers took much more than they needed simply to survive. They cut open the earth to remove tons of minerals, cut down forests for lumber to build homes, dammed the rivers, and plowed the soil to grow crops to sell at distant markets. The Navaho did not understand why white people urged them to adopt these practices and improve their lives by creating material wealth. When told he must grow crops for profit, a member of the Comanche tribe (who, like the Navaho, believed in the order of the natural environment) replied, "The earth is my mother. Do you give me an iron plow to wound my mother's breast? Shall I take a scythe† and cut my mother's hair?" (Norton, *A People and a Nation*, p. 499.)

Implied Main Idea The Navah and other tribal people did not understand why white settler urged then to adopt these practic and improve their lives by creating material wealth.

DIGGING DEEPER The paragraph on page 104 describes how being accepted to college is a source of both joy and anxiety. What other events in life might generate such conflicting emotions?

Inferring the Main Idea in Longer Readings

Longer readings, particularly those in textbooks, generally include thesis statements that express in writing the main, or controlling,

---

*tentatively: hesitantly, shyly.
†scythe: a sharp curved knife used to cut wheat.

idea of the entire reading. However, even writers of textbooks occasionally imply the main idea rather than explicitly stating it. When this happens, you need to respond much as you did to paragraphs without a topic sentence. Look at what the author actually says and ask yourself what logical inference can be drawn from the statements in the reading.

To illustrate, here's a reading that lacks a thesis statement, yet still suggests a main idea:

The Kamskys Are Coming

1   To some observers in the chess world, the Russian teenager Gata Kamsky is the most gifted chess genius of all time. To many others, however, he is a studious, hard-working young man whose name will *not* go down in chess history. At fifteen, Gata faced chess champion Alexander Ivanov in a formal match. He was then the youngest player in history to formally play an international champion. To the astonishment of everyone present, Gata won the match. The one person not astonished was Rustam Kamsky, the boy's father. Perhaps more than anyone else, Rustam is convinced of his son's greatness. And he takes full credit for it. "I am the person that deserves credit for my son being a champion."[1]

2   At the age of eight, Gata started playing chess. He played because his father insisted upon it. Today, however, the boy willingly spends up to fourteen hours a day studying chess strategies. Because Gata's eyes are weak, his father reads to him, and the two are seldom apart. With his father's full approval, Gata appears to have no outside interests, no hobbies, no friends, no dates, and no diversions. Chess is the boy's life. His father, it seems, would not have it any other way.

3   Although Rustam Kamsky insists that his son will one day reign supreme in the chess world, some chess experts disagree. They maintain that the boy needs to study with a grand master. In the past, however, such attempts have failed miserably. When, for example, Gata studied with the famous chess player Leonid Shamkovich, the lessons quickly came to a halt. According to Shamkovich, Rustam constantly interrupted. Shamkovich also insisted that no chess master of any real merit would ever tolerate the father's interference. Unfortunately, without the guidance of an experienced champion, some believe it may prove hard for the boy to advance to the heights his father expects.

---

[1]Fred Waitzken. "His Father's Pawn." *New York Times Magazine* May 13, 1990, p. 45.

4   Naturally, from Rustam's point of view, such criticism is non-sense. Only he can support the boy without jealousy or hostility. Perhaps. Only time will tell who is right.

In this reading, there is no thesis statement. No sentence or group of sentences sums up the controlling idea. However, we can draw an inference from what the author both does and does not say.

1. The author mentions that *some* observers think the boy will be famous, but *many* others do not. However, the only reasons discussed are those that explain why the boy might not succeed.
2. She details the father's interference.
3. She explains why that interference might harm the boy's career.
4. She does not mention anyone who considers such parental control beneficial.

Based on this information, we can infer the following idea: It's not clear whether Rustam Kamsky is hurting his son's career or helping it.

Appropriate and Inappropriate Inferences

As you would expect, main ideas in longer readings have to be firmly grounded in the author's actual words. For example, let's say that we had drawn the following inference: Gata Kamsky resents his father's influence on his career. If we look for support for that inference in the reading itself, we find no evidence that the boy resents his father's control.

Even more telling are the statements that contradict that inference. The boy "willingly spends up to fourteen hours a day studying chess," and he and his father are "seldom apart." It's hard to believe that someone who was resentful of his father's authority would spend this much time in his father's company. In this case, our inference is based more on a personal response—many of us balk at parental authority—than on the author's actual words.

If at any point you have doubts about whether the controlling idea you have inferred is appropriate, ask yourself these three questions:

1. What statements support this inference?
2. Do any of the author's statements contradict the inference?

3. Am I relying too much on what I think or believe and not enough on what the author actually says?

◢ EXERCISE 3

DIRECTIONS Read the following selections. Then circle the letter of the main idea you think is implied by each reading.

EXAMPLE

The Hermits of Harlem

1 On March 21, 1947, a man called the 122nd Street police station in New York City and claimed that there was a dead body at 2078 Fifth Avenue. The police were familiar with the house, a decaying three-story brownstone in a run-down part of Harlem. It was the home of Langley and Homer Collyer, two lonely recluses* famous in the neighborhood for their odd but seemingly harmless ways.

2 Homer was blind and crippled by rheumatism. Distrustful of doctors, he wouldn't let anybody but Langley come near him. Using his dead father's medical books, Langley devised a number of odd cures for his brother's ailments, including massive doses of orange juice and peanut butter. When he wasn't dabbling in medicine, Langley liked to invent things, like machines to clean the inside of pianos or intricately wired burglar alarms.

3 When the police responded to the call by breaking into the Collyers' home, they were astonished and horrified. The room was filled from floor to ceiling with objects of every shape, size, and kind. It took them several hours to cross the few feet to where the dead body of Homer lay, shrouded in an ancient checkered bathrobe. There was no sign of Langley, and the authorities began to search for him.

4 When they found him, he was wearing a strange collection of clothes that included an old jacket, a red flannel bathrobe, several pairs of trousers, and blue overalls. An onion sack was tied around his neck; another was draped over his shoulders. Langley had died some time *before* his brother. He had suffocated under a huge pile of garbage that had cascaded down upon him.

5 On several occasions, thieves had tried to break in to steal the fortune that was rumored to be kept in the house. Langley had responded by building booby traps, intricate systems of trip wires and ropes that would bring tons of rubbish crashing down on any

---

*recluses: people who live alone cut off from others.

unwary intruder. But in the dim light of his junk-filled home, he had sprung one of his own traps and died some days before his brother. Homer, blind, paralyzed, and totally dependent on Langley, had starved to death.[2]

Implied Main Idea (a.) In the end, the Collyer brothers' eccentric and reclusive ways led to their death.

b. The Collyer brothers' deaths were probably suicides.

EXPLANATION In this case, *a* is the more appropriate inference because statements in the reading suggest that the brothers' eccentricity contributed to their deaths. It was, for example, a trap of Langley's own devising that killed him. However, there is no evidence that either of the brothers chose to die.

1. Frustration

1 **External frustration** is based on conditions outside of the individual that impede progress toward a goal. All of the following are external frustrations: getting stuck with a flat tire, having a marriage proposal rejected, finding the cupboard bare when you go to get your poor dog a bone, finding the refrigerator bare when you go to get your poor tummy a T-bone, finding the refrigerator gone when you return home, being chased out of the house by your starving dog. In other words, external frustrations are based on *delay, failure, rejection, loss,* and other direct blocking of motives.

2 **Personal frustrations** are based on personal characteristics. If you are four feet tall and aspire to be a professional basketball player, you very likely will be frustrated. If you want to go to medical school, but can earn only D grades, you will likewise be frustrated. In both examples, frustration is actually based on personal limitations. Yet, failure may be *perceived* as externally caused.

3 Whatever the type of frustration, if it persists over time, it's likely to lead to aggression. The frustration-aggression link is so common, in fact, that experiments are hardly necessary to show it. A glance at almost any newspaper will provide examples such as the following:

Justifiable Autocide
BURIEN, Washington (AP)—Barbara Smith committed the assault, but police aren't likely to press charges. Her victim was a 1964 Oldsmobile that failed to start once too often.

---

[2]Adams and Riley. "Hermits of Harlem." *Facts and Fallacies*, Pleasantville, N.Y.: Reader's Digest Association, 1988, p. 226.

When Officer Jim Fuda arrived at the scene, he found one beat-up car, a broken baseball bat, and a satisfied 23-year-old Seattle woman.

"I feel good," Ms. Smith reportedly told the officer. "That car's been giving me misery for years and I killed it."

(Adapted from Coon, *Essentials of Psychology*, p. 419.)

Implied Main Idea   a. External frustration is the more painful type of frustration, and it frequently leads to aggressive feelings and actions.

b. Although there are two different types of frustration, both can, if they persist, lead to aggressive behavior.

2. Children Having Children

1   Like other 16-year-olds, Gail thinks about her clothes, her friends, and getting her homework done. But Gail has to think about something else that most 16-year-olds do not: her 6-month-old daughter. Gail is one of more than a million teenagers in the United States who get pregnant each year. Many of these girls will raise their baby as a single parent (Children's Defense Fund, 1989).

2   Today, few pregnant teenagers opt for adoption, in part because of greater acceptance of single parents (Rickel, 1989). For a girl uncertain about her identity and future, a baby can seem a "solution" to teenage dilemmas. "I want to have the baby," said one teenage mother. "It would be my own. Something that was mine and would love me" (Kaser, Kolb, and Shephard, 1988). The girls most likely to become single parents are those who are doing poorly in school, have low self-esteem and aspirations, and grow up in poor single-parent families (Furstenberg, Brooks-Gunn, and Chase-Lansdale, 1989).

3   The teen mother is thrust prematurely into adult responsibilities. "This is harder than I thought it would be," a 15-year-old confided. "My mother can't always take care of [the baby], and my friends don't want him around" (Kaser, Kolb, and Shephard, 1989). Compared to their peers who delay parenthood, teenage girls who become pregnant are more likely to drop out of school, to require public assistance, to have more children, and to have poor job prospects.

4   The children of young single mothers often have problems in school, in their social relationships, and with the law (Furstenberg, Brooks-Gunn, and Chase-Lansdale, 1989). The mother's lack of education, low income, and inexperience as a parent can cause difficulties. For example, adolescent mothers tend to talk to their infants less than older mothers do—perhaps because they don't know that infants benefit from such stimulation.

5   For children to be successful parents, they must grow up a lot faster than their peers. Recently, social programs have been developed to help teenagers—and more are needed. Family-planning and sex-education programs aim at preventing pregnancy. Counseling programs help pregnant teenagers think about their options, which include adoption, abortion, and keeping the baby. Comprehensive programs help teenage mothers stay in school by providing daycare and teaching effective parenting skills. (Rubin et al., *Psychology*, p. 242.)

Implied Main Idea a. With the help of new social programs, most teenage mothers are avoiding the problems that plagued them in the past.

b. Most teenage mothers have a difficult time raising their children.

 # Inferring Details

In addition to main ideas, writers also expect their readers to read between the lines and infer supporting details. For an illustration, read the following paragraph. Then decide which inference sums up a supporting detail that is suggested but never explicitly stated.

The buzz echoed faintly at first, a tentative, conversational hum vibrating on the back channels of the Internet: "Is it true?" asked a message posted to a public discussion group. "Did the FBI really nail Kevin Mitnick?" It did indeed. In February of 1995, federal law authorities knocked on Mitnick's Raleigh, North Carolina, apartment door at 1:30 in the morning, interrupting his long career as America's most sought after computer bad boy. "The Condor is extinct," moaned another message. The reference is to Mitnick's favorite film, *Three Days of the Condor*, a 1975 Robert Redford movie about a CIA analyst on the run from shadowy forces within the government. The evil at play in Mitnick's case, alleges the FBI, is the 31-year-old hacker's total obsession with burrowing his way into the most secret nerve centers of telephone companies and corporate computer systems. (Vic Sussman, "Gotcha! A Hard-core Hacker Is Nabbed," *U.S. News and World Report*, February 27, 1995, p. 66.)

Based on the paragraph, which inference makes more sense?

1. Although he was hunted by the FBI, Kevin Mitnick apparently had at least one fan.

2. When he got caught, Kevin Mitnick was deeply apologetic for all the trouble he had caused.

If you look back at the paragraph, it should be clear that the first inference is appropriate, whereas the second one is not. Support for inference 1 comes from the sentence that tells us that one message "moaned," "The Condor is extinct." The use of the word *moaned* and the word *extinct*—as if Mitnick belonged to an endangered species— suggests that someone felt unhappiness at his capture. However, none of the statements in the paragraph suggests that Mitnick was apologetic for his actions. Because no support for inference 2 can be found, it's not appropriate.

■ EXERCISE 4

DIRECTIONS After reading each paragraph, circle the letter of the implied supporting detail that readers are expected to supply.

EXAMPLE The incidence* of melanoma, the most dangerous and the deadliest form of skin cancer, has nearly doubled in the past ten years. That increase may be due to many factors, including lifestyle changes, migration to the Sunbelt, and better detection, but the depleted ozone layer may also be partly to blame. While it's not clear how much ozone depletion has been responsible for current melanoma cases, there's no doubt that the thinning ozone layer raises the future risk of skin cancer. (Adapted from *Consumer Reports*, 1991, p. 51.)

Implied Supporting Detail

a. It's generally believed that the ozone layer will continue to be depleted.

b. The use of pesticides and industrial pollution will further damage the ozone layer.

EXPLANATION The words *thinning* and *future risk* suggest that the decrease in the ozone layer is an ongoing process that will continue into the future, making *a* the better answer.

1. If we're really interested in saving the environment, and therefore ourselves, there are some not-so-easy things we can and must do. **About population:** On the personal level, we can stop at two, or one,

---

*incidence: the extent, or frequency, of an occurrence.

or none—and learn to love other people's children. On the government level, we can give every couple the knowledge and technology to choose the number of their children, and then give them straight, honest reasons why they should choose no more than two. The U.S. government, which used to be foremost in this field, has essentially stopped funding family planning and population education both domestically and internationally. We need to lean hard on our leaders to reverse that policy. (Donella Meadows, *In Context*, No. 26, 1991, p. 386.)

Implied
Supporting Detail

a. Big families are no longer popular in America.

b. The Earth is in danger of being overpopulated.

2. Dr. C. James Mahoney seemed incredulous* as he sat cuddling a four-month-old chimpanzee named Cory. But the reports were true: The highly regarded New York University primate research center† at which the veterinarian had worked for 18 years was being taken over by a New Mexico foundation charged by federal officials with a long list of violations of animal-welfare laws. The primate center and its 225 chimpanzees were added last week to the holdings of the Coulston Foundation, a research group that already owns or leases 540 other chimpanzees for medical tests. The foundation, based in Alamogordo, New Mexico, now has control of well over half of the chimpanzees used in medical research in the United States. Critics, including Dr. Jane Goodall, who pioneered studies of the endangered species in the wild, claim that the foundation, already cited for the deaths of at least five chimpanzees, cannot possibly care for more. (Andrew C. Revkin, "A Furor Over Chimps," *New York Times*, August 13, 1995, p. 2.)

Implied
Supporting Detail

a. Dr. C. James Mahoney was stunned at learning that he would soon be out of a job.

b. Dr. C. James Mahoney was stunned by the news that the chimps he had cared for would be turned over to the Coulston Foundation.

3. In the nineteenth century, questions about natural resources caught Americans between the desire for progress and the fear of spoiling the land. By the late 1870s and early 1880s, people eager to protect the natural landscape began to coalesce* into a

---

*incredulous: stunned, disbelieving.
†primate research center: center that studies the behavior of animals closely related to humans.
*coalesce: to come or grow together.

conservation* movement. Prominent* among them was western naturalist John Muir, who helped establish Yosemite National Park in 1890. The next year, under pressure from Muir and others, Congress authorized President Benjamin Harrison to create forest reserves—public land protected from cutting by private interests. Such policies met with strong objections. Lumber companies, lumber dealers, and railroads were joined in their opposition by householders accustomed to cutting timber freely for fuel and building material. Public opinion on conservation also split along sectional lines. Most supporters of regulation came from the eastern states, where resources had already become less plentiful; opposition was loudest in the West, where people were still eager to take advantage of nature's bounty.* (Norton et al., *A People and a Nation*, p. 509.)

Implied
Supporting Detail

    a. Because the early conservation movement was led by Easterners, many Westerners did not support it.

    b. In the East, the early conservation movement caught on quickly because people in the East had begun to see firsthand that the country's resources were not endless.

4. Although his armies were all defeated by April of 1865, Jefferson Davis, the leader of the Southern Confederacy, remained in hiding and called for guerilla* warfare and continued resistance. But one by one, the Confederate officers surrendered to their opponents. On May 10, Davis and the Confederate postmaster were captured near Irwinville, Georgia, and placed in prison. Andrew Johnson, who had assumed the presidency upon Lincoln's death, issued a statement to the American people that armed rebellion against legitimate authority could be considered "virtually at an end." The last Confederate general to lay down his arms was Cherokee leader Stand Watie, who surrendered on June 23, 1865. (Berkin et al., *Making America*, p. 439.)

Implied
Supporting Detail

    a. Because he did not know his armies were all defeated, Jefferson Davis continued to fight.

    b. In the face of defeat, Jefferson Davis would not abandon the Confederate cause.

---

*conservation: the act of protecting or preserving.
*prominent: famous.
*bounty: goodness.
*guerilla: used to characterize warfare waged by small, informal bands of soldiers.

■ **DIGGING DEEPER** The paragraph on page 112 points out that skin cancer is on the rise. Most people know this, yet a good many still sunbathe, even though tanning increases the risk of skin cancer. Why do you think people behave in a way that so obviously endangers their health?

■ **WRITING SUGGESTION** Write a paragraph or two that evokes a particular mood or emotion like gaiety, grief, despair, or joy. Describe the scene, but don't mention the mood or emotion you have in mind. Let your description imply it. Ask a classmate to infer the mood or emotion.

▶ Summing Up

Listed below are the most important points in Chapter 4. Put a check mark in the box if you think the point is clear in your mind. Leave the box blank if you think you need to review the material one more time. The page numbers in parentheses tell you where to look in order to review each point on the list.

☐ **1.** Authors don't always put main ideas of paragraphs into topic sentences. Sometimes they expect readers to read between the lines and infer the main idea. (p. 98)

☐ **2.** Appropriate inferences are based more on what the author says than on the reader's personal experience or knowledge. Inappropriate inferences do not follow from the author's words and they rely too heavily on the reader's experience and background. (pp. 99–100)

☐ **3.** Authors don't always use thesis statements to express main ideas in longer readings. Sometimes they expect readers to infer a main idea that is developed throughout the entire reading. (pp. 105–108)

☐ **4.** Like main ideas, supporting details sometimes need to be inferred by the reader. (pp. 111–112)

Working with Words

Here are some of the words defined in Chapter 4. Use the following exercises to gain practice with these words and to learn more about their history and meaning.

EXERCISE 5

DIRECTIONS Use the following words to fill in the blanks.

brandish: display or wave

pun: play on words

ecologically: having to do with the relationship between organisms and their environment

tentatively: hesitantly, shyly

recluses: people who live alone cut off from others

incidence: the extent, or frequency, of an occurrence

incredulous: stunned, disbelieving

coalesce: to come or grow together

conservation: the act of protecting or preserving, often used in the context of protecting nature from harm

prominent: famous

1. John Muir was an early leader of the _Conservation_ movement that began in the nineteenth century.

2. The government must develop an _ecologically_ sound policy to protect the environment.

3. Every time the police threatened to enter the building, the kidnapper would _brandish_ his gun.

4. Unfortunately, the _incidence_ of tuberculosis has increased.

5. For most of their lives, the two sisters lived as _recluses_, completely cut off from both friends and family.

6. He laughed wildly at his own _pun_, but nobody else really understood what he meant.

7. Under the microscope, you could see how the cells were beginning to ___Coalesce___ into a tiny, star-shaped tumor.

8. The workers looked stunned and _incredulous_ when their manager described the coming layoffs.

9. Through the bars, the monkey ___Tentatively___ put out his hand.

10. Because she was a ___prominent___ attorney, everyone was surprised when she agreed to represent a group of homeless people who could not afford her fee and who would not increase her fame.

EXERCISE 6

DIRECTIONS To answer the following questions, you'll need a hardbound dictionary.

1. The word *guerilla* comes from the word _warfare_ meaning _informal band of soldiers_

2. The origin of the word *pun* is unknown, but the word was first used in _French (gauche)_ by the writer and poet _(Burt 1937.)_
   (British psychologist

3. In addition to being a person, a *prodigy* can also be ___
   an extrodinary act or event

4. According to the dictionary, you are most likely to *brandish* a _Weapon_.

5. The word *incredulous* consists of the Latin prefix *in* meaning ___not___ and the Latin root *credulous* meaning _to believe_.

Chapter 4: Review Test

Part A   After reading each paragraph, circle the letter of the implied main idea.

1. In one study, done in the early 1970s when young people tended to dress in either "hippie" or "straight" fashion, experimenters donned hippie or straight attire and asked college students on campus for a dime to make a phone call. When the experimenter was dressed in the same way as the student, the request was granted in more than two-thirds of the instances; when the student and requester were dissimilarly dressed, the dime was provided less than half the time (Emswiller, Deaux, and Willits, 1971). In another experiment, marchers in an antiwar demonstration were found to be more likely to sign the petition of a similarly dressed requester *and* to do so without bothering to read it first. (Cialdini, *Influence*, p. 164.)

Implied Main Idea   a. The results of two different studies suggest that people don't necessarily read the petitions they sign.

  b. The results of two different studies suggest that we are more likely to help those whose clothing resembles our own.

2. Some people choose to confront conflict by engaging in **avoidance,** or not confronting the conflict at all. They simply put up with the situation, no matter how unpleasant it may be. While seemingly unproductive, avoidance may actually be useful if the situation is short-term or of minor importance. If, however, the problem is really bothering you or is persistent, then it should be dealt with. Avoiding the issue often uses up a great deal of energy without resolving the aggravating situation. Very seldom do avoiders feel that they have been in a win-win situation. Avoiders usually lose a chunk of their self-respect since they so clearly downplay their own concerns in favor of the other person's. (Roy Berko, Andrew D. Wolvin, and Darlyn Wolvin, *Communicating.* Boston: Houghton Mifflin, 1992, p. 248.)

Implied Main Idea   a. Avoiding conflict is a bad strategy for dealing with life's problems; it's often better to meet problems head-on.

  b. Although avoiding conflict can be effective in some situations, it's an ineffective strategy when the problem is persistent.

3. To be a compelling speaker, you must work to be vivid in your presentation. Good descriptions, a colorful choice of language, and a

lively style can all encourage listeners to pay attention to your message. For example, a speaker addressing a group of potential airline flight attendants can stress the importance of cabin safety with some vivid descriptions of past accidents. Humor is another useful speaking strategy. If relevant and in good taste, humor can gain and keep the listeners' attention. It may also allow them to relax. Humor was creatively used by a minister who was asked how long a good sermon should be: "I use one rule," he said. "The mind can only absorb what the seat can endure." In trying to keep your audience's attention, you may also wish to use the device of novelty—treating a subject in a unique fashion. One speaker, for instance, used novelty when he started a speech by saying, "I'm much like you in many ways. I have two arms, two legs, two hands, two eyes, and two ears. I'm different from you, however, because I'm on methadone. You see, I'm a heroin addict." (Berko et al., *Communicating*, p. 387.)

Implied Main Idea a. Good speakers use a variety of techniques to keep their listeners' attention.

      b. Good speakers are hard to find, and it's unusual to hear a speech that isn't boring.

4. For unknown presidential candidates like Jimmy Carter in 1976 and Democratic Senator Gary Hart of Colorado in 1984, the first step in winning public support is achieving name recognition. Carter was so little known that he referred to himself as "Jimmy Who?" and when Hart started his campaign, over 60 percent of the public claimed they had never heard his name. But once a candidate solves the name-recognition problem, the next task is to establish credibility as a contender. In 1984, for example, Democratic Senator John Glenn of Ohio was widely known as an astronaut and hero. However, he was unable to convince the public that he was a credible presidential candidate. Four years earlier, Republican John Connally of Texas, a national political figure of some fame, was forced out of the race for the same reason. (Adapted from John H. Aldrich, Gary J. Miller, Charles W. Ostrom, and David W. Rohde, *American Government*, Boston: Houghton Mifflin, 1986, p. 271.)

Implied Main Idea a. Without name recognition, a presidential candidate is doomed to fail.

      b. Achieving name recognition and credibility as a candidate are two key elements of any presidential campaign.

Part B After reading each passage, identify the supporting details you needed to supply to make sense out of the author's words.

5. [1]Debates about human nature are always fascinating. [2]But what initially inspired social psychologists to study the nature of helping were hair-raising stories about bystanders who fail to take action even when someone else's life is in danger. [3]The problem first made headlines in March 1964. [4]Kitty Genovese was walking home from work in Queens, New York, at 3:20 in the morning. [5]As she crossed the street from her car to her apartment, a man with a knife appeared. [6]She ran, but he caught up and stabbed her. [7]Genovese cried frantically for help and screamed, "Oh my God, he stabbed me! . . . I'm dying, I'm dying!"—but to no avail. [8]The man fled but then returned, raped her, and stabbed her eight more times, until she was dead. [9]In the still of the night, the attack lasted for over half an hour. [10]Thirty-eight neighbors heard the screams, turned lights on, and came to their windows. [11]One couple even pulled chairs up to their window and turned out the light to see better. [12]Yet nobody came down to help. [13]Until it was over, nobody even called the police. (Saul Kassin, *Psychology*. Boston: Houghton Mifflin, 1995, pp. 509–510.)

The author expects readers to infer that the story of Kitty Genovese illustrates what problem?

Peoples unwillingness to help others even in extraordinary circumstances

6. [1]In 1963, Martin Luther King, Jr., sought to increase the support of the movement for civil rights. [2]In May, he helped organize demonstrations for the end of segregation in Birmingham, Alabama. [3]The protesters found the perfect enemy in Birmingham's police commissioner, Eugene "Bull" Connor, whose beefy features and snarling demeanor made him a living symbol of everything evil. [4]Connor's police used clubs, dogs, and fire hoses to chase and arrest the demonstrators. [5]President John F. Kennedy watched the police dogs in action on television with the rest of the country and confessed that the brutality made him sick. [6]He later observed that "the civil rights movement should thank God for Bull Connor. [7]He's helped it as much as Abraham Lincoln." [8]As a result of the demonstrations, the president sent the head of the Justice Department's civil rights division to Birmingham to try to work out an arrangement between King's demonstrators and business leaders that would permit desegregation of lunch counters, drinking fountains, and bathrooms. [9]The president also made several calls to the business leaders himself, and they finally agreed to his terms. (Schaller et al., *Present Tense*, p. 235.)

The authors never explain why President Kennedy thought Bull Connor actually helped the civil rights movement. Instead, they ex-

pect you to infer that Connor helped the movement by *uniting various forces such as the federal Goverment business leader and civil right actovist against him and his beliefts.*

7. [1]On June 10, during a national address focusing on civil rights, Kennedy acknowledged that the nation faced a moral crisis. [2]He rejected the notion that the United States could be the land of the free "except for the Negroes." [3]Reversing his earlier reluctance to request civil rights legislation, he announced that he would send Congress a major civil rights bill. [4]The law would guarantee service to all Americans regardless of race in public accommodations—hotels, restaurants, theaters, retail stores, and similar establishments. [5]Moreover, it would grant the federal government greater authority to pursue lawsuits against segregation in public education and increase the Justice Department's powers to protect the voting rights of racial minorities. (Schaller et al., *Present Tense*, p. 236.)

The authors do not specifically define the moral crisis facing the nation. Instead they expect you to infer that *focusing on Civil rights* was the cause of a moral crisis in America.

8. [1]On Christmas Day, 1859, the ship HMS *Lightning* arrived at Melbourne, Australia, with about a dozen wild European rabbits bound for an estate in western Victoria. [2]Within three years, rabbits had started to spread, after a bushfire destroyed the fences enclosing one colony. [3]From a slow start at first, the spread of the rabbits picked up speed during the 1870s, and by 1900 the rabbit was the most serious agricultural pest ever known in Australia. [4]Rabbits eat grass, the same grass used by sheep and cattle, and so quickly the cry went up: "Get rid of the rabbit!" [5]The subsequent history of control attempts in Australia is a sad tale of ecological ignorance. [6]Millions of rabbits were poisoned and shot at great expense with absolutely no effect on their numbers. [7]Nowhere else has the introduction of an exotic species had such an enormous impact and spotlighted the folly of the introduction experiment. *Act in haste, and repent at leisure.* (Adapted from Krebs, *The Message of Ecology*, p. 8).

Although the author does not specifically say how the rabbits got off the estate, he expects you to infer that they _were poisoned and shot at great expense with absolutely no effect on their numbers_

9. Improving Your Memory

1   Do you, like just about everyone else, want to improve your memory? Well, the good news is that you can. All you have to do is put the following advice into practice, and you'll see immediate results.

2   For example, remembering when Christopher Columbus discovered America is easy enough if you use visualization. You could, for example, imagine Columbus standing on the beach with his ships in the harbor in the background. Fortunately, unrealistic images work just as well or better, and you could imagine Columbus's boat having the large numerals *1492* printed on its side, or Columbus reviewing his account books after the trip and seeing in dismay that the trip cost him $1,492. You could even envisage something still more fanciful: Since *1492* sounds like the words *for tea, nightie two*, you might imagine Columbus serving tea in his nightie to two Indians on the beach. A weird image like this is often easier to remember than a realistic one because its silliness makes it more distinct (Levin, 1985).

3   Visual imagery also works well for remembering single terms, such as unfamiliar words in a foreign language. The French word for snail, *l'escargot*, can be remembered easily if you form an image of what the word sounds like in English—"less cargo"—and picture an event related to this English equivalent, such as workmen dumping snails overboard to achieve "less cargo" on a boat. The biological term *mitosis* (which refers to cell division) sounds like the phrase *my toes itch*, so it is easier to remember if you picture a single cell dividing while scratching its imaginary toes.

4   Another device for memory improvement is called the method of loci, or locations. With this method, you purposely associate objects or terms with a highly familiar place or building. Suppose you have to remember the names of all of the instruments in a standard symphony orchestra. Using the method of loci, choose a familiar place, such as the neighborhood in which you live, and imagine leaving one of the instruments at the doorstep of each house or business in the neighborhood. To remember the instruments, simply take an imaginary walk through the neighborhood, mentally picking up each instrument as you come upon it.

5   Research on loci has found the method effective for remember-

ing a wide variety of information (Christen and Bjork, 1976). The same loci, or locations, can work repeatedly on many sets of terms or objects without one set interfering with another. After memorizing the musical instruments in the above example, you could still use your neighborhood to remember the names of exotic fruit, without fear of accidentally "seeing" a musical instrument by mistake. Loci can also help in recalling terms that are not physical objects, such as scientific concepts. Simply imagine the terms in some visual form, such as written on cards, or, better yet, visualize concrete objects that rhyme with each term and leave these around the mental neighborhood.

6   Imagery and visual loci work for two reasons (Pressley and McDaniel, 1988). First, they force you to organize new information, even if the organization is self-imposed. Second, they encourage you to elaborate mentally on new information. In "placing" musical instruments around the neighborhood, you have to think about what each instrument looks like and how it relates to the others in a symphony. These mental processes are essential for moving information into long-term memory. (Adapted from Kevin L. Seifert, *Educational Psychology*. Boston: Houghton Mifflin, 1991, pp. 199–201.)

What is the implied main idea of the entire reading? *How to improve memory, Simply imagine the term in Some visual form, Visualize concrete object that rhyme with each term and leave these around the mental neighborhood.*

10. **Remembrance of Things Past**

1   A whiff of perfume, the top of a baby's head, freshly cut grass, a locker room, the musty odor of a basement, the floury aroma of a bakery, the smell of mothballs in the attic, and the leathery scent of a new car—each may trigger what Diane Ackerman (1990) has called "aromatic memories." Frank Schab (1990) tested this theory in a series of experiments. In one, subjects were given a list of adjectives and instructed to write an antonym, or word opposite in meaning, for each adjective. In half of the sessions, the sweet smell of chocolate was blown into the room. The next day, subjects were asked to list as many of the antonyms as they could— again, in the presence or absence of the chocolate aroma. As it turned out, the most words were recalled when the smell of chocolate was present at both the learning and the recall sessions. The reason? The smell was stored in the memory right along with the words, so it later served as a retrieval cue.

2   The retrieval of memories is influenced by factors other than smell. In an unusual study, Duncan Godden and Alan Baddeley (1975) presented deep-sea divers with a list of words in one of two settings: fifteen feet underwater or on the beach. Then they tested the divers' recall in the same or another setting. Illustrating what is called *context-dependent memory*, the divers recalled 40 percent more words when the material was learned and retrieved in the same context. The practical implications are intriguing. For example, recall may be improved if material is retrieved in the same room in which it was initially learned (Smith, 1979).

3   Indeed, context seems to activate memory even in 3-month-old infants. In a series of studies, Carolyn Rovee-Collier and her colleagues (1992) trained infants to shake an overhead mobile equipped with colorful blocks and bells by kicking a leg that was attached to the mobile by a ribbon. The infants were later more likely to recall what they learned (in other words, to kick) when tested in the same crib and looking at the same visual cues than when there were differences. Apparently, it is possible to jog one's memory by reinstating the initial context of an experience. This explains why I will often march into my secretary's office for something, go blank, forget why I was there, return in defeat to my office, look around, and, ZAP!, suddenly recall what it was I needed.

4   Studies also reveal that it is often easier to recall something when our state of mind is the same at testing as it was while we were learning. If information is acquired when you are happy, sad, drunk, sober, calm, or aroused, that information is more likely to be retrieved under the same conditions (Bower, 1981; Eich, 1980; Eich et al., 1994). The one key complicating factor is that the mood we're in leads us to evoke memories that fit our current mood. When we are happy, the good times are most easy to recall; but when we feel depressed or anxious, our minds become flooded with negative events of the past (Blaney, 1986; Ucros, 1989). (Adapted from Kassin, *Psychology*, p. 231.)

What is the implied main idea of the entire reading? _It is possible to jog ones memory by reinstating the initial context of an experience. mood we're in leads us to evoke memories that fit our current mood._

C H A P T E R 5

Annotating Pages, Making Outlines, and Writing Summaries

 In this chapter, you'll learn

- how to annotate, or mark, the pages of textbooks.

- how to make an informal outline.

- how to use the Cornell system of note taking.

- how to write brief but complete summaries.

Chapter 5 introduces three different ways to condense and organize information in preparation for later review and study. For textbooks that don't contain a lot of new and unfamiliar information, *annotating*, or marking, pages may be all you need to do to prepare for exams. When it comes time to review, you'll just have to reread your marginal notes and marked passages.

Informal outlines are ideal for taking more detailed reading notes. They provide you with a blueprint of the author's ideas, one that reveals, even at a quick glance, the order in which those ideas were presented and their relationship to one another. *Summaries* condense, or reduce, whole articles to about one-quarter of their original length and are essential to doing research. After all, you can't possibly carry home every single reading you might use for a term paper, yet you need to know what articles might be useful in writing that paper.

After you complete Chapter 5, you'll understand three essential methods of organizing information for review, and you'll be surprised at how much easier it is to effectively prepare for exams and write term papers.

▰ Annotating Pages

Some students don't like to annotate, or mark, their textbooks because they hope to resell them. Unfortunately, those students are actually cheating themselves of the real profit that comes from writing in a text. As you underline important words in a passage, put asterisks next to key statements, or jot potential test questions in the margins of your textbook, you not only prepare those pages for later exam reviews, you also increase your chances of remembering what you read. When you underline words and make your marginal jottings, you're giving your mind a second chance to review and absorb the author's message. That extra review ensures remembering.

To illustrate what your annotated pages should look like when you finish reading, here's a passage that we looked at in Chapter 3. Look carefully at the underlined words. Notice, too, the comments and the potential test question (TQ) written in the margin. These marginal jottings model for you the kind of annotating you should be doing while you read, if you want to remember the author's ideas long after you've closed your textbook.

Illusion of the Perfect Mate

No such thing as perfect mate

1 The illusion that you have found the perfect partner—one who will be all things to you and vice versa—will carry you through courtship. But the reality is very different. You have not found the perfect mate—there isn't one. Anyone you marry will come with a minus quality, and the one quality that is lacking may become the only one you regard as important (Sammons, 1984).***

Results of Ann Landers's survey: 52% "no," 48% "yes"

2 Columnist Ann Landers (1977) asked her readers, "If you had it to do over again, would you marry the same person?" She received 50,000 responses. Fifty-two percent replied "no," and 48 percent said "yes." Marital happiness is hard to predict because the drug of the premarital period—love—alters your view of the partner; but this view is only an illusion.

TQ: Why is marital happiness hard to predict?

During courtship we hide undesirable aspects of personality.

3 Your illusion of the perfect mate is helped along by some deception on the part of your partner, who is showing you only his or her best side. At the same time, you are presenting only favorable aspects of yourself to the other person. Such deceptions are usually not deliberate but are an attempt to withhold undesirable aspects of one's self for fear that the partner may not like them.

Example of student who hides drinking until after marriage; once wife finds out, it's over.

4 For example, one male student said he knew he drank too much but that if his date found out, she would be disappointed and maybe drop him. He kept his drinking hidden throughout their courtship. They married and are now divorced. She said of him, "I never knew he drank whiskey until our honeymoon. He never drank like this before we were married." (Adapted from Knox, *Choices in Relationships*, pp. 230, 234.)

If you needed to review the above selection for an exam, you would just study the marginal jottings along with the underlined sentences. In doing so, you would be reviewing the essential elements of the selection.

Although annotating pages is an excellent way to aid remembering and to prepare for exams, a word of caution is in order. Your objective in marking a passage for review is to highlight content and relationships selectively while reducing the amount of text you need to reread. To meet this objective, you have to analyze and evaluate the material you're reading. Otherwise, you could end up with pages that are marked too heavily or too lightly. Here are some guidelines you can follow to help you annotate pages effectively.

1. **Underline selectively.** Instead of underlining every word in a sentence, underline only the words necessary to communicate the meaning. To select key words, imagine you are sending a telegram. What are the fewest words you need to make your meaning clear? Underline only those words.

2. **Underline and annotate after a second reading.** Unless you're reading fairly simple material, it's a good idea to underline and annotate during a second reading. The second time around, you're more likely to know what's important and what's not.

3. **Combine underlining with marginal jottings.** To sum up the essential elements of a passage, don't think you need to rely just on underlining or just on marginal annotations. Often a combination of the two works best. Look, for example, at paragraph 2 of the sample selection. To get the key points of the paragraph, you need to read the underlined portions along with the marginal notes.

4. **Develop your own code of symbols for annotating pages.** In addition to underlining, there are lots of other symbols you can use to annotate pages. You can, for example, use asterisks (***) to suggest importance, exclamation points (!!!) to indicate surprise, circles to highlight specialized vocabulary, and boxes to call attention to key words. Combined with underlining, such symbols give you a precise system that allows you to evaluate the author's message and note your own personal responses.

5. **Identify sources of confusion.** When you run across a difficult passage, don't get bogged down trying to decipher its meaning. If you're confused, mark the passage for a second reading, using a symbol like *RR* (reread). You might also try to pinpoint in the margins what it is that troubles you; for example, "What does the author mean when he says that our language limits what we can know or see?"

6. **Identify test questions.** In the margins, formulate the kinds of questions you think your instructor might ask on an exam; for example, "TQ: What did Ann Landers discover in her survey of married couples?"

7. **Record your personal responses.** Whenever you can, jot down your responses to the author's words. After reading that the per-

fect mate doesn't exist, you might disagree and mention in the margin that you think it's possible to find one. The more you relate what you read to your personal experience, the more likely you are to understand and remember the author's message.

The following chart identifies several symbols you can use to underline and annotate pages. Feel free, however, to make up your own symbols or to adapt the ones listed here to suit your particular needs. Whatever symbols you decide on, just be sure to use them consistently, so you know exactly what each one represents.

	Symbols for Underlining and Annotating Pages
═══ ═══ ═══	**Double underlining** to highlight the main idea of the entire reading
── ── ──	**Single underlining** to highlight main ideas in paragraphs
1, 2, 3, 4	**Numbers** to itemize and separate a series of supporting details
(1830)	**Circles** to highlight key points, specialized vocabulary, key terms, statistics, and dates
?	**Question marks** to indicate confusion
!	**Exclamation points** to indicate your surprise at the author's statements
～～～	**Squiggly lines** under words you need to look up in a dictionary
↘	**Arrows** to identify cause and effect relationships

‖	**Vertical lines** to emphasize passages longer than a sentence or two
***	**Asterisks** to identify a crucial piece of information
RR	Symbol to indicate passages in need of a second reading
RP	Symbol to identify ideas for research papers
TQ	Symbol to identify the possible source of a test question
See p. 27 or compare p. 27	**Cross-reference notes** to compare closely related statements in the text
Charles Darwin	**Boxes** to indicate names you need to remember

EXERCISE 1

DIRECTIONS Read each annotated passage. Then circle the letter of the passage that you think is most effectively annotated.

EXAMPLE

a. **Severe punishment** can be extremely effective in stopping behavior. If a child sticks a finger in a light socket and gets a shock, that may be the last time the child ever tries it. More often, however, milder forms of punishment only temporarily suppress a response, and if the response is rewarded in any way, the punishment may be particularly ineffective. Responses suppressed by **mild punishment** almost always reappear later. If a child sneaks a snack from the refrigerator before dinner and is punished for it, the child may pass up snacks for a short time. But since snack sneaking was also rewarded by the sneaked snack, the child will probably try sneaky snacking again, sometime later.

Severe punishment can be extremely effective in stopping behavior.

b. **Severe punishment** can be extremely effective in stopping behavior. If a child sticks a finger in a light socket and gets a shock, that may be the last time the child ever tries it. More often, however, milder forms of punishment only temporarily suppress a response, and if the response is rewarded in any way, the punishment may be particularly ineffective. Responses suppressed by **mild punishment** almost always reappear later. If a child sneaks a snack from the refrigerator before dinner and is punished for it, the child may pass up snacks for a short time. But since snack sneaking was also rewarded by the sneaked snack, the child will probably try sneaky snacking again, sometime later.

Although severe punishment can stop behavior, most milder forms only temporarily suppress it.

TQ: What type of punishment is more effective in stopping behavior?

This was true for me when I was a kid.

c. **Severe punishment** can be extremely effective in stopping behavior. If a child sticks a finger in a light socket and gets a shock, that may be the last time the child ever tries it. More often, however, milder forms of punishment only temporarily suppress a response, and if the response is rewarded in any way, the punishment may be particularly ineffective. Responses suppressed by **mild punishment** almost always reappear later. If a child sneaks a snack from the refrigerator before dinner and is punished for it, the child may pass up snacks for a short time. But since snack sneaking was also rewarded by the sneaked snack, the child will probably try sneaky snacking again, sometime later.

EXPLANATION Passage *a* is too heavily underlined. It's as if every word were important, and that is very seldom the case. Also, there are no marginal notes for this passage. Passage *b*, on the other hand, is too lightly underlined, and the marginal note doesn't paraphrase the main idea. Instead, it paraphrases and explains the introductory sentences. Passage *c*, however, is correctly annotated. The marginal notes sum up the main idea, identify a potential test question, and record a personal response. Now it's your turn to choose the selection that's been most effectively underlined and annotated.

1. a. The search for a cheap, quick, and long-lasting insecticide was completed in 1939, when a Swiss chemist, Paul Muller, confirmed the bug-killing properties of dichlorodiphenyltrichloroethane (DDT). Used on everything from the potato beetle to disease-bearing lice and fleas (as well as in World War II to fumigate troops' bedding and clothing), DDT was heralded as a huge success for twentieth-century agriculture. But within 20 years, many insects developed strains resistant to the poison. Meanwhile, it wreaked havoc on the food chain by killing off beneficial insects and predators. In the end, DDT was not a boon to the

potato beetle and lice

fumigate troops' bedding

human race. If anything, it proved a disaster, the proportions of which are still becoming known.

b. The search for a cheap, quick, and long-lasting insecticide was completed in 1939, when a Swiss chemist, Paul Muller, confirmed the bug-killing properties of dichlorodiphenyltrichloroethane (DDT). Used on everything from the potato beetle to disease-bearing lice and fleas (as well as in World War II to fumigate troops' bedding and clothing), DDT was heralded as a huge success for twentieth-century agriculture. But within 20 years, many insects developed strains resistant to the poison. Meanwhile, it wreaked havoc on the food chain by killing off beneficial insects and predators. In the end, DDT was not a boon to the human race. If anything, it proved a disaster, the proportions of which are still becoming known.

TQ: Who confirmed the bug-killing properties of DDT?

TQ: What were the negative side effects of DDT?

DDT proved to be a disaster.

c. The search for a cheap, quick, and long-lasting insecticide was completed in 1939, when a Swiss chemist, Paul Muller, confirmed the bug-killing properties of dichlorodiphenyltrichloroethane (DDT). Used on everything from the potato beetle to disease-bearing lice and fleas (as well as in World War II to fumigate troops' bedding and clothing), DDT was heralded as a huge success for twentieth-century agriculture. But within 20 years, many insects developed strains resistant to the poison. Meanwhile, it wreaked havoc on the food chain by killing off beneficial insects and predators. In the end, DDT was not a boon to the human race. If anything, it proved a disaster, the proportions of which are still becoming known.

Yes, evidence of cancer link

Informal Outlining

MONIQUE: I like to outline chapters that are very detailed. Outlining helps me understand how the information fits together.

FRANKLIN: Outline! You mean where every A has to have a B or it's all wrong? I could never outline a whole chapter. I'd rather not take notes than worry about which letter or number to use.

Like Franklin, many students are intimidated by outlining. They worry about whether to use capital or lowercase letters, Roman or Arabic numbers,† sentences or phrases. But, in fact, those questions apply only to the formal outlines some instructors assign as part of writing a paper or giving a speech.

---

†Roman numerals: I, II, III; Arabic numerals: 1, 2, 3.

Those questions do *not* apply to the kind of informal outlining suggested here. When you outline for purposes of review, your goal is to develop a clear and detailed blueprint of the author's ideas, one that shows *you* the order in which the ideas were presented and their relationship to one another. Exactly how you do this—with numbers, letters, or any other kind of symbol—is up to you.

If you want to create a useful outline, one that concisely and completely records the essential information of a chapter, stop worrying about proper outline format, about whether to use capital or lowercase letters, sentences or phrases. Instead, put into practice the following pointers for successful outlining.

1. **Start with the chapter title.** The chapter title usually identifies the topic being discussed. Sometimes the title even identifies the overall purpose or objective of the chapter. The title is an important element in your outline, one that ties together all the individual parts. To clarify the relationship between the chapter as a whole and its individual sections, be sure to put the title at the very top of the page. This position makes it clear that everything else in the outline explains some aspect of the topic or point referred to in the title.

2. **Indent to show relationships.** Under the title, list the main idea of each chapter section. Then indent and list any supporting details essential to explaining the main ideas.

Chapter Title

1. **Main Idea**
   a. **Supporting Detail**
   b. **Supporting Detail**
   c. **Supporting Detail**
      1. **Additional Detail**
      2. **Additional Detail**

2. **Main Idea**
   a. **Supporting Detail**
   b. **Supporting Detail**

3. **Main Idea**
   a. **Supporting Detail**
   b. **Supporting Detail**

As the above illustration indicates, an outline is not the same as a list. When you make an outline, you have to indent. Indentation is one of the main ways to indicate whether different ideas carry equal weight. Main ideas of chapter sections, for example, should all be aligned in the same position to indicate their relationship in the chapter.

3. **Be consistent about the symbols you use to show relationships.** Letters, numbers, and, for that matter, even dashes (—) or asterisks (**) can help you itemize key points from the chapter. Whichever symbols you use, be sure to use them consistently within the outline. Don't switch back and forth, sometimes using numbers for supporting details and sometimes using letters. In the long run, this kind of inconsistency will only confuse you.

4. **Be selective.** When you outline, try to reduce the original text as much as possible, retaining essential details and eliminating nonessential details. When adding supporting details to your outline, consciously decide what you need to include and what you can safely leave out. To give you a clearer picture of how you should apply these four pointers, here's an outline based on the Alfred Adler and Karen Horney readings in Chapter 3.

Chapter Title: Theories of Personality

1. Alfred Adler believed that superiority was the primary goal of the psyche, but his definition of superiority was quite complex.
   a. Adler thought of superiority as the desire to be competent, complete, and strong rather than the need to lord it over others.
   b. Sometimes superiority takes the form of lust for power.
   c. Thought of superiority as innate and part of struggle for survival.
      (1) How individuals undertake quest for superiority depends on culture, history, and lifestyle.
2. Karen Horney believed that the primary characteristic of American culture was hypercompetitiveness—an overwhelming desire to compete and win.
   a. Horney believed that this tendency was "a fertile ground for the development of neurosis."
   b. Side effects of hypercompetitiveness
      (1) View others as evil
      (2) In sexual relations, need to dominate
      (3) Have a neurotic need to prove superiority

As you can see, the outline mixes sentences and phrases. It also doesn't use any Roman numerals. Nevertheless, it's still an effective outline because it (1) highlights important points, (2) shows relationships, and (3) eliminates nonessential details.

■ EXERCISE 2

DIRECTIONS Here is an expanded version of a selection introduced in Chapter 3. After you reread it, fill in the blanks left in the outline. To get you started, the first two blanks have already been completed.

A New First Lady

1   In the nineteenth and early twentieth centuries, presidents' wives did not engage in political activity. Even if they were privately active, as in the case of President Warren G. Harding's wife, publicly they played the role of the dutiful wife whose opinions perfectly matched those of her husband.

2   With the election of Franklin D. Roosevelt to office in 1933, however, the image of the First Lady underwent a dramatic change. The first truly active First Lady, Eleanor Roosevelt embraced the idea of a caring government committed to helping the poor, minorities, and women, and she made no secret of her desire for social changes.

3   Throughout her husband's presidency, Eleanor Roosevelt did everything she could to make herself the voice of people in need. She crisscrossed the country meeting, listening to, and talking with coal miners, waitresses, farmers, housewives—a cross section of American society. Those who missed her personal visits could read her daily newspaper column, "My Day," or write to her. And thousands did write, generally describing their hardships and asking for help. It was not uncommon for her to receive as much personal mail as the president. Rarely able to provide any direct assistance, Eleanor Roosevelt's replies emphasized hope and explained changes being made by the New Deal. Within the White House, she was a constant goad to her husband and New Dealers not to neglect the poor, women, and minorities.

4   Eleanor Roosevelt took the lead in supporting women. She worked publicly and privately to reduce discrimination in the government and throughout the country. In 1933, she helped to convene a special White House conference on the needs of women, and with the help of other women in the administration, she labored to ensure that women received more than just token consideration from New Deal agencies and the Democratic party.

5   Eleanor Roosevelt did everything she could to promote the work of women journalists. For example, she held news conferences just for women reporters. And because women were banned from the National Press Club and its annual Gridiron feast, she helped to create the "Gridiron Widow's party," which recognized the important work of women journalists. With Eleanor Roosevelt as role model and supporter, the New Deal provided more opportunities for women in government and politics than had any program at any previous time in American history.

6   Eleanor Roosevelt was just as determined to affirm the equality and the significant contributions of African-Americans. Working with black educators and administrators like Mary Bethune of the National Youth Administration, she sought to generate new opportunities for blacks. In 1939, she graphically demonstrated her commitment to racial equality when the Daughters of the American Revolution refused to allow renowned black opera singer Marian Anderson to sing at their concert hall in Washington, D.C. In a highly visible protest, Eleanor Roosevelt resigned her membership in the DAR and helped arrange a larger, public concert on the steps of the Lincoln Memorial. Marian Anderson's performance before Lincoln's statue attracted more than 75,000 people. (Berkin et al., *Making America*, pp. 785–786.)

Title   A New First Lady

Main Idea   Eleanor Roosevelt was the first truly active First Lady; she was committed to helping the poor, minorities, and women.

Supporting Details

1. She constantly tried to make herself a voice for people in need.
   a. crisscrossed the country talking to miners, waitresses, and farmers
   b. *wrote a column called "My Day"* _____
   c. *received thousands of letters describing hardships* _____
   d. Her replies emphasized hope and explained New Deal changes.

2. _____

   _____

   a.   convened a special White House Conference on Needs of Women in 1933.

   b. _____

   _____

3. _____

_____

   a. held news conferences just for women journalists

   b. _____

_____

_____

4. _____

_____

   a. Working with Mary Bethune and others, she tried to provide opportunities for blacks.

   b. In 1939, showed her commitment to racial equality when Daughters of the American Revolution refused to let black opera singer Marian Anderson sing at their concert hall.

     (1) _____

_____

     (2) _____

_____

Exercise 3

DIRECTIONS Reread the following selection from Chapter 3. Then fill in the blanks in the accompanying outline.

Studying Leadership

1 At the University of Michigan, researchers have been studying leadership behavior. The studies of the Michigan researchers suggest that in the context of business management, leadership behavior falls into two categories: job-centered behavior and employee-centered behavior.

2   Leaders who practice job-centered behavior closely supervise their employees in an effort to monitor and control their performance. They are primarily concerned with getting a job done and

less concerned with the feelings or attitudes of their employees—unless those attitudes and feelings affect the task at hand. In general, they don't encourage employees to express their opinions on how best to accomplish a task.

3   In contrast, leaders who practice employee-centered behavior focus on reaching goals by building a sense of team spirit. An employee-centered leader is concerned with subordinates' job satisfaction and group cohesion. Employee-centered leaders are also willing to let employees have a voice in how they do their jobs.

4   The Michigan researchers felt that job-centered and employee-centered behaviors represent a single continuum, with one of the two basic behaviors at each end. That is, they believed that if leaders become more job centered, they simultaneously become less employee centered, and vice versa. They also felt that leaders who were employee centered would generally be more effective as managers than leaders who were primarily job centered. That is, their employees would perform at a higher level and also be more satisfied. (Adapted from Van Fleet, *Contemporary Management*, p. 332.)

Title Studying Leadership

Main Idea _____

_____

_____

Supporting Details   1. _____

_____

   a. _____

_____

   b. _____

2. _____

_____

   a. _____

_____

   b. _____

3. _____

_____

a. _____

_____

_____

b. _____

_____

Introducing the Cornell System

If you want to make your informal outline an even more powerful tool for exam reviews, you should use the Cornell system of note taking. Invented by Dr. Walter Pauk, a professor at Cornell University in Ithaca, New York, the Cornell system has been proven to be an effective format for taking and reviewing both lecture and reading notes.

To create the Cornell format, take an $8\frac{1}{2} \times 11$-inch piece of note paper and draw a vertical line down the left side of the page about two and a half inches from the edge. However, don't continue the line to the bottom of the page; instead, end it about two inches from the bottom. Then, where you ended the vertical line, draw a horizontal line all the way across the width of the page. The result should look something like this:

Format for the Cornell method

1. **Use the right column for your outline.** While you're reading, use the right-hand side of the page for your outline. Leave the left column blank.

2. **Use the left column for recall cues.** When you start to review for exams, start filling up the left-hand column with **recall cues.** Recall cues are individual words or phrases meant to jog your memory and help you to recall a cluster of ideas. For example, the words "superiority" and "hypercompetitiveness" would be perfect recall cues for the theories of Alfred Adler and Karen Horney.

   The more you review for exams, the less you should be looking at your actual notes. Instead, look at the recall notes and test yourself to see how well you remember the ideas these recall cues represent.

3. **Use the bottom section to summarize and synthesize.** As exam time comes closer and you feel more in control of the material, it's time to start filling in the bottom section of the page. This is the place to briefly sum up in a sentence or two the key concepts, theories, or studies that you think will be important for your exams. It's also the place to synthesize, or combine, different points of view. Here to illustrate are the notes from page 134. This time, they appear in the context of the Cornell system of note taking.

Recall cues	Chapter Title: Theories of Personality
Adler's theory of superiority	1. Alfred Adler believed that superiority was the primary goal of the psyche, but his definition of superiority was complex.
competent, complete, and strong	a. Adler thought of superiority as the desire to be competent, complete, and strong, rather than the need to lord it over others.
lust for power	b. Sometimes superiority takes the form of lust for power.
innate	c. Thought of superiority as innate and part of struggle for survival.
culture, history, and lifestyle	(1) How individuals undertake quest for superiority depends on culture, history, and lifestyle.

Summary: Alfred Adler was convinced that human beings were motivated by the quest for superiority, but, in his terms, superiority was not the desire to lord it over others. It was the desire to be competent, complete, and strong.

Recall Cues	
hypercompetitiveness	2. Karen Horney believed that the primary characteristic of American culture was hypercompetitiveness—an overwhelming desire to compete and win.
"fertile ground"	a. Horney believed that this tendency was "a fertile ground for neurosis."
side effects	b. Side effects of hypercompetitiveness
	(1) View others as evil
	(2) In sexual relations, need to dominate
	(3) Have a neurotic need to prove superiority

Synthesis: Both Horney and Adler see one particular characteristic as essential to understanding human behavior. They differ, however, as to what that characteristic is. For Adler, it is the quest for superiority—the desire to feel complete, strong, and whole. For Horney, it is hypercompetitiveness, at least in American culture. Hypercompetitiveness is the overwhelming desire to compete and win.

As the notes indicate, the bottom section of the page can be used to summarize *or* synthesize, depending at what stage you are in your understanding of the material.

Tested over time, the Cornell method of note taking guarantees a deeper understanding of the material you're studying, which is exactly what you want when you are preparing for exams.

EXERCISE 4

DIRECTIONS Turn to page 93 in Chapter 3 and reread the selection about America's water resources. Then take notes using the Cornell method. Write your notes on the right side of the page. Put recall cues in the left column. In the bottom section, briefly summarize the two environmental acts described in the reading.

Recall Cues	Protecting the Nation's Water Resources
	1.
	a.
	(1)
	(2)
	b.
	(1)
	(2)
	(3)
	(4)
	c.
	(1)

Summary:

Writing Summaries

In the preceding exercise, for the Cornell system of note taking, you wrote one or two sentences summarizing key information in the reading on water pollution. However, as a college student, it's quite likely that you'll need to write longer summaries. For example, when you do research, you'll need to summarize articles that might be useful for your term papers. In short, the ability to write good summaries is an extremely valuable skill for college students to possess.

Summaries are less detailed than outlines, and they reduce a reading to about one-third or one-quarter of its original length. This severe reduction in length is accomplished by including the main idea of the entire reading and *only* the most crucial supporting details.

Brief as they are, the writing of summaries can't be rushed. To determine which statements are essential to an author's meaning, you need to thoroughly understand the material. Usually that means reading it at least twice, asking yourself as you read, "What's the main idea here?" and "What supporting details are most crucial to explaining or proving it?" Prior to writing your summary, annotate the passage and cross out anything you think you won't need—anecdotes, repetitions, extra or extended examples, minor facts and figures. However, make your deletions in pencil just in case you change your mind later and decide you want to include a particular detail you had originally crossed out.

Once you've thoroughly digested the material you plan to condense, the actual summary writing is not particularly difficult. Just keep these four pointers in mind:

1. **Make your first paragraph count.** The first paragraph of your summary should paraphrase the main idea of the entire reading and include any significant background information.

2. **Make distinctions between the essential and the absolutely essential.** When creating an outline, you need to distinguish among essential details. For example, if an author explains a main idea with three separate examples, all of the examples might be crucial to an outline written in preparation for an exam. But if you're writing a summary, you should decide which of those examples *best* illustrates the author's point. That's the one to include in your summary. Leave out the other two.

3. **Check connections between sentences.** Writing summaries requires you to combine information from different parts of the

original text. As a result, the original connections between sentences can get lost without new connections being created. For that reason, it's important to read your summary aloud and check to hear how your sentences flow together. If they don't flow easily and you can't figure out why one sentence follows another, you may need to add some transitions in order to clarify the connections between sentences. Transitions are verbal bridges that help readers move easily from one thought to another. For a list of the most common transitions, see the following chart:

Common Transitional Signals

Transitions indicating an addition to the original train of thought:

also, in addition, further, furthermore, lastly, moreover, first, second, secondly, too

Transitions indicating that the author is changing, challenging, or contradicting the original train of thought:

although, after all, but, by contrast, however, nevertheless, on the contrary, yet, still, despite that fact

Transitions signaling that the author is pointing out similarities:

similarly, likewise, by the same token, in the same vein

Transitions that introduce examples and illustrations:

for example, for instance, specifically, in other words, that is

Transitions that introduce the effects of some cause:

as a result, consequently, thus, therefore, hence, in response

Transitions that help readers follow a sequence in time:

in the meantime, next, soon, after a while, in time, of late, thereafter, afterwards, finally

Transitions that repeat a point already made:

in short, in brief, in conclusion, in other words, on the whole, in summary, to reiterate, to sum up

---

For more on transitions, see Chapter 6.

4. **Revise, if necessary.** If the summary you're writing is to be handed in for an assignment, then you probably should prepare another draft in order to double check your word choice, grammar, and punctuation.

If you are turning in your summary, also make sure that you add the author and title of the selection. Sometimes instructors want that information in a heading or a footnote, but often you'll be expected to weave it into the opening sentence, so it's a good idea to ask for specific directions.

Here is a selection that illustrates how to prepare a passage for summarizing. Note how all essential information has been highlighted and all nonessential information has been deleted.

Power

Power: capacity of people to control or influence others' actions

Sociologists use the term *power* to refer to the capacity of people or groups to control or influence the actions of others, whether those others wish to cooperate or not. Sociologists study power to determine not only who exercises it, but also why it is exercised and who benefits from its use. Of the three main types of desirables—wealth, power, and prestige—power is the hardest to measure.

Most studies of power are nothing more than an average of guesses about where power is found. Many forms of power are so well hidden that only the power-holders know their source. Because it is so hard to measure, the subject of power—who holds it and how it is used—is a source of much debate in sociology.

2 theories of who holds power

C. Wright Mills example of theory 1

Some sociologists maintain that power in America is concentrated in the hands of a few people who have a common background and who tend to act together (Domhoff, 1983, 1978). C. Wright Mills (1956) suggested that America is run by a "power elite" and sets its total number at no more than 300 people. Other sociologists believe that power in America is divided among many groups and people (Rose, 1967; Riesman, 1961).

Sociologists do agree that real power may not always lie where we think it does. The mayors of some cities, for example, are sometimes mere figureheads* who simply look impressive. The actual decisions are made by a handful of business leaders who stay behind the scenes. And some decisions are made at the lowest level, where the work is really carried out. Such is the case with the police officer on the beat or the teacher in the classroom.

---

*figureheads: people in positions of leadership who have no real authority.

(John Poponoe, *Sociology*. Englewood Cliffs, N.J.: Prentice Hall, 1989, p. 218.)

Now read the summary based on the selection:

> Power—the capacity of people or groups to control the actions of others—is hard to measure and is therefore a source of debate among sociologists. Some sociologists, like C. Wright Mills, believe that power is concentrated in the hands of only a few who share a common background and act together. Other sociologists believe that power is divided among many different groups and people. On one point, however, there is agreement: Power is not always where we think it is.

As you can see, this summary deletes many portions of the original text. Gone, for example, is most of the introduction; the only piece left is the author's definition of power. Eliminated, too, are the examples from the last paragraph, used to illustrate the point that real power may not always lie where we think it does. The examples can be safely deleted because it's easy enough to come up with illustrations of this point.

■ **DIGGING** Who do you think holds power in America? Which one of the theories
DEEPER outlined on page 148 makes the most sense to you, and why?

◄ EXERCISE 5

DIRECTIONS After reading the following selection, look over each of the three summaries. Circle the letter of the one that most effectively meets the guidelines on pages 146–147 for summary writing.

1. Erich Fromm's Theory of Human Nature

The psychologist Erich Fromm was born in Frankfurt, Germany, in 1900, the only child of a deeply orthodox* Jewish family. At the age of thirteen, Fromm began to study the Talmud,† beginning an interest in religious literature and an admiration of the German mystic* "Meister" Eckhart (1260?–1327?) that remained throughout his life. In his later years, Fromm did not formally practice religion, but he referred to himself as an "atheistic mystic," and it is clear that Fromm's early religious experiences left a distinct mark on his personality and work. The moral and committed tone of his

---
*orthodox: following to the letter the tenets of a particular faith or religion.
†Talmud: collection of ancient Jewish writings on which Jewish law is based.
*mystic: a person who enters a trancelike state in order to become more spiritual.

writings has a quality that has been described as reminiscent of the Old Testament prophets. He was deeply interested in religion, and both his earlier and later writings reflect this concern.

Erich Fromm began with the thesis (1941) that *freedom* is a basic human condition that poses a "psychological problem." As the human race has gained more freedom by transcending* nature and other animals, people have become increasingly characterized by feelings of separation and isolation. Thus, a major theme of Fromm's writings is the concept of loneliness. To be human is to be isolated and lonely, because one is distinct from nature and others, and it is loneliness, according to Fromm, that radically separates human nature from animal nature. Unlike other animals, we know we are going to die, and this knowledge leads to feelings of despair.

Fromm believed that human beings have two ways to respond to the problem of freedom. They can work with one another in a spirit of love to create a society that will optimally fulfill their needs, or they can "escape from the burden" of freedom into "new dependencies and submission" by giving themselves over to a strong leader. From Fromm's perspective, relying on a leader helps the individual escape feelings of isolation, but it does not creatively meet the needs of humanity or lead to optimum* personality development.

a. **Erich Fromm's Theory of Human Nature**

Born in Frankfurt, Germany, Erich Fromm was the only child of a deeply religious Jewish family. At the age of thirteen, Fromm began to study the Talmud and developed an interest in religious literature. He was particularly taken with the writings of German mystic Meister Eckhart. Although Fromm did not formally practice any established religion, he referred to himself as an "atheistic mystic."

Fromm believed that a sense of freedom is part of the human condition and the source of a profound psychological problem. As human beings have gained more freedom by overcoming their animal nature, they have become increasingly isolated and lonely. The feeling of loneliness finds its fullest expression in the problem of death because we, unlike the animals, know that we're going to die and that knowledge leads to despair.

In response to the problem of loneliness, Fromm believed that human beings could work together in a spirit of love to create a

---

*transcending: overcoming.
*optimum: most favorable.

society that would fulfill their needs or escape into "new dependencies and submission" by giving themselves over to the control of a powerful leader who would dominate their lives. Although this response might eliminate loneliness, it stifles personality development.

b. **Erich Fromm's Theory of Human Nature**

According to Erich Fromm, the condition of freedom is an essential part of being human, yet it causes intense psychological distress. The more we separate ourselves from the world of nature and identify ourselves as free beings, the more likely we are to experience feelings of loneliness and separation. These feelings of loneliness and separation are most powerfully expressed in our despair at the thought of death.

From Fromm's perspective, human beings could resolve this problem in two ways: (1) They could work together in a spirit of love and create a society that met their needs, or (2) they could escape from freedom by giving themselves over to the control of a powerful leader. Fromm cautioned, however, that the second alternative would stunt personality development.

c. **Erich Fromm's Theory of Human Nature**

Erich Fromm began with the thesis that freedom is a basic condition of human nature. To be human is to be isolated and therefore in despair. Unlike the animals, we know that we are going to die.

■ **DIGGING DEEPER** In 1941, Fromm wrote about the threat of giving ourselves over to a powerful leader as a way of escaping loneliness. What historical events do you think might have influenced his thinking?

 EXERCISE 6

DIRECTIONS In Exercise 7, you'll be asked to write a summary of the following selection. In preparation, read this selection twice. The second time you read it, mark the selection to highlight important information and cross out any material you think is not absolutely essential.

Interpreting Your Dreams

To unlock dreams, Sigmund Freud identified four dream processes that he believed disguise the hidden meanings of dream images. The first is called **condensation.** Through condensation, a single character in a dream may represent several people at once. A character in a dream that looks like a teacher, acts like your father, talks like your mother, and is dressed like your employer might be a condensation of the authority figures in your life.

A second way of disguising dream content is **displacement.** Displacement may cause the most important emotions or actions of a dream to be redirected toward safe or seemingly unimportant targets. Thus, a student angry at his parents might dream of accidentally wrecking their car instead of directly attacking them.

A third dream process is **symbolization.** Freud believed that dreams are often expressed in images that are symbolic rather than literal* in their meanings. To uncover the meaning of dreams, it helps to ask what feelings or ideas a dream image might symbolize. Let's say, for example, that a student dreams of coming to class naked. A literal interpretation would be that the student is an exhibitionist!* A more likely symbolic meaning might be that the student feels vulnerable in the class or is unprepared for a test.

A process called **secondary elaboration** is the fourth method by which the meaning of dreams is disguised. Secondary elaboration is the tendency to make a dream more logical, and to add details when remembering it. (Coon, *Essentials of Psychology,* p. 256.)

EXERCISE 7

DIRECTIONS Write a summary of the selection in Exercise 6, "Interpreting Your Dreams."

Dream — identified four dream
process, and hiden images, frist their
Condensation which comes in different
figures, second is displacement an
emotion, or action be redirected to

---

*literal: realistic, factual.
*exhibitionist: somebody who likes to show off and draw attention to him- or herself.

Unimportant target. third process is
symbolization are expressed in images
rather than being realistic.
fourth is secondary elaboration is
the method by which dream is
disquised, it is also more logical
and add details when remembering it.

◢ Summing Up

Listed below are the most important points in Chapter 5. Put a check
mark in the box if you think the point is clear in your mind. Leave
the box blank if you think you need to review the material one more
time. The page numbers in parentheses tell you where to look to
review each point in the list.

☐ **1.** *Annotating*, or marking, textbook pages is an excellent method
of organizing information for review. It's most effective if you're
reading a textbook that doesn't contain a lot of unfamiliar and
highly detailed information. To annotate effectively, you need to
underline selectively and develop your own code of symbols. (pp.
126–130)

☐ **2.** When you *outline* for purposes of review, your goal is to develop
a clear and detailed blueprint of an author's ideas, one that
shows you the order in which they were presented and their relationship to one another. (pp. 132–135)

☐ **3.** The *Cornell system of note taking* has proven itself to be an effective format for taking and reviewing notes. To use the Cornell
system, you need to divide each page of your notebook into two
columns with space left at the bottom. Each section is used for
a different purpose. (pp. 139–144)

☐ **4.** *Summaries* are less detailed than outlines. They reduce a reading
to about one-third or one-quarter of its original length. This severe reduction in length is accomplished by including the main
idea and *only* the most crucial supporting details. (pp. 146–149)

Working with Words

Here are some of the words defined in Chapter 5. Use the following exercises to gain practice with these words and to learn more about their history and meaning.

EXERCISE 8

DIRECTIONS Use the following words to fill in the blanks. *Note:* You will have to use some of the words twice, and you may have to make a plural word singular or vice versa.

figureheads: people in positions of leadership who have no real authority

orthodox: following to the letter the tenets of a particular faith or religion

mystic: a person who enters a trancelike state in order to become more spiritual

transcending: overcoming

optimum: most favorable

literal: factual, realistic

exhibitionist: a person who behaves in a shocking manner in order to draw attention to him- or herself

1. A(n) ___orthodox___ Jew strictly observes the laws of the Talmud.

2. Many conservationists worry that by ___transcending___ nature, we have lost our sense of connection to the earth and we will, in time, suffer for that loss.

3. She was a(n) ___exhibitionist___ who had a penchant for wearing bizarre clothing that made her the object of everyone's attention.

4. Everyone knows that Queen Elizabeth and Prince Philip of England are ___figureheads___ who possess no real power.

5. That plant will produce a flower only under ___optimum___ conditions.

6. Her _literal_ interpretation of the poem completely distorted its meaning.

7. As a psychologist, Carl Jung had a touch of the _Mystic_ about him; unlike Freud, he believed that the spirit was more important than the body.

8. At some point, you have to go beyond the _factual_ level and start to figure out what the words suggest as well as mean.

9. The pandas' new habitat provided the _optimum_ conditions for mating, and the zookeepers were hoping the rare animals would multiply.

10. Committed as she was to helping others, Eleanor Roosevelt was still more of a _figureheads_ than a power in her own right.

EXERCISE 9

DIRECTIONS To complete the following sentences, use a hardbound dictionary.

1. The plural form of _optimum_ is _optima_ or _optimums?_

2. The word _literal_ comes from the Latin word _littera_, meaning _letter_.

3. When it's used in the context of computer science, the word _literal_ means _a word or symbol that represents a particular constant rather than a variable._

4. If a sailor uses the word _figurehead_, he's not referring to a person; rather, he's talking about _Carved figure on the Prow of a ship._

Tuesday text 156 –

◢▰ Chapter 5: Review Test

1. Read the following selection. Then fill in the blanks in the accompanying outline.

Managing Conflict

Conflict is a natural part of life. It can have negative or positive results, depending on how people respond to it. What many people don't realize, however, is that there are several different strategies they can use to manage a conflict

Negotiation

Negotiation is the art of bargaining to reach an agreement. Negotiation requires that each person know what the other party wants or needs. The ultimate goal of negotiation is to find a compromise that will, to some degree at least, satisfy both sides.

Avoidance

As the term *avoidance* suggests, some people react to conflict by refusing to acknowledge it. If the situation is of short-term or minor importance, this tactic can work. However, as a consistent strategy, avoidance is likely to cause more problems than it solves.

Accommodation

A person who resolves conflict through accommodation puts the other person's needs ahead of his or her own. In effect, the person deals with conflict by giving in. Accommodation is a useful strategy if the other person's needs really are more important. Unfortunately, accommodators tend to follow the same pattern no matter what the situation. They simply refuse to stand up for their rights.

Smoothing Over

The goal of smoothing over is to give the impression that conflict has been resolved even if it hasn't. Occasionally, smoothing over can be effective. If, for example, the relationship involved is more important than the situation that needs to be resolved, smoothing over may be the right strategy. But like accommodation and avoidance, smoothing over can cause problems when it's overused.

Integration

Integration is a lot like negotiation. The main difference is that integrators, unlike negotiators, believe that both sides can participate in a win-win solution. From the integrator's point of view, both parties can end up feeling that their needs have been met. This sense of mutual success is based on the realization that the relationship between the parties is the most important element of the entire situation. Not surprisingly, integration is the most time consuming of all of the conflict-management strategies.

Main Idea _life entails a number of Conflict which can be resolved in several way_

Supporting Details

1. _negotiation involves bargaining to reach an agreement_

   a. *Each person has to know what the other one wants or needs.*

   b. _The ultimate goal is to reach a satisfactory Compromise._

2. *People who engage in avoidance simply refuse to acknowledge conflict.*

   a. _if the situation is of short-term or minor importance, it may work._

   b. _as a consistent strategy, avoidance is likely to be unsuccessful._

3. _a person who resolves Conflict through accommodation put the other persons needs ahead of his or her own._

a. *Accommodation is a useful strategy if the other person's needs really are more important.*

b. accommodators tend to follow the same pattern no matter what the situation.

4. Smoothing over can be effective.

a. *If the relationship is more important than the situation, smoothing over can work.*

b. but like accommodation and avoidance, smoothing over can cause

Problems when overused.

5. Integration and Negotiation are similar

a. from the integrator's point of view both parties can end up feeling that their need been met.

b. Integration is the most time consuming of all the conflict-management strategies.

2. Read, annotate, and then summarize the following selection.

Term Limits

One illustration of Americans' antagonism toward legislators is the movement toward **term limits.** Fifteen states have passed laws that place a limit on the number of years legislators can serve in office. Those laws are aimed at both state legislatures and Congress. The length of term limits varies from state to state, but typically members of a state house of representatives can serve eight years, and a member of a state senate can serve eight to twelve years.

Despite overwhelming support from voters, term limits for members of Congress may never take effect. The Supreme Court has yet to make a final ruling, but a lower federal court has determined that it is unconstitutional for a state to place term limits on members of Congress. The legal reasoning is simple: The Constitution specifically sets qualifications for representatives and senators. (A representative must be at least twenty-five years old and a citizen for at least seven years; a senator must be at least thirty years old and a citizen for nine years. Both must be residents of the state in which they are elected.) Accordingly, if a state sets a term limit for members of Congress, it is in effect amending the Constitution on its own by adding qualifications. The Supreme Court has, however, ruled term limits on state legislators to be constitutional. (Adapted from Janda et al., *The Challenge of Democracy*, p. 366.)

Several State

■ **DIGGING DEEPER** Do you support term limits? Why or why not?

■ **WRITING SUGGESTION** Write a paragraph that synthesizes and summarizes the theories of Adler, Horney, and Fromm. To get started, look over the synthesis statement on page 143 of this chapter. It sythesizes only the theories of Horney and Adler, but you can expand it to include that of Fromm. Use the expanded synthesis statement as your topic sentence. For your supporting details, summarize each theory in a sentence or two.

C H A P T E R 6

Recognizing Five Common Patterns of Organization

 In this chapter, you'll learn

- **how to identify five of the most common patterns, or methods, authors use to organize supporting details.**

- **how to use those patterns to determine which details are essential and which are not.**

- **how to respond to a reading that combines, or mixes, two or more patterns.**

To effectively annotate, outline, or summarize a reading, you have to decide which information is truly essential to explaining the main idea. Fortunately, you can make that task easier if you are able to recognize the pattern or patterns of organization an author has used in his or her writing. This chapter introduces five of the most common organizational patterns: sequence of dates and events, sequence of steps, comparison and contrast, cause and effect, and, finally, classification. It also shows you how recognizing each of these patterns can help you decide what's important in a paragraph or reading.

 ## Patterns of Organization

Pattern 1: Sequence of Dates and Events

Authors who write about history and government frequently use a **sequence of dates and events** to explain or argue their claims. They present, that is, a series of dates and events listed according to the order in which they occurred. Here's an example of that pattern in a paragraph:

> After Thomas Jefferson graduated from college, his career advanced quickly and steadily. Jefferson graduated from the College of William and Mary in 1762 and was admitted to the bar in 1767. He became a member of the Second Continental Congress in 1775 and was chairman of the committee that wrote the Declaration of Independence. From 1785 to 1789, he was the U.S. minister to France, and, from 1790 to 1793, he served as the U.S. secretary of state. Jefferson served as vice president from 1797 to 1801; and on March 4, 1801, he was inaugurated as the third president of the United States.

In the first sentence, the author makes the claim that "[Jefferson's] career advanced quickly and steadily." Aware that the phrase "quickly and steadily" can have different meanings for different people, the author provides a sequence of dates and events in order to illustrate and clarify that claim.

As you would expect, the dates and events pattern can easily be used to organize readings longer than a paragraph. Here, for example, is a reading from Chapter 3. Note how the supporting details rely on dates and events to explain the author's main idea.

The Trail of Tears

Throughout the nineteenth century, the Cherokees proved themselves to be highly inventive and enterprising. They also showed a willingness to adapt and excel at whatever they learned from white settlers. Unfortunately, their success did not save them from being evicted from their tribal lands.

In 1820, the tribe established a system of government modeled on that of the United States. It elected a principal chief, a senate, and a house of representatives.

In 1821, Sequoya, a Cherokee warrior who had been crippled in a hunting accident, produced a workable alphabet of Cherokee characters. The Cherokees studied the alphabet enthusiastically, and within months thousands could read and write the new alphabet. By 1828, the Cherokees were producing their own weekly newspaper, and the readership of the paper was growing faster than the papers could be produced.

Unfortunately, in the same year, the Georgia legislature outlawed the Cherokee government. Gold had been discovered on tribal lands almost ten years before, and greedy land speculators were determined to take control of those lands, even if it meant illegally evicting the Cherokee people. In 1832, the U.S. Supreme Court ruled in favor of the Cherokees' right to their lands. But that decision was ignored by federal authorities, and, in 1838, federal troops drove about 20,000 Cherokees west on a forced march for three hundred miles. During the march so many Cherokees died from hunger, disease, and exposure that the route they followed came to be called the "Trail of Tears."

Once you recognize that a paragraph or an entire reading is organized according to the dates and events pattern, you also know that all or most of the dates and events in the reading are essential details. Although the final test of any supporting detail is the question, "Do I need this detail to understand or explain the main idea?" the sequence of dates and events pattern strongly suggests that each event marked by a date is essential to explaining the main idea.

Although the presence of several dates and events organized in a sequence is a surefire clue to the dates and events pattern, you should also look for the following transitions. They, too, are clues to this pattern.

◄ Transitions That Mark Dates and Events ►

After

From _____ to _____

In _____

Then

Finally

Before

In the years

During the years

In the years that followed

In the following years

Previously

A year later

Between the years _____ and _____

Following

At that point

■ **EXERCISE 1**

DIRECTIONS Read the following selections. Paraphrase the main idea of each one. Then identify the event or events connected with each date. *Note:* One date can mark two events.

1. **The Conquest of Peru**
The conquest of Mexico in 1519 by Hernando Cortez and a small band of Spanish explorers produced huge quantities of gold and silver, more than Europe had ever seen. Inspired by dreams of similar wealth and glory, the Spanish explorer Francisco Pizarro decided to conquer the Incan empire of Peru. Pizarro fulfilled his dreams but at a tragic cost to the Incan people.

In 1529, Charles I, king of Spain, granted Pizarro the right to conquer and rule Peru, allowing him to raise a small Spanish military force. In 1531, Pizarro set sail for Peru, with a force of about 180 men.

Upon arrival in 1532, Pizarro's small band was able to land unopposed because the Incas assumed that the fair-skinned Spaniards were returning Incan deities.* In less than a year, Pizarro quickly took control of the Incan empire and imprisoned Atahualpa, the Incan emperor. Atahualpa tried to renegotiate his freedom by offering the Spaniards a roomful of gold, but, in 1533, while the gold was being collected, Pizarro had Atahualpa strangled to death. By 1537, the Incan empire was engulfed in civil war, and, by 1538, the empire lay in ruins.

Main Idea _the spanish explorer Francisco Pizarro decided to conquer incan empire of Peru._

Dates and Events 1529: _Charles I, gave Prizarro the right to conquer and rule Peru_

1531: _Pizarro set sail for peru_

1532: _In less than a year Pizarro quickly took control of the incan empire and imprisoned Atahualpa, Atahuapa renegotiate his freedom by offering the Spani_

1533: _Pizarro had atahualpa strangled to death._

1537: _incan empire was engulfed in civil war._

1538: _the empire lay in ruins._

2. The Scandal Called Watergate

The name of a hotel, "Watergate" has also come to designate a major political scandal that forced the resignation of then U.S. president Richard Nixon.

---

*deities: gods.

The scandal that was to rock the nation began on June 17, 1972, when five men were caught trying to burglarize the offices of the Democratic National Committee. The arrest of the five men led to an investigation that uncovered a White House plan of espionage against political opponents. Deeply involved in that plan were two top White House aides, John Erlichman and H. R. Haldeman.

On April 30, 1973, Richard Nixon accepted the resignations of Haldeman and Erlichman. At the same time, Attorney General Elliot Richardson appointed a special prosecutor, Harvard Law School professor Archibald Cox, to conduct a full-scale investigation of the Watergate break-in.

On May 20, 1973, the Senate Committee on Presidential Activities opened hearings, and on July 16, 1973, White House aide Alexander Butterfield exploded a bombshell. He told the committee that Nixon had taped all the conversations that went on in his office.

Nixon refused to turn the tapes over to the investigating committee, and on October 20, 1973, he ordered the dismissal of prosecutor Cox. After a storm of public protest, Nixon agreed in June of 1974 to turn over the tapes. After members of the committee had examined the tapes closely, they discovered that eighteen-and-one-half minutes had been mysteriously erased. Once again, there was a public outcry.

By July 20, 1974, the House Judiciary Committee had approved three actions of impeachment. Rather than face almost certain disgrace, Richard Milhous Nixon resigned as president in August of 1974.

Main Idea _____

_____

_____

Dates and Events June 17, 1972: _____

_____

April 30, 1973: _____

_____

May 20, 1973: _____

_____

July 16, 1973: _____

_____

October 20, 1973: _____

June 1974: _____

_____

July 20, 1974: _____

_____

August 1974: _____

Pattern 2: Sequence of Steps

Particularly in the sciences, writers often need to tell their readers how something works, functions, or develops. When that is their purpose, authors are likely to describe a sequence of steps.

When a sequence of steps organizes a paragraph, the supporting details trace the individual steps or stages that make up some larger process or activity. Here, for example, the author describes the individual steps that go into taking a picture:

> A simple box camera is made up of four essential parts: shutter, lens, box, and film. When a picture is "taken," the shutter opens and allows the light to enter. The lens, a circular piece of glass with a curved face, focuses the light and allows it to pass through the box. The light-sensitive film at the back of the box then receives and records the image.

In longer readings, writers who use the sequence of steps pattern give more attention to each step. Sometimes, they devote an entire paragraph to one step, or stage. The second paragraph in the following selection is a good illustration.

Laboring to Give Birth

During the process of labor, the uterus contracts rhythmically and automatically to force the baby downward through the vaginal canal. The contractions occur in a relatively predictable sequence of stages.

The **first stage of labor** usually begins with relatively mild and irregular contractions of the uterus. As contractions become stronger and more regular, the cervix (the opening of the uterus) widens, or dilates, enough for the baby's head to fit through. Toward the end of this stage, which may take from eight to twenty-four hours for a first-time mother, a period of **transition** begins. The cervix nears full dilation, contractions become more rapid, and the baby's head begins to move into the birth canal. Although this period generally lasts for only a few minutes, it can be extremely painful because of the increasing pressure of the contractions.

The **second stage of labor** is from complete dilation of the cervix to birth. It usually lasts between one and one-and-one-half hours. During the **third stage of labor,** which lasts only a few minutes, the afterbirth (the placenta and umbilical cord) is expelled. (Adapted from Seifert and Hoffnung, *Childhood and Adolescent Development,* pp. 131–132.)

Note that the discussion of the first stage of labor occupies an entire paragraph. This is not unusual for readings in which the author has the space to explore each step or stage in detail.

To get the most out of a paragraph or reading organized around a sequence of steps, make sure you can (1) identify the longer process being described and (2) explain each individual step in the correct order.

Words like *steps, stages, phases,* and *process* are all clues to the sequence of steps pattern, but so too are transitions like the ones listed below.

■ Transitions That Identify a Sequence of Steps ■	
First, second, third	Toward the end
Finally	By the time
Then	At this point
Next	In this stage
Afterwards	In the final stage

■ EXERCISE 2

DIRECTIONS The following selections use a sequence of steps pattern. Read each selection and then answer the questions following each selection.

1. Stages of Sleep

The changes that come with sleep can be measured with an **electroencephalograph** (e-LEK-tro-en-SEF-uh-lo-graf), or brain-wave machine, commonly called an **EEG.** The brain gives off tiny electrical signals that can be amplified and recorded. With the help of an EEG, researchers have identified four different sleep stages:

Stage 1 As you lose consciousness and enter **light sleep,** your heart rate slows down. Breathing becomes irregular; the muscles of your body relax. This sometimes triggers a reflex muscle contraction called a **hypnic jerk** (HIP-nik), which is normal. In stage 1 sleep, the EEG is made up mainly of small, irregular waves. Persons awakened at this time may or may not be aware that they were asleep.

Stage 2 As sleep deepens, the EEG begins to show short bursts of activity called **sleep spindles,** and body temperature drops. Sleep spindles seem to mark the true boundary of sleep. Within four minutes after spindles appear, the majority of persons who are awakened recognize that they had been asleep (Bonnet and Moore, 1982).

Stage 3 In stage 3, new brain waves called **delta waves** begin to appear. Delta waves are very large and slow. Delta waves signal deeper sleep and a further loss of consciousness.

Stage 4 In stage 4, the brain-wave pattern becomes almost pure delta waves, and the sleeper is in a state of oblivion.* If you sound a loud noise during stage 4, the sleeper will awaken in confusion and may not remember the noise. (Adapted from Coon, *Essentials of Psychology,* pp. 144–145.)

a. What process does the author describe? _Stages of Sleep, and their are four Stages_

b. What is the main idea? _With EEg researchess have indentified 4 stages of sleep_

c. Describe each stage of sleep.

   Stage 1: _light Sleep_

---

*oblivion: unconsciousness.

*your body relax and heart
rate slow.*

Stage 2: *Sleep spinder, with in four
minute your sleep deepen*

Stage 3: *delta wave, signal sleep*

Stage 4: *detla pattern - if by a loud
noise during stage, the deeper will
awaken in confusion and may not
remembering the noise.*

*half
heart*

2. Developing a New Product

Developing a new product is both time-consuming and expensive. Before a new product is introduced, it goes through seven different phases of product development.

Idea Generation   Idea generation involves looking for product ideas that will help a firm achieve its objectives. Although some organizations get their ideas largely by chance, firms trying to maximize product effectiveness usually develop systematic approaches for generating new-product ideas. Ideas may come from marketing managers, researchers, engineers, competitors, advertising agencies, management consultants, private research organizations, or customers.

Screening   During screening, ideas that do not match organizational resources and objectives are rejected. At this stage, firms must ask whether they have the expertise to develop and market a product. Management may reject a good idea because the company lacks the necessary skills and abilities. The largest number of product ideas are rejected during the screening phase.

Concept Testing   During concept testing, a small sample of potential buyers is presented with a product idea, through either a written or an oral description. The purpose at this stage is to determine the buyers' attitudes and initial buying intentions regarding the product. Concept testing is a low-cost means for an organization to determine consumers' initial reactions to a product idea prior to investing considerable resources in product research and development (R&D).

Business Analysis Business analysis provides a tentative outline of a product's position in the marketplace, including its probable profitability. During this stage, the firm considers how the new product, if it were introduced, would affect the firm's sales, costs, and profits. Marketing personnel usually work up preliminary sales and cost projections at this point, with the help of R&D and production managers.

Product Development In the product-development phase, the company must find out first if it is technically feasible to produce the product and then if the product can be made at costs low enough to justify a reasonable price. If a product idea makes it to this point, it is transformed into a working model, or *prototype.*

Test Marketing Test marketing is the limited introduction of a product in several towns or cities chosen to represent the intended market. Its aim is to determine buyers' probable reactions. The product is left in the test markets long enough to give buyers a chance to repurchase the product if they are so inclined.

Commercialization During commercialization, plans for full-scale manufacturing and marketing must be refined and completed, and budgets for the project must be prepared. In the early part of the commercialization phase, marketing management analyzes the results of test marketing to find out what changes in the marketing mix are needed before the product is introduced. (Adapted from Pride, Hughes, and Kapoor, *Business.* Boston: Houghton Mifflin, 1993, pp. 368–369.)

a. What process does the author describe? _How to_ _develope a new product._

b. What is the main idea? _____

_____

c. Describe each stage of product development.

Stage 1: _Idea Generation, idea that_ _____

will help a firm to achieve its objective.

Stage 2: Screening - Firm must ask whether they have the expertise to develope and market a product regarding the product.

Stage 3: Concept testing - to determine the buyers attitudes and initial buying intention

Stage 4: Business Analysis,

Stage 5: Product Development

Stage 6: Test marketing

Stage 7: Commercialization

Pattern 3: Comparison and Contrast

Writers use the comparison and contrast pattern to highlight the similarities and differences between two topics. In paragraphs that use this pattern, supporting details may identify similarities (*compare*) or point out differences (*contrast*). In some paragraphs, they may do both.

In the following paragraph, the author wants to tell readers how much the Great Plains changed between the nineteenth and twentieth centuries. To make that main idea clear and convincing, the supporting details concentrate on differences in the Great Plains before and after 1900.

Topic Sentence   Between the nineteenth and twentieth centuries, the huge area in America known as the Great Plains underwent startling changes. At the beginning of the nineteenth century, there were few settlements, and one could walk for miles without seeing a house. By the end of the century, settlements were springing up all over, and more and more men and women were seeking their fortunes in the section that had been known as the "Great American Desert." In 1800, the plains were covered by herds of buffalo. These huge, dumb animals were the natural cattle of the plains, and the Native Americans living on the plains hunted them because their flesh could be eaten and their hides made into clothing. By 1900, the buffalo were fast disappearing, and the tribes—among them Apache, Sioux, and Navajo—who had roamed freely over the plains in pursuit of the buffalo, had been forced to live on reservations.

To illustrate the "startling changes" mentioned in the topic sentence, the author of the above paragraph describes differences in the Great Plains between the beginning and the end of the nineteenth century.

The only significant difference between paragraphs that use the comparison and contrast pattern and longer readings that use the pattern is the degree of development. In longer readings, authors have more time to describe similarities and differences in greater detail. Authors are also more likely to describe both similarities *and* differences. The following selection is a good illustration of that point. Although the authors open by describing some similarities between boys and girls, they go on to describe some definite differences.

Gender Differences

 During the first two years, boys and girls generally do not differ in competence and only sometimes in performance. It appears that what babies can do under good conditions has relatively little to do with their gender, at least during the first year or so of infancy. Boys and girls sit upright at about the same age and stand and walk at about the same time. All the major milestones,* in fact, develop at about the same rate.

How infants use their time, however, is another matter. Almost as soon as they can move, boys show more activity. Even before birth, late in pregnancy, they move about in their mothers' wombs more than girls do. The trend continues after birth: One-year-old boys engage in more gross motor activity than one-year-old girls do (Teitelbaum, 1976). Boys move around more, using whatever locomotor skills they have developed thus far, whereas girls spend more time quietly using fine motor skills to investigate the contents of the kitchen wastebasket, for instance. Presumably

---

*milestones: important events.

these gender differences stem at least partly from different encouragement by parents and perhaps also from the children's own desires to model "correct" sex-role behavior. But given the very young age of the children, some of the differences may be genetically based.

By age two—and onward throughout early childhood—boys and girls tend to show different motor abilities, even in optimal, testlike situations. In general, girls excel more often at fine motor skills; for example, they can usually build a tower of blocks sooner, taller, and with fewer mistakes than boys can . . . (Ames et al., 1979). Girls also excel more often at skills involving balance and rhythm, such as the dancing sometimes done in nursery school classrooms. Boys excel more often wherever speed or strength is required: They usually run faster outdoors and pound the play dough harder at nursery school. (Seifert and Hoffnung, *Childhood and Adolescent Development,* pp. 173–174.)

Based on the title of this excerpt, experienced readers would know immediately that they needed a clear understanding of the differences between boys and girls. The major portion of the reading does, after all, focus on difference. But experienced readers would also realize that the similarities between the two groups cannot be ignored. Those similarities and differences described in the supporting details suggest the implied main idea: In infancy, boys and girls are very similar except for how they use their time.

Topic sentences or thesis statements like "Spartan society was very different from the society of Athens" or "In the old West, there wasn't all that much difference between cowboys and cowgirls" are strong indications of the comparison and contrast pattern of development. In addition, the presence of transitions like those listed below is also a signal to look out for similarities and differences.

Transitions That Signal Comparison or Similarity	
Similarly	In the same manner
Likewise	In like manner
In much the same vein	Along the same lines
By the same token	Just like

Transitions That Signal Contrast or Difference

However	Nevertheless	In reality
But	Unfortunately	On the contrary
And yet	Whereas	In opposition
On the one hand	In contrast	Conversely
On the other hand	Nonetheless	
Still	Despite that fact	

■   **WRITING**   Write a paper explaining how you are similar to or different from
SUGGESTION   some member of your family.

EXERCISE 3

DIRECTIONS   Read the following selections and answer the accompanying questions.

1. Convergent and Divergent Thinking

One way in which schoolchildren differ is in their use of convergent and divergent thinking. **Convergent thinking** refers to focused, deductive* reasoning that leads to a particular solution to a problem. Solving an arithmetic problem requires convergent thinking; so does working a jigsaw puzzle. A lot of school learning requires convergent thinking because there is often just one right answer, which students are supposed to figure out. The prevalence of convergent thinking in school, in fact, may partly explain why nearly all children can use this style of thinking at least some of the time. Over the years, they simply receive a lot of training in it.

But some children seem especially disposed to using convergent thinking widely. Such children seek out and prefer structured learning tasks, such as those offered by books of puzzles or by complex building toys. They may even engage in structured activities at the expense of freer, more open-minded recreation, such as hanging around with friends.

Divergent thinking refers to the production of a wide variety of ideas, regardless of how unusual or disconnected they may be.

---

*deductive: using general laws or principles to understand particular cases.

It closely resembles the notion of "creativity" but lacks any emphasis on quality. Divergent thinking simply diverges, and in doing so it can end up as either bizarre or uniquely valuable. Divergent thinkers tend to produce ideas fluently and elaborately, and they tend to form associations among ideas relatively flexibly. Most of us use this style of thinking from time to time; it is illustrated by our answers to open-ended questions such as, "How many uses can you think of for a brick?" (Guilford, 1967).

Some children seem predisposed to think divergently. And they do not necessarily use their divergent thinking only in situations that explicitly encourage it. Throughout childhood and youth, some children produce ideas fluently even on timed tests of creativity, in spite of the stress that such tests can create. For them, divergent thinking is just as likely in situations that are untimed, relaxed, and fun (Borland, 1988; Runco and Okuda, 1988). (Adapted from Seifert and Hoffnung, *Childhood and Adolescent Development*, pp. 429–430.)

a. What two topics are discussed in this selection?

_____ *Convergent thinking* _____

_____ *Divergent thinking* _____

b. What, if any, similarities do the authors mention?

_____ *None* _____

_____

c. What, if any, differences do the authors mention?

_____

_____

d. The authors use the comparison and contrast pattern to explain what main idea?

_____

_____

2. Are There Differences Between the Sexes?

When asked whether man or woman was more intelligent, the famous English writer Samuel Johnson gave an appropriate reply: "Which man? Which woman?" Keeping in mind that there is much commonality in the attributes of males and females, let's take a brief look at recent findings about sex differences.

On the average, boys are taller, heavier, and more physically active than girls, and the size of this difference increases from infancy through adolescence (Eaton and Enns, 1986). Boys' greater activity level is most evident when they are playing informally rather than in structured classroom settings.

There are also sex differences in several physical skills (Smoll and Schutz, 1990). In general, males are better than females at catching, they can throw a ball faster and farther, and they have greater gripping strength. In athletic performance, small sex differences begin to emerge in childhood and increase substantially when boys reach puberty. As Janet Hyde (1990) notes, however, athletic performance is greatly affected by training and diet. In the world Olympic Games, today's top women swimmers surpass the record-breaking speeds set by men in the 1950s. Although men have also improved their swimming speed, the gender gap has narrowed over time. Physiologist Brian Whipp of UCLA reports that world-class women marathon runners are increasing their speed at rates twice as fast as men (cited in Dye, 1992). If this trend continues, top women marathon runners could be on a par with men by 1998.

Around the world, males tend to be more aggressive than females in both childhood and adulthood. Boys are more likely than girls to fight, to taunt and insult others, and to fantasize about aggressive themes (Perry, Perry, and Weiss, 1989). Most murderers are men, as are most people who physically abuse their spouse. Opinion polls show that men tend to have more favorable attitudes toward violence than women do in a wide range of spheres: Men are more likely to favor capital punishment, to endorse military intervention in international disputes, and to oppose gun control (Smith, 1984). Men show greater interest in aggressive sports like boxing and football. (Rubin et al., *Psychology,* pp. 292–293.)

a. What two topics are discussed in this selection?

_____

b. What, if any, similarities do the authors mention?

_____

_____

_____

c. What, if any, differences do the authors mention?

_____

_____

_____

d. The authors use the comparison and contrast pattern to explain what main idea?

_____

_____

▪ **DIGGING DEEPER**   Reread the quotation from Samuel Johnson on page 175. What point was Johnson trying to make?

▪ **WRITING SUGGESTION**   Write a paper in which you use the comparison and contrast pattern to describe your transition from child to adult. What are the similarities between who you are now and who you used to be? What are the differences?

Pattern 4: Cause and Effect

At one time or another, all writers use a cause and effect method of paragraph development. They describe how one event or series of events (the cause or causes) led to another event or series of events (the effect or effects). For example, in the following paragraph, the author explains how two events helped cause America to abandon its position of neutrality during World War I.

Topic Sentence   For three years prior to America's entry into World War I, Americans had wavered in their desire to give up their neutral position; but the Germans' resumption* of submarine warfare and the Zimmerman telegram helped change neutrality into hostility, and America went to war. In the two months that preceded President Wilson's war message, eight vessels had been sunk by German submarines, and forty-eight American lives were lost. The hostility created by the sinking of the vessels was further increased when it was revealed that German Foreign Secretary Alfred Zimmerman

_____

*resumption: the act of beginning or starting again.

had proposed in a message to the Mexican government that Mexico should join with Germany if a German-American war broke out.

As is typical for most paragraphs using the cause and effect pattern, the topic sentence outlines the cause and effect relationship in general terms. It tells you that two causes—the resumption of submarine warfare and the Zimmerman telegram—led to one effect—America's entry into the war. The supporting details then describe those two causes in greater depth.

As a reader responding to this paragraph, you need to have a clear grasp of the cause and effect relationship stated or implied in the paragraph. However, you also have to know if the paragraph focuses more on causes or on effects. Once you recognize the author's emphasis, be sure that you can clearly describe those causes or effects with some specificity. For example, you could not claim to understand the above paragraph unless you could answer the question raised by the topic sentence and answered in the supporting details: What was the Zimmerman telegram?

In longer readings using the cause and effect pattern, the thesis statement may or may not introduce the cause and effect relationship under discussion. Sometimes writers use the thesis statement to comment on a particular event. Then the supporting details describe its causes or effects, or both.

This is certainly true of the following selection, in which the thesis statement introduces the Salem witchcraft trials and tells us how cataclysmic, or devastating, they were. Then the supporting details describe the effects of the trials and one possible cause.

The Witchcraft Trials of Salem

 Like their contemporaries elsewhere, seventeenth-century New Englanders believed in the existence of witches. If people could not find rational explanations for their troubles, they tended to suspect they were bewitched. Before 1689, 103 New Englanders, most of them middle-aged women, had been accused of practicing witchcraft. Although most such accusations occurred singly, on occasion a witchcraft panic resulted when one charge set off a chain reaction **Thesis Statement** of similar charges. However, nothing else in New England's history ever came close to matching the Salem village cataclysm.

The crisis began in early 1692, when a group of adolescent girls accused some older women of having bewitched them. Before **Effects** the hysteria spent itself ten months later, nineteen people (including several men, most of them related to accused female witches)

had been hanged, one person pressed to death by heavy stones, and more than a hundred people jailed.

Possible Cause Historians have proposed various explanations for this puzzling episode, but one possible cause of the witchcraft accusations and resulting trials was the economic problems rife* in New England at the time. No residents of Salem village could have had sharper feelings of economic insecurity than the young and relatively poor girls who issued the initial accusations. As the most powerless people in a town that was apparently powerless to affect its fate, the girls offered their fellow New Englanders a compelling explanation for the seemingly endless chain of troubles afflicting them: Their village was under direct attack from the devil and his legion* of witches. (Adapted from Norton et al., *A People and a Nation*, pp. 46–47.)

Although longer readings using the cause and effect pattern may, like paragraphs, concentrate on causes *or* effects, they are quite likely to discuss both, and you need to respond accordingly. If an author describes causes *and* effects, make sure you pay attention to the specific details of both.

▪ Transitions That Describe Cause and Effect Relationships ▪

Consequently	Therefore
As a result	Thus
In response	In the aftermath
In reaction	Hence

▪ Verbs That Connect Cause and Effect ▪

Produces	Engenders
Brings about	Creates
Generates	Sets off
Initiates	Leads to
Causes	Results in
Fosters	Stimulates

---

*rife: occurring widely.
*legion: large number, multitude.

EXERCISE 4

DIRECTIONS Read the following selection and answer the accompanying questions.

1. Alzheimer's Disease

Alzheimer's (ALLS-hi-merz) disease is one of the most fearsome and devastating problems of aging. The senility it causes afflicts about 5 to 10 percent of all people over age 65, or about 2 million Americans at present.

Alzheimer's victims at first have difficulty remembering recent events. Then they slowly become more disoriented,* suspicious, and confused. In time, they lose the ability to work, cook, drive, or use tools. As their condition worsens, victims can no longer read, write, and calculate. Eventually, they are mute, bedridden, and unable to walk, sit up, or smile (Roach, 1985).

Researchers are urgently seeking the causes of Alzheimer's disease. It is now known that highly selective damage to nerve cells in the brain is probably to blame. Especially important is the presence of unusual webs and tangles in nerve cells leading to and from the hippocampus—an area of the brain important for learning and memory (Hayman et al., 1984). (Coon, *Essentials of Psychology*, p. 511.)

a. In your own words, what is the main idea of the selection?

How Alzheimer's Disease affect
the life of older people ita
devastating problems

b. Circle the number of the correct statement.

1. The author focuses on causes.

2. The author focuses on effects.

(3.) The author focuses on causes and effects.

c. List any effect or effects described in the reading.

difficulty remembering recent event
unable to work, disoriented
mute, bedridden or even smile

---

*disoriented: confused about time and place.

d. List any cause or causes described in the reading.

Nerve cell damage in the brain
Unusual web and tangles in nerve cell leading
to and from hippocampus - an area of the Brain
for learning and memory.

2. Breaking the Bad Habit of Poor Posture

At the risk of sounding like your mother, I am going to tell you to "stop slouching and stand (sit) up straight." Not that poor posture will cause some dread disease or turn you into a laughingstock. But perpetually allowing your body to stand or sit in misaligned positions can exact an unpleasant toll on your physical well-being and possibly your social stature.

Body language says a lot to the world about your self-image. A person who stands up straight conveys a message of self-confidence and competence, while someone who stands with slouched shoulders and a sagging gut appears depressed and self-conscious. Poor posture can make you look older and fatter than you are.

Poor posture can also set you up for all kinds of chronic or recurring aches and pains, especially neck and back pain, and it can drain your energy and increase fatigue. Slouching creates up to fifteen times as much pressure on your lower back as standing up straight does. When you slump, your diaphragm collapses, there is less room for your lungs to expand, and the resulting shallow breathing means there is less oxygen available to nourish your body.

In children, posture problems, which tend to become more noticeable during adolescence, may be caused by a congenital* or developmental abnormality. The child may have a spinal deformity that warrants medical attention and correction. The child's doctor may recommend a consultation with a specialist in pediatric orthopedics.†

But experts in physical therapy say that in most cases bad posture in adults is a bad habit, and, like any habit, it can be broken and replaced with another: good posture.

Contributing Causes

Although some people slouch because they have a poor self-image, more often inadequate muscle strength in the upper body

---

*congenital: existing at birth.
†pediatric orthopedics: a special branch of medicine dealing with the skeletal system of children.

and weak stomach muscles play major roles. A person may be a runner or biker with incredibly strong legs and hips, but, unless another activity is pursued that strengthens the upper body, muscles there may be surprisingly weak.

For some, the physical demands of their jobs—the need to sit in one place hour after hour, having to carry heavy loads or bend over often—put strain on the body and prompt them to slouch in a misguided effort to relieve the stress.

Being overweight can also take a toll on your posture by adding to the demands on your skeletal structure and increasing fatigue when you stand or walk. Pregnant women who fail to maintain good muscle tone, especially in their backs and the upper body, are more likely to acquire the postural distortion and severe back strain that can accompany their expanding abdomens. And women who walk around in very high heels much of the time can end up with abnormally arched backs, distorted to keep them from falling over. (Jane E. Brody, "Breaking the Bad Habit of Poor Posture," *New York Times*, April 21, 1993, p. C-12.)

a. In your own words, what is the main idea of the selection?

_____

_____

b. Circle the number of the correct statement.
   1. The author focuses on causes.
   2. The author focuses on effects.
   3. The author focuses on causes and effects.

c. List any effect or effects described in the reading.

_____

_____

_____

d. List any cause or causes described in the reading.

_____

_____

_____

Pattern 5: Classification

If you read business, science, or sociology texts, you are bound to encounter the classification pattern. Writers in all three subject areas frequently need to show how some larger group can be divided or broken down into smaller subgroups or categories, each with its own set of characteristics.

The following paragraph illustrates the classification pattern. Notice how the topic sentence identifies the larger group to be classified, whereas the supporting details name and describe each category.

Topic Sentence   The air that surrounds the earth can be divided into four main layers. The layer closest to the earth, the troposphere, is characterized by turbulence* and cloud formations. The layer above the troposphere is called the stratosphere, and it extends for fifty miles above the earth. Above the stratosphere is the layer called the ionosphere, which is dominated by short-wave radiation of the sun. Since 1901, scientists have been aware that radio signals coming from the earth are reflected by the ionosphere. The layer that extends to the very limits of our atmosphere is called the exosphere and is composed mostly of hydrogen atoms.

As is typical for the classification pattern, the topic sentence identifies the larger group that is being divided into subgroups or categories. It also announces the number of categories to be described—four. Then the supporting details take over and more specifically describe the four subgroups, identifying the characteristics of each one.

Easy to recognize, this pattern is also relatively easy to understand. Simply be sure you know these three elements: (1) the larger group being subdivided, (2) the number of categories created, and (3) the names (if they appear) and characteristics of each group.

Longer readings organized around the classification pattern are similar to paragraphs that describe a system of classification. However, the longer the reading, the more likely it is that the author will expand the pattern to (1) mention some similarities or differences between the groups and (2) end with a comment that applies equally to all of the categories described. The following selection illustrates both of these additions.

---

*turbulence: unrest or disturbance.

Types of Power

Thesis Statement <u>Most people agree that there are five basic types of power: legitimate, reward, coercive, expert, and referent power.</u>

First Category **Legitimate power** is power created and conveyed by the organization. It is the same as authority. A boss can generally tell subordinates how they should be doing their jobs, how they should allocate* their time at work, and so forth. Orders and requests from someone with legitimate power may be carried out by subordinates but only to the minimum extent needed to satisfy the boss.

Second Category A second type of power is **reward power**—the power to grant and withhold various kinds of rewards. Typical rewards in organizations include pay increases, promotions, praise, recognition, and interesting job assignments. The greater the number of rewards a manager controls and the more important they are to subordinates, the more reward power the manager has.

Third Category **Coercive power** is the power to force compliance* through psychological, emotional, or physical threats. In some settings, such as the military and prisons, coercion may take the form of physical force. In most settings today, though, coercion is practiced more subtly, through verbal reprimands, disciplinary layoffs, *Similarity* fines, demotions, the loss of privileges, and excessive public criti- *Between Two* cism. As with reward power, the more punitive* elements a man- *Identified* ager can bring to bear and the more important they are to subor- *Categories* dinates, the more coercive power he or she has. However, the use of coercion also tends to increase hostility and resentment.

Fourth Category **Expert power** is power based on knowledge and expertise. A manager who knows the best way to deal with a difficult customer or a secretary who knows the ins and outs of the organization's bureaucracy has expert power. The more important the knowledge is and the fewer people who are aware of it, the more expert power the person has.

Fifth Category The fifth type of power is **referent power.** It is referent power that generally sets leaders apart from nonleaders. This type of power is based on imitation and charisma.* If a child dresses and talks like his favorite rock singer, the rock singer has referent power over the child. If an ambitious middle manager starts to emulate a successful top manager (dressing like her, going to the same restaurants for lunch, playing the same sports, and so on), the top manager has referent power. . . .

---

*allocate: distribute.
*compliance: obedience.
*punitive: punishing.
*charisma: personal magnetism or charm.

Comment Applying
to All Categories
Of course, most leaders use several different bases of power at the same time. For example, no matter how effective an individual is as a leader, she will sometimes find it necessary to rely on legitimate power. Indeed, many managers who lack leadership characteristics are still somewhat effective by using legitimate and reward power together. Likewise, leaders are often successful by combining expert and referent power. (Van Fleet and Peterson, *Contemporary Management,* pp. 328–329.)

Responding to a longer reading that uses classification is really no different from responding to a paragraph based on that pattern. You still need a clear understanding of three essential elements: (1) the larger topic being classified, (2) the number of categories created, and (3) the names and characteristics used to describe each category.

If the author spends a good deal of time comparing and contrasting the different categories, then you should look carefully at any points of similarity or difference. However, in the case of the preceding example, the reference to a similarity between *coercive* and *reward* power is too brief to be considered important.

However, the final paragraph of the selection contains a piece of significant information. It tells us that the different kinds of power usually are used in combination rather than in isolation. With longer readings that describe a system of classification, read the final paragraph carefully. It frequently contains information relevant to an understanding of all the categories mentioned in the classification.

■ Exercise 5

DIRECTIONS Read the following selections and answer the accompanying questions.

1. ### Contemporary Functions of Dating

Since most people regard dating or "getting together" as a natural part of getting to know someone else, the functions of dating are sometimes overlooked. Actually, there are at least five functions—confirmation of a social self, recreation, companionship, socialization, and mate selection.

Confirmation of a Social Self
One of the ways we come to be who we are is through interaction with others who hold up social mirrors in which we see ourselves and get feedback on how we are doing. When you are on a first

date with a person, you are continually trying to assess how that person sees you. (Does he or she like me? Will he or she want to be with me again?) When the person gives you positive feedback through speech and gesture, you feel good about yourself and tend to view yourself in positive terms.

Recreation

Dating, hanging around, or getting together is fun. These are things we do with our peers, away from our parents, and we select the specific activities because we enjoy them. "I get tired of studying and being a student all day," a straight-A major in journalism said. "Going out at night with my friends to meet guys really clears my head. It's an exciting contrast to the drudgery of writing term papers."

Companionship

A major motivation for dating is companionship. The impersonal environment of a large university makes a secure dating relationship very appealing. "My last two years have been the happiest ever," remarked a senior in interior design. "But it's because of the involvement with my fiancé. During my freshman and sophomore years I felt alone. Now I feel loved, needed, and secure with my partner." . . .

Socialization

Dating offers the experience of learning how to initiate conversation and the opportunity to develop an array of skills in human relationships such as listening and expressing empathy. It also permits an individual to try out different role patterns like dominance or submission and to assess the "feel" and comfort level of each. . . .

Mate Selection

Finally, dating may serve to pair off two people for marriage. For those who want to get married, dating is a process of finding a person who has a similar agenda and the desired characteristics.

Which dating function is important will vary from person to person and for a particular person over time. "I've gone full circle," said one banking employee. "Dating used to be for fun that led to companionship and marriage. But I'm recently divorced and am not interested in marriage. I'm dating just for the fun again with no goal whatsoever of getting involved with anyone." (Knox, *Choices in Relationships*, pp. 160–162.)

a. What larger topic is divided into smaller subgroups or categories?

<u>Contemporary functions of dating</u>

b. How many categories are listed? <u>5</u>

c. Name and describe each category.

① <u>Confirmation of social self</u>: How someone else see you. (2) recreation: Select the specific activities because we enjoy them 3 <u>Companionship</u>: major motivation for dating. 4 <u>Socialization</u>: develop an array of skills in human relationships. mate Selection: for those who want to get married.

d. Does the author at any point compare or contrast some of the categories? <u>yes.</u>

e. Circle the number of the correct statement.

1. The last paragraph introduces a new category.

②. The last paragraph makes a comment that applies to all of the categories.

2. Marketing Surveys

Companies trying to predict future sales frequently use surveys or questionnaires. Valuable marketing tools, surveys can be divided into three different categories.

Through a **customer forecasting survey,** marketers can ask customers what types and quantities of products they intend to buy during a specific period. This approach may be useful to a business that has relatively few customers. For example, a computer chip producer that markets to less than a hundred computer manufacturers could conduct a customer survey. PepsiCo, though, has millions of customers and cannot feasibly use a customer survey to forecast future sales.

In a **sales-force forecasting survey,** members of the firm's sales force are asked to estimate the anticipated sales in their territories for a specified period of time. These territorial estimates are then combined to arrive at a tentative forecast. A company may survey the sales staff for several reasons. The most important reason is that the sales staff is closer to customers on a daily basis than other company personnel; therefore, the sales staff should know more about customers' future product needs. Moreover, when sales representatives assist in developing the forecast, they are likely to work toward its achievement.

When a company wants an **expert forecasting survey,** it hires experts to help prepare the sales forecast. Drawing on their experience and their analyses of available information about the company and the market, the experts prepare and present their forecasts or answer questions regarding a forecast. Using experts is expedient* and relatively inexpensive. However, because they work outside the firm, experts may not be as motivated as company personnel to do an effective job. (Adapted from Pride and Ferrell, *Marketing.* Boston: Houghton Mifflin, 1993, pp. 132–133.)

a. What larger topic is divided into smaller subgroups or categories?

   Marketing Survey

b. How many categories are listed? ___3___

c. Name and describe each category.

   Customer forecasting servey ?

   _____

   _____

   _____

   _____

   _____

d. Do the authors at any point compare or contrast some of the categories? *yes*

e. Circle the number of the correct statement.

   1. The last paragraph introduces a new category.

   2. The last paragraph makes a comment that applies to all of the categories.

---

*expedient: practical, appropriate for a particular purpose.

■ **WRITING SUGGESTION** Write a paper in which you divide some larger group—friends, teachers, shoppers, wives or husbands, for example—into smaller categories, each with its own set of characteristics. If you can, give each subgroup a name, e.g., casual shoppers, obsessed shoppers, and holiday shoppers.

 ## Mixing Patterns

Although you will encounter readings that rely on one pattern or another, be prepared for those readings that combine, or mix, patterns. Overall, authors are more inclined to mix patterns than to keep them separate. Look, for example, at the following selection. Which two patterns do you think it combines?

Imagery and Stress

Thesis Statement

Imagery can be used to fight stress. Just as small doses of disease organisms injected into our bodies can inoculate, or protect, us against certain diseases, small doses of stressful situations introduced into our mental imagery can inoculate us against specific stressful situations (Meichenbaum, 1985).

If you want to use imagery to reduce stress, start by constructing mental pictures around a potentially threatening situation, and be sure to include in your imagery the event you most fear in that situation. For example, if you are apprehensive about a speech you have to make, you might imagine yourself having a complete mental block in the course of that speech. Then let yourself feel the anxiety, embarrassment, and physical responses (e.g., sweaty palms, heart palpitations, and shortness of breath) that would accompany such a mental block.

The final and key step in stress inoculation is to think through exactly what you might do if the worst happened in a situation. For example, in the case of a mental block during a speech, you might look down at your notes and start reading them aloud until your thinking has cleared. Imagining a solution for your anxiety will ultimately make you feel more confident and help you relax. (Adapted from Williams and Long, *Manage Your Life*, p. 204.)

This reading begins by describing a cause and effect relationship: Imagining potentially stressful situations in small doses can have the effect of reducing stress. The reading then outlines a sequence of steps or actions one can take to gain confidence and reduce stress. In this case, both patterns are necessary in order to clarify the thesis statement.

Particularly in longer readings, authors are likely to mix, or combine, paragraphs, and you should be alert to that possibility. You also need to respond to mixed patterns by identifying the key elements of each one.

■ EXERCISE 6

DIRECTIONS Read the following selection and identify the two patterns that are combined in the reading.

The Civil Rights Act of 1964

 In 1961, a new administration headed by President John F. Kennedy came to power. At first, Kennedy did not seem to be committed to civil rights. His stance changed as the movement gained momentum and as more and more whites became aware of the abuse being heaped on sit-in demonstrators, freedom riders (who tested unlawful segregation on interstate bus routes), and those who were trying to help blacks register to vote in southern states. Volunteers were being jailed, beaten, and killed for advocating activities that whites took for granted.

In late 1962, President Kennedy ordered federal troops to ensure the safety of James Meredith, the first black to attend the University of Mississippi. In early 1963, Kennedy enforced the desegregation of the University of Alabama. In April 1963, television viewers were shocked to see marchers in Birmingham, Alabama, attacked with dogs, fire hoses, and cattle prods. (The idea of the Birmingham march was to provoke confrontations with white officials in an effort to compel the national government to intervene on behalf of blacks.) Finally, in June 1963, Kennedy asked Congress for legislation that would outlaw segregation in public accommodations.

Two months later, Martin Luther King, Jr., joined in a march on Washington, D.C. The organizers named their activity "A March for Jobs and Freedom," signaling the economic goals of black America. More than 250,000 people, black and white, gathered peaceably at the Lincoln Memorial to hear King speak. "I have a dream," he told them, "that my little children will one day live in a nation where they will not be judged by the color of their skin but by the content of their character." Congress had not yet enacted Kennedy's public accommodations bill when he was assassinated on November 22, 1963. His successor, Lyndon B.

Johnson, considered civil rights his top legislative priority. Within months, Congress enacted the Civil Rights Act of 1964, which included a vital provision barring segregation in most public accommodations. Congressional action was, in part, a reaction to Kennedy's death. But it was also almost certainly a response to the brutal treatment of blacks throughout the South. (Janda et al., *The Challenge of Democracy*, pp. 565–567.)

a. sequence of dates and events
b. sequence of steps
c. comparison and contrast
d. cause and effect
e. classification

⊁⃞ Summing Up

Listed below are the most important points in Chapter 6. Put a check mark in the box if you think the point is clear in your mind. Leave the box blank if you need to review the material one more time. The page numbers in parentheses tell you where to look in order to review each point on the list.

☐ **1.** If you're taking a course in history or government, you're bound to encounter some readings that rely on the *sequence of dates and events pattern*. To explain or illustrate the main idea, the author will list a series of dates and events according to the order in which they occurred. As you might expect, the dates and events are usually essential details. (pp. 161–163)

☐ **2.** Particularly in science textbooks, writers need to tell readers how something works, functions, or develops. To make their point, they use a *sequence of steps pattern*, in which the supporting details describe each individual step or stage according to the order in which it occurs. (pp. 166–167)

☐ **3.** Authors in every discipline frequently need to compare and contrast two topics. They need, that is, to describe similarities or differences. When you encounter the *comparison and contrast pattern* of organization, be sure you can identify the two topics under discussion and briefly summarize the similarities or differences mentioned by the author. (pp. 171–173)

☐ **4.** The *cause and effect pattern* is perhaps the most common pattern found in writing. Writers of every kind occasionally need to explain how one event (the cause) leads to another event (the effect). In fact, authors frequently need to describe how several causes lead to one event or vice versa. To get the most out of a reading relying on the cause and effect pattern, be sure you can identify all the causes and effects mentioned. (pp. 177–179)

☐ **5.** The *classification pattern* usually opens with an explanation of how some larger group can be broken down into smaller categories or subgroups. Then the supporting details take over and help readers make sense out of the main idea by describing each category or subgroup. (pp. 183–185)

☐ **6.** Particularly in longer readings, authors are likely to combine two or more patterns. Once you identify the patterns being used to organize the supporting details, sift out the key elements of each pattern. (pp. 189–190)

◢◣◉ Working with Words

Here again are some of the words defined in Chapter 6. Use the following exercises to gain practice with these words and to learn more about their history and meaning.

◢▬ EXERCISE 7

DIRECTIONS Use the following words to fill in the blanks.

punitive: punishing

deities: gods

oblivion: unconsciousness

deductive: using general laws or principles to understand particular cases

resumption: the act of beginning or starting again

rife: occurring widely

legion: large number, multitude

disoriented: confused about time and place

congenital: existing at birth

turbulence: state of being agitated or disturbed

1. The infant suffered from a _Congenital_ defect, but the surgeon was convinced she could fix it.

2. In the hopes of reaching a state of _Oblivion_, he drank three martinis in quick succession.

3. The headlines announced the _resumption_ of warfare after the ceasefire.

4. As their many myths reveal, the ancient Greeks worshipped a number of different _deities_.

5. Rumors of war were _rife_ throughout the country.

6. The lack of air made her anxious and _disoriented_.

7. The prison warden's severe ___*punitive*___ measures had driven the prisoners to riot.

8. The committee tested her ability to use ___*deductive*___
reasoning as an aid to problem solving.

9. Surrounded by a ___*legion*___ of fans, the rock
star couldn't have been happier.

10. The ___*turbulence*___ in the air forced the airplane to
swoop and dive.

■ **EXERCISE 8**

DIRECTIONS Use a hardbound dictionary to answer the following
questions.

1. The word *turbulence* frequently refers to air. However, it can also

refer to _____.
Note: To answer this question, you may have to look at the entry
for *turbulent.*

2. In medicine, the word *compliance* refers to _____

_____.

3. The word *allocate* comes from the Latin word *locus,* mean-

ing _____.

4. The word *expedient* can mean "practical" and "appropriate for a par-

ticular purpose." However, it can also mean _____

_____.

5. The word *milestone* can refer to an important event. However, it

can also refer to _____.

◤ Chapter 6: Review Test

DIRECTIONS Read each selection. Then circle the letter that identifies the pattern or patterns of organization used in the selection.

1. Schizophrenia usually strikes in late adolescence or early adulthood, shattering and destroying its victims' lives. As a result of the disease, schizophrenics may appear tired and apathetic, withdrawn from the outside world. But inwardly they are in terrible turmoil. They suffer from hallucinations, think they hear voices, and believe that their thoughts are controlled by electronic devices. Even though they can have long periods of apparent sanity, schizophrenics generally find it all but impossible to establish normal social relationships. They cannot pursue or maintain careers. Although 25 to 30 percent of all patients fully recover from a first attack of schizophrenia, the majority remain chronically ill throughout their lives.

   a. sequence of dates and events

   b. sequence of steps

   c. comparison and contrast

   (d.) cause and effect

   e. classification

2. Your behavior is influenced by the conscious and subconscious parts of your mind. The **conscious mind** is the mental activity you are aware of and generally control. The ability to recall specific information about a letter typed last week is an example of the conscious part of the mind at work. So is recalling someone's phone number or address. The **subconscious mind** is a vast storehouse of forgotten memories, desires, ideas, and frustrations, according to William Menninger, founder of the famed Menninger Foundation. He notes that the subconscious mind can have a great influence on behavior. It contains memories of past experiences as well as memories of feelings about past experiences. The subconscious is active, continuously influencing conscious decision-making processes.

   a. sequence of dates and events

   b. sequence of steps

   c. comparison and contrast

   d. cause and effect

   (e.) classification

3. The Democrats and the Republicans claim to be very different. Yet, many observers believe that the parties are really quite similar when compared with other countries' parties. Specifically, both parties support capitalism and both reject government ownership of the means of production. A study of Democratic and Republican positions on four economic issues—ownership of the means of production, the government's role in economic planning, redistribution of wealth, and providing for social welfare—found that Republicans consistently oppose increased government activity, while Democrats consistently support it. Comparing these findings with data on party positions in thirteen other democracies, the researchers found about as much difference between the American parties as is usual within two-party systems. However, both American parties tend to be more conservative on economic matters than parties in other two-party systems. (Janda et al., *The Challenge of Democracy*, p. 277.)

a. sequence of dates and events

b. sequence of steps

c. comparison and contrast

d. cause and effect

e. classification

4. Petroleum, also known as "crude oil," is the end product of a lengthy biological process. Its formation begins when organic matter like fish and plant life accumulates on the ocean floor. As the layers build up and bury one another, they produce heat, much like the layers in a compost pile. When the temperature rises, the organic matter is converted into a mixture of oil, gas, and water. Because of its watery form, that mixture is free to migrate upward through highly porous rocks like sandstone. But once the mixture encounters a hard rock like shale, it builds up into pools and the elements in the mixture begin to separate. The oil moves to the surface of the rock, and the gas goes on top of the oil.

a. sequence of dates and events

b. sequence of steps

c. comparison and contrast

d. cause and effect

e. classification

5. The Road to Revolution

The British believed that taxing the colonies was the obvious way to meet the costs of administering the colonies; the colonists did not agree. Like most people, they did not want to be taxed. And they especially did not want to be taxed by a distant government in which they had no representation. Nevertheless, a series of taxes (including a small tax on all printed matter) was imposed on the colonies by the Crown. In each instance, public opposition was widespread and immediate.

A group of citizens—merchants, lawyers, prosperous traders—created an intercolonial association, the Sons of Liberty. This group destroyed taxed items and forced their official distributors to resign. In October 1765, residents of Charleston, South Carolina, celebrated the forced resignation of the colony's stamp distributor by displaying a British flag with the word *Liberty* sewn across it. On the night of December 16, 1773, colonists reacted to a British duty on tea by organizing the Boston Tea Party. A mob boarded three ships and emptied 342 chests of that valuable substance into Boston Harbor. The act of defiance and destruction could not be ignored. "The die is now cast," wrote George III. "The Colonies must either submit or triumph."

In an attempt to reassert British control over its recalcitrant colonists, Parliament passed the Coercive (or Intolerable) Acts (1774). One act imposed a blockade on Boston until the tea was paid for; another gave royal governors the power to quarter British soldiers in private American homes. The taxation issue became secondary; more important was the conflict between British demands for order and American demands for liberty. The Virginia and Massachusetts assemblies summoned a continental congress, an assembly that would speak and act for the people of all the colonies.

All the colonies except Georgia sent representatives to the First Continental Congress, which met in Philadelphia in September 1774. The objective was to restore harmony between Great Britain and the American colonies. In an effort at unity, all colonies were given the same voting power—one vote each. A leader, called the president, was elected. (The terms *president* and *congress* in American government trace their origins to the First Continental Congress.) In October, the delegates adopted a statement of rights and principles, many of which later found their way into the Declaration of Independence and the Constitution. By early 1775, however, a movement that the colonists themselves were calling a revolution had already begun. (Janda et al., *The Challenge of Democracy*, pp. 63–66.)

a. sequence of dates and events

b. sequence of steps

c. comparison and contrast

d. cause and effect

e. classification

PART 2

Becoming a Critical Reader

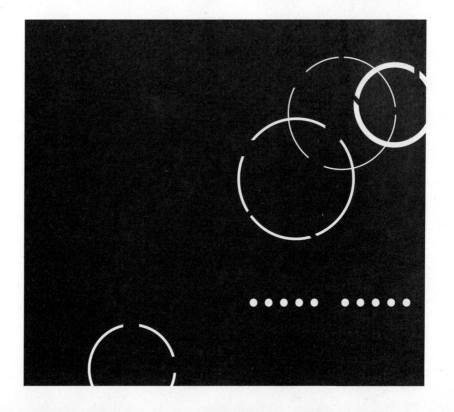

C H A P T E R   7

Focusing on Facts and Opinions

 In this chapter, you'll learn

- **how to distinguish between facts and opinions.**

- **how to recognize connotative and denotative language.**

- **how to know if a statement blends fact with opinion.**

- **how to evaluate the opinions an author presents.**

Critical readers know the difference between facts and opinions and are careful to distinguish between the two. They are also alert to those statements that blend fact and opinion and don't allow themselves to absorb an author's point of view without conscious consideration. Not surprisingly, then, the goal of Chapter 7 is to give you a solid understanding of how facts and opinions differ. Once you can distinguish between the two, you're ready to take the next step and evaluate an author's opinions, deciding how effectively or ineffectively the writer defends his or her point of view.

 # Distinguishing Between Fact and Opinion

Statements of **fact** provide information about people, places, events, and ideas, and they can be verified or checked for accuracy. Facts, however, do not reveal the author's personal perspective or point of view. The following sentences are all statements of fact:

- American Samoa consists of seven islands in the South Pacific.
- In 1961, Trans World Airlines was the first commercial airline to introduce in-flight movies.
- The Treaty of Versailles ended World War I.
- On May 17, 1954, the U.S. Supreme Court ruled on *Brown v. The Board of Education.*
- John Wilkes Booth assassinated Abraham Lincoln on April 14, 1865.

Look up facts like these in different places and you'll discover the same information. Established facts usually don't vary with place or person. For example, if you check Martin Luther King Jr.'s date of birth in New York or San Francisco, with a local librarian at home or a history teacher in Fairbanks, Alaska, the date will remain the same: January 15, 1929.

Shifting Facts

Facts do occasionally change over time as new discoveries or methods of experimentation come to light. This is especially true in science, history, and medicine, fields in which information considered factual is often based on existing levels of knowledge. As scientists and historians gain a more precise knowledge of the world, the facts on which they base their theories sometimes undergo a change.

For example, it was once considered a fact that the sun revolved around the earth. But in the sixteenth century, a Polish astronomer named Nicolaus Copernicus used the laws of planetary motion to challenge that "fact." Copernicus proved that, *in fact,* the earth revolves around the sun.

Generally, however, facts are fairly fixed pieces of information that can be verified through research and *proved* accurate or inaccurate, true or false.

Statements of Fact

- **can be checked for accuracy or correctness.**
- **can be proved true or false.**
- **are not affected by the writer's background or training.**
- **rely heavily on measurements, dates, and statistics.**

Opinions

Statements of **opinion** reflect the author's perspective on the subject discussed. Shaped by an author's personal experience, training, and background, opinions on the same subject can change from person to person, group to group, or place to place. For an illustration, ask a group of teenagers how they feel about high school dress codes. Then ask their parents. Don't be surprised if you uncover a marked difference of opinion.

Unlike facts, opinions cannot be **verified,** or checked, with outside sources. They are too **subjective,** too personal, to be checked in reference books or historical records. The following are all statements of opinion:

- Madonna is an artist of extraordinary talent.
- Although John F. Kennedy gets most of the credit, it was Lyndon Johnson who truly advanced the cause of civil rights.
- Killing animals for sport is wrong, and hunters should be ashamed of themselves.
- This country needs better gun control laws.

Because opinions reflect an individual's personal responses to people, events, and ideas, you cannot prove them true or false, accurate or inaccurate, right or wrong. This is not to say, however, that opinions cannot be judged or evaluated in any way. As you'll learn from the discussion that follows, opinions can and should be evaluated.

Statements of Opinion

- **cannot be checked for accuracy or correctness.**
- **cannot be proved true or false.**
- **are shaped by the writer's background or training.**
- **use verbs and adverbs that suggest doubt: seems, appears, probably, arguably.**

■ **DIGGING DEEPER** Do you agree that hunters should be ashamed of themselves? Why or why not?

EXERCISE 1

DIRECTIONS Label each statement *F* for fact or *O* for opinion.

EXAMPLE The first commercially printed Christmas cards were produced in London in 1843. __*F*__

EXPLANATION The date of the first commercially printed Christmas card can readily be verified and is not in any way affected by someone's personal point of view.

1. All this uproar about animal rights is nonsense. Animals don't have rights. __*O*__

2. The word *amen* appears 13 times in the Old Testament; it appears 119 times in the New Testament. __*F*__

3. The word *coffin* comes from the Greek word *kophinos*, meaning "basket." __*F*__

4. The group Guns 'N Roses doesn't deserve to be called musicians. Those people don't make music; they make noise. __*O*__

5. Martin Luther King Jr.'s "Letter from a Birmingham Jail" was pub-

lished in 1963 by the American Friends Service Committee, a Quaker organization. _F_

6. Teenagers today are obsessed with money and success. They don't care about making the world a better place. _O_

7. The atomic weight of carbon is closer to 12 than to 14. _F_

8. Women's stomachs are less effective than men's when it comes to absorbing alcohol and neutralizing its effects. _F_

9. Rap music is here to stay. _O_

10. Queen Victoria of England died on January 22, 1901; at her death, she had been queen for almost 64 years. _F_

Recognizing Connotative and Denotative Language

Denotative language consists of words that have little or no power to sway our emotions. Words like *table, chair,* or *tree* are all examples of denotative language, language that is highly **objective,** or impersonal. Authors rely on denotative language when they don't want to reveal their own feelings or don't wish to affect the feelings of their audience.

As you might guess, statements relying primarily on denotative language are likely to be factual. The following statements, for example, all rely on denotative language, and all are statements of fact rather than opinion:

- Seven fifteen-year-old boys stood at the bus stop.
- In 1926, Gertrude Ederle became the first woman to swim the English Channel.
- *Aesop's Fables** is a collection of stories written by Aesop, a Greek storyteller.

Fact of Denotative Language

---

*fables: short stories that convey a moral and often contain speaking animals.

In contrast to denotative language, **connotative language** consists of words that evoke positive or negative associations called "connotations." Words like *traitor, idiot, hero,* and *champion* are all examples of highly connotative language. Connotative language sways our emotions and encourages us to feel or think in a certain way. It also reveals an author's point of view. Describe someone as a "traitor" or an "idiot," and you encourage your audience to respond negatively to the person you're describing. Characterize someone as a "hero" or a "champion," and you encourage your audience to react with positive feelings.

In general, statements that include words with strong connotations are more than likely statements of opinion. The following statements, for example, are all opinions, and they all include connotative language:

- *The Bridges of Madison County* has got to be the dreariest tearjerker ever written.
- When Hillary Rodham Clinton made her appearance, she was her usual brilliant and articulate self.
- With his agile* grace, Fred Astaire made dancing look easy.

The Importance of Context

Change the context, or setting, of a word, and it's possible to make it more connotative than denotative. For example, the word *stories* in the following sentence evokes little more than its **denotation**— its dictionary meaning with no emotional charge attached to it.

Aesop's Fables is a collection of stories written by a Greek storyteller.

However, look what happens when the context of the word *stories* changes:

In an effort to deny Jean a promotion, a jealous coworker spread *stories* about her character.

With this change in context, the word *stories* no longer refers to "an account of events"; instead, it becomes a synonym for "lies" and takes on a negative connotation. This example illustrates a key point about labeling language connotative or denotative: *Context is crucial.* Don't assume that a word carrying only a denotation in one

---

*agile: able to move quickly and lightly.

sentence will always be lacking connotations. Like meaning, the associations attached to a word can vary with the context.

EXERCISE 2

DIRECTIONS Read each sentence, looking carefully at the italicized word or words. Then fill in the blank with one of the following letters: *D* to indicate that the word or words carry no association other than the dictionary meaning; *C+* to indicate that the word or words have positive connotations; or a *C−* to indicate that the word or words have negative connotations.

EXAMPLE Gertrude Stein was a *twentieth-century author* who spent most of her life in France. ___*D*___

EXPLANATION The phrase *twentieth-century author* does not carry with it any positive or negative associations. It simply identifies the time in which Stein lived.

1. Woodstock is a village in New York State, which was the scene of the *greatest rock music festival* in the history of rock and roll. __C+__

2. "Zulu" is a *general name* for some 2.5 million Bantu-speaking peoples who live in South Africa. __D__

3. The Amazon River is the *second longest river* after the Nile. __D__

4. Nuclear weapons are the *plague of the twentieth century.* __C+__

5. In the nineteenth century, Marshall "Wild Bill" Hickok was *fearless* in his pursuit of outlaws. __C−__

6. *Famed revolutionary hero* Emiliano Zapata was *beloved* by the poor of Mexico. __D__

7. Gospel music is the kind of *intense joyful music* that *makes the spirit sing.* __C+__

8. Francisco Goya was a Spanish painter of the *late eighteenth and nineteenth centuries.* __D__

9. John James Audubon was a nineteenth-century *painter and naturalist.** _D_

10. John D. Rockefeller, founder of the Standard Oil Company, was famous for his charity work, but he was also known as a *"robber baron,"* whose business methods were remarkably *ruthless.* _C_

■ **WRITING SUGGESTION** Describe someone—a friend, family member, teacher, or employer—in purely denotative language. That is, describe his or her height, weight, hair color, and so on. Then rewrite your description to make your word choice more connotative than denotative. For example, "David is six feet tall and weighs 160 pounds" might become "David is tall and slender with an easy, athletic grace."

EXERCISE 3

DIRECTIONS In the following sentences, decide whether the italicized words have a positive (+), negative (−), or neutral (O) connotation. Then fill in the blank with the appropriate symbol.

EXAMPLE She enjoyed *flaunting* her newly found wealth. __−__

EXPLANATION The word *flaunting* suggests that someone is "showing off," and because most people don't want to be considered show-offs, the word *flaunting* has negative connotations.

1. He was *obsessed* by the memory of his dead wife. His house had become a shrine to her memory. __−__

2. Even from a distance, she could recognize his *sturdy,* muscular form. __O__

3. The campgrounds were empty of *visitors.* __O__

4. The *cuddly* little kitten brought life back into the house. __+__

5. The way she *gobbled* her food destroyed his romantic mood. __−__

---

*naturalist: someone who studies and writes about nature.

6. Every time the professor made a joke, the student *grinned* his approval. ___

7. In his usual *plodding* manner, he explained every detail of the procedure. ___

8. Whenever she made a mistake, he would *smirk* at her. ___

9. The book lay on the *table.* ___

10. He refused to *haggle* over money. ___

Blending Fact and Opinion

Recognizing whether an author uses connotative or denotative language will certainly help you distinguish between facts and opinions. Just as important, it will help you recognize statements in which the two blend together. Read the following sentence; would you label it fact or opinion?

> At least thirty-eight states have sensibly decided to give terminally ill patients the right to refuse medical treatment.

At first glance, that example appears to be just a statement of fact. Although it might take a little research, you could certainly check how many states actually give terminally ill patients the right to suspend treatment. Look closely, however, at the word *sensibly* and consider its positive connotations. Wouldn't most people prefer to believe they are behaving "sensibly," or with good judgment? With that one word, then, the author suggests a **bias,** or personal leaning. The author approves of the decision and encourages readers to do the same.

Critical readers, however, would think twice before they made that opinion their own. They would, in effect, be careful not to let connotative language lure them into accepting someone else's opinion without question. Critical readers are conscious of the way an author's choice of words can implicitly interpret, or evaluate, events. They know full well that the same set of facts can convey different messages, depending on the language an author uses, and they try to stay attuned to the way language affects meaning.

Remember the statement on page 205 about the fifteen-year-old boys at the bus stop? Look now at how the message of that statement changes with the choice of words.

Negative connotations.

1. A *gang* of *shifty-looking* teenage *wise guys loitered* at the bus stop.

2. A *lively* group of *good-natured, high-spirited* teenagers stood at the bus stop.

Positive connotations

In the first sentence, the italicized words carry negative connotations. Reading that sentence, you might think trouble will erupt at any moment. However, that's probably not your response to the second sentence. In this sentence, the italicized words carry positive connotations. They suggest youthful high spirits rather than the desire to do mischief.

Reading critically would probably be a good deal easier if authors kept statements of fact and statements of opinion neatly divided. But they don't. Whether consciously or unconsciously, writers of all kinds—and textbook authors are no exception—can't always avoid coloring a fact with an opinion. Your job as a critical reader is to make sure you recognize when and where fact and opinion blend together. That way, you won't mistakenly absorb an opinion you haven't seriously considered.

■ EXERCISE 4

DIRECTIONS Some of the following statements are purely factual. Others blend fact and opinion. Put an *F* in the blank next to the factual statements. Put a *B* in the blank next to statements that blend fact and opinion. For those sentences you mark with a *B*, underline the word or words that led you to your conclusion.

EXAMPLE Leslie Marmon Silko's *Ceremony* is the <u>deeply moving</u> story of a young Native American held prisoner during World War II. __*B*__

EXPLANATION In this statement, the author provides factual information about the book's plot. The words *deeply moving* convey the author's opinion of the book.

1. According to the Television Advertising Bureau, an extraordinary 98.2 percent of all American households have a television set. __*B*__

2. Psychiatrist Bruno Bettelheim spent many years studying the hidden meaning of fairy tales. __F__

3. There actually are people who have tattoos covering 98 percent of their body. __B__

4. Diane Nash was only twenty-two years old when she led the campaign to desegregate the lunch counters in Nashville, Tennessee. __B__

5. In 1944, Russian troops entered eastern Czechoslovakia, and the nightmare of life under the Communist rule began. __B__

6. The great religion of Islam originated in the city of Mecca, which lies near the Red Sea. __B__

7. After World War I, victorious Britain and France greedily divided up the Turkish empire. __B__

8. Surprisingly, Muhammad, the founder of Islam, devoted a number of his sermons to the subject of women's rights. __B__

9. After World War II, Britain turned Palestine over to the United Nations, which in 1948 voted to create the state of Israel. __F__

10. In 1908, Jack Johnson became the first African-American to win the world heavyweight championship. __F__

 ## Looking for an Argument

Don't be fooled by the title of this section. In this context, looking for an argument has nothing to do with being cantankerous, or disagreeable. Instead, the title refers to the first thing critical readers do once they have identified an author's opinion: They try to discover the author's method of arguing, or supporting, that opinion.

Critical readers are rightfully skeptical, or distrustful, of opinions that are not backed up by the appropriate evidence. They know the difference between an *assertion* and an *argument.* An assertion is an unsupported opinion, a claim that's made without being justified in any way. An argument, however, introduces an opinion *and* supplies the evidence or reasons needed to make it convincing. In general, critical readers prefer arguments to assertions. They would, for example, be appropriately skeptical of an unjustified opinion like the one expressed in the following passage:

> During World War II, Japanese-Americans were shabbily treated by the U.S. government. Without reason, their lives were destroyed. The treatment of Japanese-Americans during World War II was and is a terrible scar on our reputation as a democratic country.

The writer of this passage obviously believes that Japanese-Americans were badly treated by the U.S. government during World War II. Unfortunately, that opinion is not accompanied by any supporting details that might convince readers to share or at least consider the opinion. Instead, the author restates, in slightly more specific terms, the opening opinion. This tactic is called a **circular argument.**† If you catch an author using it, you should be wary of sharing his or her point of view without further study and research.

Look now at the next example. The opinion is the same. What's different is the author's attempt to *argue* that opinion rather than simply assert it.

Opinion

Fact 1

Facts 2 and 3

Facts 4 and 5

Opinion

During World War II, Japanese-Americans were shabbily treated by the U.S. government. In 1942, President Roosevelt issued an executive order forcing 120,000 people of Japanese ancestry to relocate from the West Coast. Although there was no evidence that Japanese-Americans had collaborated* with the enemy, the U.S. Supreme Court upheld Roosevelt's order. After being forced to abandon their homes and give up their professions, Japanese-Americans were herded into detention centers, where they lived behind barbed wire surrounded by guards. The treatment of Japanese-Americans during World War II was and is a terrible scar on our reputation as a democratic country.

Notice that this passage begins and ends with the same opinions expressed in the earlier passage. But, unlike the first, the second

---

†For more on circular arguments, see page 294.
*collaborated: cooperated with occupying enemy forces.

passage provides an argument that makes those opinions convincing. Given this kind of evidence, a reader is bound to respect and perhaps even share the author's opinion.

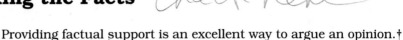 Checking the Facts

Providing factual support is an excellent way to argue an opinion.†
However, it's important that you look carefully at the facts provided
and ask some critical questions like the following:

Question 1: Are the facts relevant? The author of the following
passage offers her opinion: She believes that testing for the AIDS
virus should be mandatory* for all health care workers. Would you
be satisfied with the justification she supplies?

> Health care workers must be tested for the virus that causes AIDS.
> At present, more than 100,000 people have already died from
> AIDS-related illnesses. In addition, current figures from the na-
> tional Centers for Disease Control show that thousands more are
> already infected with HIV, the virus that causes AIDS, and will
> probably develop full-blown AIDS.

To make her opinion about AIDS testing convincing, the author
needs factual statements that support a cause and effect connection
between infected health care workers and the spread of the virus
that causes AIDS. Those facts would be relevant and would help
justify her position.

But those are not the facts the author supplies. Instead, she offers
facts relevant to the claim that AIDS is a serious epidemic. Unfortunately, those facts are irrelevant, or unrelated, to her demand for
mandatory testing. Critical readers would be dissatisfied with the
argument she supplies and remain unconvinced.

Question 2: Are the facts current? Critical readers would be
equally dissatisfied with the argument in the next passage. Here the
author claims that radon gas is not a threat. Notice how he argues
that opinion.

> The threat of radon gas is not as serious as we have been led to
> believe. In 1954, a team of government researchers studying the
> effects of radon in the home found no relationship between high
> levels of the gas in private dwellings and the incidence of lung
> cancer.

---

†For more information on opinions backed by reasons, see Chapter 9.
*mandatory: required by authority.

Here we have an author writing in the 1990s, trying to prove a point with a study almost a half-century old. To be considered effective evidence for an opinion, research usually needs to be more up-to-date.

Question 3: Are the necessary sources identified? Many writers use the results of studies to argue their opinion. However, the argument is considerably less persuasive if no specific names, dates, or institutions are cited, or mentioned.

> For decades now, people have avoided eating too many eggs for fear of developing heart disease. But all that caution was probably unnecessary; eating eggs every day of the week is apparently no health risk. In the past year, several studies have shown that eating two eggs per day does not raise cholesterol levels.

There very well may be "several studies" that support the author's conclusion. But before being persuaded, critical readers would want to know who conducted those studies, when they took place, and, above all, who funded them. They would not be satisfied with a vague phrase like "several studies." After all, if some of those studies were funded by a group called "Poultry Farmers of America," the studies might not be altogether trustworthy.

Question 4: Is the expert really an expert? If an author cites an expert to argue an opinion, he or she should also make it clear why that person is in a position to pass judgment. In effect, the author should give you the expert's credentials, or qualifications. Unidentified "experts" like the one cited in the following passage should arouse your suspicion.

> Despite the doom and gloom sayers who constantly worry about the state of the environment, the earth is actually in pretty good shape. As Dr. Paul Benjamin recently pointed out, "Nature is perfectly capable of taking care of herself; she's been doing it for hundreds of years."

The author uses Dr. Paul Benjamin to support her claim and convince readers that environmentalists worried about the earth are wrong. However, for all we know, Dr. Benjamin might be a dentist. Without additional knowledge about his credentials, we shouldn't be too quick to be swayed by his opinion. In particular, we need to know more about Dr. Benjamin's personal background and biases. If, for example, he's done a lot of work for a company frequently cited for damaging the environment, then his ability to stay objective, or neutral, is suspect.

Question 5: Are the facts sufficient? Many opinions are **gener-**

alizations. Generalizations are statements that group together and sum up or draw conclusions about a number of individual events or experiences. All of the following opinions are generalizations:

- For far too many children, television has replaced books.

- Initially, the reunification of Germany was a cause for joy, but lately there are signs of discontent as well.

- Divorce has become an epidemic in this country.

- It's a lovely day.

Like other statements of opinion, generalizations require factual statements that are both relevant and current. However, for **broad generalizations**—generalizations meant to account for large numbers of people, events, or experiences—the *number* of factual statements becomes especially important.

Critical readers, for example, would not readily accept the following opinion. It presents a broad generalization justified by only two examples.

Flying is no longer a safe way to travel. In the past six months alone, there have been two terrible crashes.

Given the hundreds of planes that fly every day over a six-month period, it makes no sense to say that flying is unsafe because of two crashes. To make that generalization convincing, you would have to cite many more examples as evidence.

As a critical reader, you should be skeptical of a broad generalization backed by only one, two, or even three examples. Such generalizations are called **hasty generalizations,** and experienced readers know they should not be trusted. If an author does offer a broad generalization on the basis of only one or two examples, withhold judgment until you can do a little research on your own.

You should also think twice about any generalization that uses or implies words like *all, always, never,* and *in every case.* Most generalizations have exceptions. Few hold for *all* cases *all* of the time.

■ **DIGGING DEEPER** On page 212, the author uses the word "herded" to describe how Japanese-Americans were taken to detention camps. What associations do you have with this word, and why did the author choose it?

EXERCISE 5

DIRECTIONS For each of the following passages, decide whether the author's argument is effectively argued or ineffectively argued and write *Effective* or *Ineffective* in the blank. If you write *Ineffective* in the blank, circle the letter of the statement that explains the reason for your answer. *Note:* In some cases, two different reasons may apply, so you may need to circle two letters.

EXAMPLE In our stupidity and greed, we are devastating* our environment and destroying the planet we live on. Our heedless* pollution of the air, water, and earth must stop. We cannot continue to treat the environment as we have in the past. If we do, we will end up inhabiting a wasteland.

Ineffective

a. hasty generalization

(b.) circular argument

c. sources of studies not identified

d. dated facts

e. irrelevant facts

f. expert's qualifications not identified

EXPLANATION The author of this example uses strong language to express her point of view. However, she doesn't provide any evidence for her position. Instead, she makes the same point in different words, offering readers little more than a circular argument.

1. Unfortunately, some people still believe that African-Americans endured slavery without protest. But nothing could be further from the truth. In 1800, for example, Gabriel Posser organized an army of a thousand slaves to march on Richmond. However, a state militia had been alerted by a spy, and the rebellion was put down. Posser was ultimately executed for refusing to give evidence against his co-conspirators. In 1822, Denmark Vesey plotted to seize Charleston, but he, too, was betrayed by an informer. Probably the most serious revolt occurred in 1831 under Nat Turner. It resulted in the execution of Turner and more than a hundred black rebels.

E

---

*devastating: laying waste, destroying.
*heedless: thoughtless.

a. hasty generalization

b. circular argument

c. sources of studies not identified

d. dated facts

e. irrelevant facts

f. expert's qualifications not identified

2. Employers looking for an edge in matching applicants to jobs would do well to use handwriting analysis. After all, handwriting analysis, like medicine, is an art and a science. Handwriting analysis can reveal a great deal about a person's character. Graphology (as handwriting analysis is called) can evaluate the whole personality. In the future, more and more employers are going to use handwriting analysis to screen applicants. It is a valuable tool.

Ineffective

a. hasty generalization

b. circular argument

c. sources of studies not identified

d. dated facts

e. irrelevant facts

f. expert's qualifications not identified

3. If current retirement patterns continue, the proportion of working people to retired people will diminish, and social security benefits may be endangered. In 1937, twelve workers contributed to the benefits for each retired person. Forty-three years later, in 1980, only three workers contributed to the benefits of each retired person. By the year 2030, the Bureau of Labor estimates that only two workers will be contributing to the benefits of each retired person.

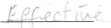
Effective

a. hasty generalization

b. circular argument

c. sources of studies not identified

d. dated facts

e. irrelevant facts

f. expert's qualifications not identified

4. Joe Hill, the popular songwriter for the 1920s labor movement, was unjustly tried, convicted, and executed for the crimes of robbery and

murder. Hill was not guilty, and justice was not served by his death. He was a martyr to the labor movement. He never should have been convicted.

ineffective

a. hasty generalization
b. circular argument
c. sources of studies not identified
d. dated facts
e. irrelevant facts
f. expert's qualifications not identified

5. The possible connection between lung cancer and high levels of radon gas in the home has been highly publicized. As a result, many homeowners have spent huge sums of money ridding themselves of radon. Yet the dangers of radon gas have been overrated. In June of 1968, the New Jersey Department of Health published a study of 750 people who had lived for sixty years in high-radon residences. In homes with the highest levels of radon, the incidence of lung cancer was actually lower than it was in the general population.

date is out dated.

ineffective

a. hasty generalization
b. circular argument
c. sources of studies not identified
d. dated facts
e. irrelevant facts
f. expert's qualifications not identified

6. We need bilingual* classrooms in our schools. Without them, children from other countries will be at a disadvantage and held back in their education. In the words of Dr. Beatrice Trove, "Putting a non-native speaker in an all English-speaking classroom is a waste of everyone's time and money."

ineffective

a. hasty generalization
b. circular argument

---

*bilingual: having the ability to speak two languages.

   c. sources of studies not identified

   d. dated facts

   e. irrelevant facts

   (f.) expert's qualifications not identified

7. Americans may talk about getting tougher on criminals, but, in fact, many are reluctant to use the death penalty. At present, capital punishment is legal in thirty-six states, and 2,210 convicted felons are waiting to be executed. But twenty-three of those thirty-six states have not had an execution in twenty years. Of the 117 executions that have taken place, 72 percent occurred in four states: Texas, Louisiana, Florida, and Georgia. And not one of those four states has executed even 10 percent of the felons it sentenced to death.

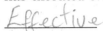 *Effective*

   a. hasty generalization

   b. circular argument

   c. sources of studies not identified

   d. dated facts

   e. irrelevant facts

   f. expert's qualifications not identified

8. Children taught at home get a better education than do children in public schools. According to a 1990 study conducted by the Washington-based National Education Association, two-thirds of the seventeen-year-olds in public high schools did not know when the Civil War occurred. And one-half of all high school seniors did not recognize the name of Winston Churchill or Joseph Stalin.

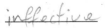 *ineffective*

   a. hasty generalization

   b. circular argument

   c. sources of studies not identified

   d. dated facts

   (e.) irrelevant facts

   f. expert's qualifications not identified

9. Environmentalists continue to warn of the dangers associated with acid rain. But how real is the threat? Many different studies suggest that acid rain may be no threat at all. In fact, a 1964 study shows little or no connection between the presence of acid rain and any significant environmental damage.

 *ineffective*

a. hasty generalization

b. circular argument

c. sources of studies not identified

d. dated facts

e. irrelevant facts

f. expert's qualifications not identified

10. The food stamp program in this country is scandalously abused. In the last week alone, the local papers reported three separate cases of people who illegally obtained and used food stamps. In each case, the individuals involved earned more than $30,000 a year.

Effective

a. hasty generalization

b. circular argument

c. sources of studies not identified

d. dated facts

e. irrelevant facts

f. expert's qualifications not identified

Summing Up

Listed below are the most important points in Chapter 7. Put a check mark in the box if you think the point is clear in your mind. Leave the box blank if you need to review the material one more time. The page numbers in parentheses tell you where to look in order to review each point on the list.

☐ **1.** *Statements of fact* provide information about people, places, events, and ideas, and can be verified for accuracy. (p. 202)

☐ **2.** It's possible for facts to change over time, and a fact in one century may not be a fact in another as existing levels of knowledge and methods of experimentation change. (pp. 202–203)

3. *Statements of opinion* reflect an author's personal point of view and are shaped by his or her training, experience, and background. (pp. 203–204)

4. *Denotative language* consists of words that have little or no power to sway our emotions. Denotative language is highly objective or impersonal, relying primarily on the dictionary meanings of words to inform rather than persuade. (p. 205)

5. *Connotative language* consists of words that evoke positive or negative associations. Connotative language is used to sway readers' emotions and often reveals an author's point of view. (p. 206)

6. Context has to be taken into account when trying to establish if a word has positive or negative connotations. (pp. 206–207)

7. Opinions cannot be proven right or wrong, but they can be evaluated. Readers can and should judge opinions as effectively or ineffectively argued, and readers should be skeptical of opinions that offer little or no justification or evidence. (pp. 211–213)

8. Critical readers know that all facts aren't equally convincing. To test an author's factual support, they ask questions like the following: Are the facts relevant? Are they current? Are the necessary sources identified? Are the facts sufficient? (pp. 213–215)

Working with Words

Here are some of the words defined in Chapter 7. Use the following exercises to gain more practice with these words and to learn more about their history and meaning.

EXERCISE 6

DIRECTIONS Fill in the blanks with one of the following words. *Note:* You will have to use two of the words more than once.

fables: short stories that convey a moral and often contain speaking animals

agile: able to move quickly and lightly

naturalist: someone who studies and writes about nature

collaborated: cooperated with occupying enemy forces

mandatory: required by authority

devastating: laying waste, destroying

heedless: thoughtless

bilingual: speaking two languages

1. After World War II, people who _Collaborated_ with the enemy were called *quislings*, after Vidkun Quisling, the Norwegian leader who worked for the Nazis and against his own people.

2. AIDS is a _devastating_ disease that has brought terrible suffering and pain to people from all walks of life.

3. While the _naturalist_ was studying the habitat of the lovely blue heron, she saw a passenger pigeon, a bird long considered extinct.

4. _Heedless_ of his own health and safety, he had a penchant for dangerous sports like bungee jumping.

5. In _Fables_, animals are treated as sentient beings—creatures capable of thought and feeling.

6. Those regulations are considered ___Mandatory___, and you are required by law to obey them.

7. After a few months in Spain, he hoped to become __bilin gual__.

8. The athlete was not ___agile___ enough to leap over the net with ease.

9. Lots of children like to read ___Fables___; they may not understand the stories' moral meanings, but they like the animals.

10. Her ___heedless___ remark made members of the group angry.

EXERCISE 7

DIRECTIONS To answer the following questions, you'll need a hard-bound dictionary.

1. The word *collaborate* can mean to work with the enemy or to __work To gether__.

2. Read the following sentence. Then look up *fable* and find a meaning that fits the context of the sentence.

   The newspaper owners didn't care if the stories were true or if they were *fables;* all they cared about was selling newspapers.

   In this sentence, *fables* means ___Falsehood___.

3. In addition to referring to stories with talking animals, the word *fables* can refer to stories about ___legendary person and exploits.___

4. Which of the following is a synonym for *heedless*?
   a. cruel
   b. careless
   c. pointless

⚡ Chapter 7: Review Test

Part A   Label each statement *F* for fact or *O* for opinion.

1. a. Lee Harvey Oswald did not act alone to assassinate President Kennedy. _O_ ✓

   b. There is much debate over whether Oswald was part of a conspiracy to kill President Kennedy. _O_

2. a. It is illegal to jaywalk. _F_

   b. Jaywalking is amoral. _O_

3. a. The plane was huge. _O_

   b. The plane was 407 feet long and 50 feet high. _F_

4. a. Lex Luthor was a fiendishly smart criminal. _O_

   b. Lex Luthor was a criminal with an IQ of over 200. _F_

Part B   Label each statement *F* for fact, *O* for opinion, or *B* for both.

5. Wounded Knee is a creek in South Dakota; in the nineteenth century, it was the site of a battle between the United States and the Dakota Sioux Indians. _F_

6. The magnificent Sojourner Truth was an escaped slave justly famous for her fight against slavery. _B_

7. Richard Rodgers gave us some of the best musical comedies ever to grace the Broadway stage. _B_

8. George Gershwin wrote "Rhapsody in Blue." _F_

9. Treated badly while he lived, American singer and actor Paul Robeson has finally been honored for his outspoken criticism of racism in America. _B_

10. *Peter Pan* is a play for both children and adults. _O_

Part C   In the blank following each paragraph, indicate if the author's opinion is effectively argued (*E*) or ineffectively argued (*I*). If you write *I* in the blank, circle the letter of the statement that identifies the reason for your answer. If two reasons apply to your answer, circle two letters.

11. If we continue to pollute the environment as we have in the past, we may live to regret it. In 1995, experts advising governments on climate change issued a clear statement on the role of human activity in global warming. In their words, "Human activity is a likely cause of the warming of the global atmosphere."[1] According to Dr. M. L. Wigley, a climatologist at the National Center for Atmospheric Research in Boulder, Colorado, the "scientific justification" for this claim is "not subject to argument." If we continue to send greenhouse gases like carbon dioxide into the atmosphere at the same rate we do currently, we can expect to see an increase in temperatures that will negatively affect our water and food supply.

   a. hasty generalization
   b. circular argument
   c. sources of studies not identified
   d. dated facts
   e. irrelevant facts
   f. expert's qualifications not identified

12. Many people are needlessly worried about the presence of mercury in dental fillings. But their worries are groundless. Several independent studies have shown that the mercury in dental fillings is not a health hazard. As one expert put it, "This is the kind of story the media loves to print, yet there is no proof that small amounts of mercury in a person's mouth can lead to any form of disease."

   a. hasty generalization
   b. circular argument
   c. sources of studies not identified

---

[1]William K. Stevens, "Global Warming Experts Call Human Role Likely," *New York Times*, September 10, 1995, p. 1.

d. dated facts

e. irrelevant facts

f. expert's qualifications not identified

13. Andrew Jackson, the seventh president (1829–1837) of the United States, was called "Old Hickory" by his admirers. However, for good reason, Native Americans were not fond of Andrew Jackson, whom they called "Long Knife." As a soldier in the U.S. Army, Jackson played tribe against tribe. He broke treaties with the Indians almost as fast as he made them. But it was as president that he truly lived up to his name. Jackson was responsible for the policy of "removal" that illegally forced Native Americans off their tribal lands. In 1836, thousands of Indians died on a forced march that has come to be known as the "Trail of Tears."

a. hasty generalization

b. circular argument

c. sources of studies not identified

d. dated facts

e. irrelevant facts

f. expert's qualifications not identified

14. Student loans should be eliminated. My neighbor's two children got student loans through the federal government, and both went on to get good jobs and earn high salaries. Yet neither one of them ever thought about repaying the loans.

a. hasty generalization

b. circular argument

c. sources of studies not identified

d. dated facts

e. irrelevant facts

f. expert's qualifications not identified

15. An increasing number of colleges and universities have introduced courses that focus on analyzing and interpreting television programs. This suggests to me that education in America has reached an all-time low. What could be sillier than sitting in a classroom and talking about television programs. What will students write their term papers on—"The Politics of *Rose-*

anne"? There's no way students can benefit from watching more television.

a. hasty generalization

b. circular argument

c. sources of studies not identified

d. dated facts

e. irrelevant facts

f. expert's qualifications not identified

16. Currently, America's labor unions are seeing hard times. In a 1995 report, the Economic Policy Institute says that corporate profits were the highest in 25 years, and more and more of those profits are going to industry stockholders. According to *Business Week* magazine, industries are also under pressure to invest more in research and development.

a. hasty generalization

b. circular argument

c. sources of studies not identified

d. dated facts

e. irrelevant facts

f. expert's qualifications not identified

17. When it comes to success, a high IQ is not the only factor that should be taken into account. A 1994 study done at Bell Laboratories, a think-tank near Princeton, New Jersey, found that the most valued and most productive electrical engineers were not those with the highest IQs. The most valued engineers were those who, in addition to a general competence in their work, knew how to make people feel comfortable and at ease. This study reinforces the work of researcher Howard Gardner, who for years has been emphasizing the importance of "personal" or "emotional intelligence." Convinced that emotional intelligence is essential to personal and professional achievement, the Yale Child Study Center has introduced courses designed to develop it.

a. hasty generalization

b. circular argument

c. sources of studies not identified

d. dated facts

e. irrelevant facts

f. expert's qualifications not identified

18. When Attorney William M. Kunstler died in 1995, the legal world lost one of its greatest heroes. There never will be another William Kunstler, a man who fought like a tiger in the name of justice. No one in the current crop of famous lawyers is his match, and he appears to have left no heirs to his tradition of hard work and devotion to the law. A first-rate intellect who could match wits with any opponent, Kunstler had a presence in the courtroom that commanded attention, and his passing is to be mourned.

a. hasty generalization

b. circular argument

c. sources of studies not identified

d. dated facts

e. irrelevant facts

f. expert's qualifications not identified

19. The notion that rollerblading is dangerous is silly and completely contradicted by the research on rollerblading. A 1975 study on rollerblading, conducted just about the time rollerblades came on the market, indicates that rollerblading is no more dangerous than ice skating or running. Yes, injuries do occur, but not out of proportion to the number of people enjoying the sport.

a. hasty generalization

b. circular argument

c. sources of studies not identified

d. dated facts

e. irrelevant facts

f. expert's qualifications not identified

20. It's time to stop thinking of intelligence as a score on an IQ test. There are many different types of intelligence, and those gifted in one area may or may not be gifted in another. But there's no such thing as a person lacking in intelligence. This is a point Howard Gardner, a psychologist at the Harvard School of Education, has been making for years. As Gardner, the author of a highly acclaimed book on intelligence called *Frames of Mind*, said recently, "There are hundreds and hundreds of ways to succeed, and many, many different abilities that will help get you there."[1]

a. hasty generalization

b. circular argument

c. sources of studies not identified

d. dated facts

e. irrelevant facts

f. expert's qualifications not identified

---

[1]Daniel Goleman, "Rethinking the Value of Intelligence Tests," *New York Times Education Supplement*, November 3, 1986.

C H A P T E R 8

Understanding Tone and Purpose

 In this chapter, you'll learn

- **why it's important to identify an author's tone.**

- **how to use tone as a clue to an author's purpose.**

- **how to evaluate the role of tone in persuasive writing.**

- **how to recognize an ironic tone.**

To express their ideas effectively, authors frequently need to assume different tones in their writing. An author who writes a textbook, for example, might assume a cool and neutral tone. However, that same author might well shift to a chatty, friendly tone when writing an editorial for the school newspaper.

Critical readers pay close attention to an author's use of tone. They know that recognizing tone can tell them a good deal about an author's purpose, or intention, in writing. They know, too, that tone can be a powerful tool of persuasion, and they don't let themselves mindlessly accept an author's opinion simply because it's expressed in a bold and confident tone.

 ## Identifying an Author's Tone

Just like a person's speaking voice, a writer's style can reveal a particular **tone,** or attitude. And just like tone of voice in speech, tone in writing can vary with the writer's audience, purpose, or subject matter.

For example, someone who writes a letter to the editor complaining about a host of new state taxes might assume an openly argumentative or an angry tone. After all, the taxes aren't going to disappear, so the letter writer is free to express his or her fury. However, a local environmental group circulating a newsletter about the importance of water and soil conservation might purposely use a friendly and informal tone in order to win people over to its cause.

For an illustration of tone in writing, read the following paragraph. Then decide which of the following words accurately describes the author's tone: serious, outraged, or lighthearted.

Before Ren and Stimpy, before Bill and Ted, before Wayne and Garth, and, yes, before Beavis and Butt-head, there was a short-lived television series called *Police Squad*. The series was the brainchild of the now famous Zucker brothers, who, along with their colleague Jim Abrams, created *Airplane!*, the Rosetta Stone† of silly stupid comedy. It's only the Zucker brothers here on this one, but their effort has suffered little from the absence of the third member of the trio (who has gone on to equally silly fare in making *Hot Shots* and its sequel). *Naked Gun 33 1/3: The Final Insult* isn't every bit as insanely madcap and over-the-top as *Airplane!* or the original *Police Squad* series were, but it's close enough not to matter. (David Etkin, *The Yale Herald,* March 25, 1994, p. 19.)

†Rosetta Stone: a stone tablet that was discovered in 1799 near Rosetta, Egypt. It provided the key to Egyptian hieroglyphics, a form of writing using pictures.

In this example, references to Beavis and Butt-head, and Wayne and Garth, along with phrases like "silly stupid comedy," all suggest a lighthearted, comical tone.

But look now at the next example. It's also a review, this time of a book; yet, notice the change in tone.

> In *Dark Sun*, Richard Rhodes provides a detailed account of how scientist Edward Teller and his allies obtained presidential authorization to create the hydrogen bomb. Mr. Rhodes draws on a vast variety of sources, combining previous scholarship with fresh material from memoirs, interviews, FBI files, and recently released Soviet documents. Illuminating issues through the play of personalities, Rhodes writes with a sharp eye for anecdote, character, and political context. He also has a talent for lucid* explanations of technical issues. The resulting work is a fascinating and vivid account of both the cold war and the arms race, one that is as chilling as it is enthralling.*

In this case, the author assumes a serious tone, one appropriate to the subject matter—the making of the hydrogen bomb. Although much of the language has positive connotations—"fascinating," "vivid," and "enthralling"—none of it inclines readers to laughter, although it does encourage readers to admire Mr. Rhodes's work.

Be Prepared for an Emotionally Neutral Tone

You can't assume that you'll always be able to determine an author's attitude through the tone he or she assumes while writing. Sometimes authors purposely assume an **emotionally neutral tone,** one that conceals how they feel about both the topic and the audience.

An emotionally neutral tone is typical of the writing that appears in most textbooks or in reference works, such as encyclopedias, government reports, bulletins, almanacs, and dictionaries. For the most part, readers of this material neither expect nor want authors to be emotionally involved with their subject. Readers are looking for the facts and ideas considered essential to understanding a particular subject, issue, or theory, and they don't want the author to take sides. Conscious of their readers' expectations, writers of textbooks and reference works usually keep their distance, as the following excerpt illustrates:

*lucid: clear.
*enthralling: fascinating.

In the eighteenth century, the English publisher John Newbery (1713–1767) became the first to print attractive, inexpensive books for children. Containing stories, verses, puzzles, riddles, maxims,* and lessons, the books sold in England for sixpence each in little paper-covered editions. His best-known publications are *The History of Little Goody Two Shoes* (1765), erroneously* credited to the British author Oliver Goldsmith; *A Little Pretty Pocketbook* (1744); and *Mother Goose's Melody* (c. 1765), reprinted in Boston in 1785. Until the late eighteenth century, no clear distinction had been made between instruction and entertainment in children's literature. Most stories and poems written for children were designed to convey useful information or moral advice. (Funk & Wagnall's New Encyclopedia, p. 134.)

In this example, the author writes about the publishing history of children's books. Unlike some subjects—divorce, civil rights, homelessness, or cruelty to animals—this topic does not inspire powerful emotion. In addition, there's the context of the passage: The author is writing for an encyclopedia, and writers of reference works traditionally keep their tone as emotionally neutral as possible. Their primary goal is to dispense information *without* interpreting or evaluating it in any way.

To create the tone of this passage, the author uses several devices. He relies primarily on denotative language and makes no reference to his own personal experiences. Nor does he try to narrow the gap between writer and reader by mentioning himself ("I would suggest here . . .") or by addressing the reader ("You only need to consider . . .").

Allusions and Tone

Allusions are references to people, places, and events that authors use to help create both tone and meaning. Look back at the paragraph on page 231, and you'll see an allusion to Wayne and Garth, two comic characters who got their start on the television show *Saturday Night Live.* You'll also see an allusion to the animated television stars of MTV, Beavis and Butt-head, along with an allusion to Bill and Ted, two characters in the movie *Bill and Ted's Excellent Adventure.* In fact, it's largely through allusions that the author of this paragraph creates his comical tone.

In the following passage, the author creates a far more serious

---

*maxims: sayings that reveal a lesson about life.
*erroneously: mistakenly.

tone and, here again, the use of an allusion—in this case to Lady Macbeth—is critical to both tone and meaning:

> Obsessed by guilt, the young woman was a modern-day Lady Macbeth. She couldn't stop thinking about the mistakes she'd made and the deadly harm they had brought to others.

As most of you probably remember, Lady Macbeth in Shakespeare's play *Macbeth* was overcome by her guilt at participating in murder. In the above passage, the author's allusion to Lady Macbeth helps create a serious tone. It also reinforces the message of the passage— the young woman is horrified by the consequences of her behavior.

Allusions help authors communicate with readers, but they only work if readers respond by figuring out what the allusion contributes to the author's point. Anytime you encounter an allusion in writing, try to figure out what the author wants to suggest by using it. If the allusion doesn't mean anything to you, look it up in a dictionary or ask your teacher about it so that you don't miss out on a valuable source of information.

■ **WRITING SUGGESTION** Write two different paragraphs describing your attitude toward life. Do you, for example, tend to take things seriously? Or do you try to laugh off life's stresses and strains? In the first paragraph, assume a serious tone to describe your philosophy of life. In the second, use a humorous tone.

■ EXERCISE 1

DIRECTIONS After reading each passage, circle the letter of the words that best describe the author's tone.

EXAMPLE My mother, Anne America Dempsey Watts, loved life too much to relish planning for her own end. But after losing two brothers, she was motivated to get her affairs in order. When Mama died recently at the age of 67, she managed to "go in style." She hadn't done everything by the book, but she had taken sufficient steps so that her surviving children could manage closing her affairs. Her example prompted me to write this article.

If there are people in your life that you love—or people that you emphatically don't love, and would prefer to keep at a distance even when you die—you need to complete certain plans and actions so that your preferences are clearly stated to your survivors, and are also legally binding. (Emily Card, "Writing Your Will," *Ms*, July 1984, p. 88.)

How would you describe the author's tone?

(a.) serious and concerned

b. casual and funny

c. emotionally neutral

EXPLANATION Although the author's style is informal, she makes no reference to comical characters or situations. Her language is conversational, but it's not designed to evoke laughter. Thus *b* is not an appropriate answer. The phrase *emotionally neutral* also does not adequately describe the author's highly personal tone. *Serious and concerned* is the best answer because the author's language implies that she feels deeply about her topic.

1. Young people should have the right to control and direct their own learning, that is, to decide what they want to learn, and when, where, how, how much, how fast, and with what help they want to learn it. To be still more specific, I want them to have the right to decide if, when, how much, and by whom they want to be *taught* and the right to decide whether they want to learn in a school and, if so, which one and for how much of the time. No human right, except the right to life itself, is more fundamental than this. A person's freedom of learning is part of his freedom of thought, even more basic than his freedom of speech. (John Holt, "Escape from Childhood," *Taking Sides*. Guilford, Conn.: Dushkin Press, 1991, p. 27.)

How would you describe the author's tone?

a. cool and confident

(b.) passionate and determined

c. emotionally neutral

2. The purpose of markets is to encourage the exchange of goods and services between buyers and sellers. In some cases, money changes hands; in others, only goods and services are exchanged. The exchange of goods and services directly, without money, is called **barter.** Barter occurs when a plumber fixes a leaky pipe for a lawyer in exchange for the lawyer's work on a will; when a Chinese citizen provides fresh vegetables to an American visitor in exchange for a pack of American cigarettes; and when children trade baseball cards. Most markets involve money because goods and services can be exchanged more easily with money than without it. (Adapted from William Boyes and Michael Melvin, *Economics.* Boston: Houghton Mifflin, 1991, p. 57.)

How would you describe the author's tone?

a. serious and concerned

b. lighthearted

c. emotionally neutral

3. The biggest surprise for me at my fifteenth high school reunion was discovering who had become the most successful member of my class (the person with the loftiest position and salary). It wasn't the valedictorian† or the kid with the highest SAT scores. It wasn't the editor of the school paper or the debate champ. And it wasn't the star of the football team. It was a friend of mine who had average grades and few extracurricular accomplishments but who was one of the most likable members of our class. He had a certain social poise and a special ability to put people at ease. Sometime after college he had become right-hand man to a powerhouse in the burgeoning* cable TV industry. By his early thirties, when our reunion rolled around, my friend already was an executive vice president of one of America's biggest cable companies.

My friend is a telling case in point of the importance for life success of "emotional intelligence," a different way of being smart. (Daniel Goleman, "The New Thinking on Smarts," *USA Weekend,* September 8–10, 1995, p. 4.)

How would you describe the author's tone?

a. angry and impassioned

b. informal yet serious

c. emotionally neutral

4. A secretary complains that her boss is a pain in the *derrière*; an undertaker (or *mortician*) asks delicately where to ship the *loved one.* These are euphemisms—mild, agreeable, or roundabout words used in place of coarse, painful, or offensive ones. The term comes from the Greek *eu,* meaning "well" or "sounding good," and *pheme,* "speech."

---

†valedictorian: the student who delivers the farewell speech at graduation.
*burgeoning: growing, increasing.

Many euphemisms are so delightfully ridiculous that everyone laughs at them. (Well, almost everyone: The people who call themselves the National Selected Morticians usually manage to keep from smiling.) Yet euphemisms have very serious reasons for being. They conceal the things people fear the most—death, the dead, the supernatural. They cover up the facts of life—of sex and reproduction and excretion—which inevitably remind even the most refined people that they are made of clay, or worse. They are beloved by individuals and institutions (governments, especially) who are anxious to present only the handsomest possible images of themselves to the world. (Hugh Rawson, "Euphemisms," *Dictionary of Euphemisms and Other Double Talk.* New York: Crown Publishers, 1981.)

How would you describe the author's tone?

a. amused but angry

b. humorously serious

c. emotionally neutral

DIGGING DEEPER What other examples of euphemisms can you think of? In what situations do you find yourself using euphemisms? Do you think we would be better off without them? Why or why not?

WRITING SUGGESTION Write a paper in which you argue for or against the use of euphemisms.

Tone and Purpose

The more practiced you become at identifying tone, the better you'll be at recognizing an author's **purpose,** or intention, in writing. Although there are many different reasons why authors write—to criticize, describe, explain, prove, celebrate, expose, and so on—most of those reasons or purposes fall under two general headings: writing meant to inform or explain and writing meant to persuade or convince. A strongly emotional tone usually suggests that the writer is intent on persuasion, while an emotionally neutral tone usually indicates that the writer wants to inform more than persuade.

The Importance of Purpose

Identifying an author's purpose is important because, to a large degree, the author's purpose determines how critically you need to read. After all, your time is limited. You cannot check every source or ponder every word. With informational writing, you can more safely relax and read to understand the author's message. The chances are good that the writer is describing events or ideas without telling you how to interpret or view them. In fact, a writer whose primary purpose is to inform is more likely to give you different explanations of the same events so that you will be able to develop your own opinions.

However, the more an author leans toward persuasion, the more willing you must be to **evaluate,** or judge, the author's language and reasoning. You have to consider whether the connotations of words are encouraging you to hold a particular point of view—a view you may not really support. Similarly, you have to pay close attention to the balance between fact and opinion, and make sure the facts the author uses are both relevant and sufficient.

The author's purpose shapes or determines the reader's response. The clearer it becomes that an author is intent on persuasion, the more ready the reader must be to read closely and critically.

Informative Writing

Writers whose purpose is to inform will usually state or suggest a main idea that describes but does not judge events, people, or experiences. In the following statement, for example, the writer describes a book about Greek culture. Notice, however, that the author does not evaluate it in any way:

> In the book *Black Athena*, Charles Bernal argues that the Greeks were deeply indebted to the Egyptians for almost every aspect of their culture.

Writers of readings designed to inform rely heavily on specific examples, statistics, studies, dates, and figures. They lean more heavily on fact than on opinion, and their language tends to be more denotative than connotative. Overall, writers of informative readings try to keep themselves and their point of view out of their writings. Although they might pass along opinions, those opinions won't be their own. They will be the opinions of experts or authorities that readers need to know about to fully understand a topic or issue. Here's a good example of writing meant primarily to inform:

> A number of factors cause children to become seriously overweight or obese (that is, at least 30 percent over normal weight). Children and parents can control some of these but not others. Two factors beyond human control are *heredity* and *age.* Like it or not, thinness and fatness do run in families. Overweight children tend to have overweight parents, and underweight children tend to have underweight parents (LeBow, 1984). And most people inevitably put on fat more during some periods of life than others. Late childhood and early puberty form one of these periods; at this time, most children gain fat tissue out of proportion to increases in other tissues, such as muscle and bone. (Seifert and Hoffnung, *Childhood and Adolescent Development,* p. 390.)

In this example, the topic is obesity in children, and the authors briefly describe two of its causes: heredity and age. Notice, however, that they themselves do not express a point of view about their subject. Nor do the authors suggest that readers should adopt a particular point of view. Their primary purpose is dispensing information. It is not persuasion.

Informative Writing

- states or suggests a main idea that describes events, people, or experiences without judging them.

- leans more heavily on fact than on opinion.

- relies more on denotative language and is sparing with highly charged words.

- reveals little about the writer's point of view.

- avoids using pronouns like I or we.

- frequently describes opposing points of view on the same subject or issue without affirming one or the other.

Persuasive Writing

Writers whose primary purpose is to persuade will usually start off with a topic sentence or thesis statement that expresses an opinion.

That opinion is likely to identify (1) some action that needs to be taken, (2) a belief that should be held, or (3) some value judgment that should be shared. Here again is a sentence describing Charles Bernal's book, *Black Athena.* Notice how this author offers her readers a value judgment:

> Charles Bernal has expended enormous energy on *Black Athena,* but he is absolutely wrong to say in conclusion, as he does, that he has rewritten the history of the eastern Mediterranean.[1]

Although writers interested in persuading their readers may also supply them with factual statements, those statements will frequently include some connotative language. Generally, writers of persuasive readings do not try to keep themselves or their point of view out of their work. They are more than likely to refer to themselves with the pronoun "I" or to their readers with the pronoun "we." Writers of persuasive readings are also likely to tell their readers about the negative effects they can expect if some particular event, attitude, or point of view isn't changed or altered. Here's a good example of a passage written primarily to persuade:

> I have been fat all of my life, and I am thoroughly sick of apologizing for it. This is my personal declaration of independence from all you skinny people out there who have insisted how much better off I would be if I lost a few pounds. Unfortunately, we live in a culture that places far too much emphasis on being thin. This emphasis leads to the kind of desperate and dangerous dieting I have engaged in for most of my adult life, and I am not alone in this obsession with losing weight. At some time in their lives, at least 80 percent of the American population has been on a diet to lose weight, even though studies show the majority of diets fail (Fett and Dick, 1991). We would probably all be a lot better off if we spent time improving our souls instead of dieting to improve our bodies.

In this example, the author wants to communicate an opinion: "We live in a culture that places far too much emphasis on being thin." And it's clear that she hopes her readers will share that opinion once they read what she has written. In addition to telling her readers what unpleasant effects the emphasis on thinness can have—it leads to desperate and dangerous dieting—she also includes them in her point of view: "*We* would probably all be a lot better off if we spent time improving our souls instead of our bodies."

---

[1]Emily Vermeale, "The World Turned Upside Down," *New York Review of Books,* March 26, 1992, p. 43.

Persuasive Writing

- expresses an opinion that suggests (1) an action needs to be taken, (2) a belief should be held, or (3) some value judgment should be shared.

- includes language with strong connotations.

- frequently reveals the author's personal opinion or point of view.

- tells readers about the negative effects or results they can expect if some event, attitude, or point of view doesn't change.

- is more likely than informative writing to use the pronouns *I* or *we.*

- frequently criticizes opposing points of view.

Balancing Information and Persuasion

Many reading selections lean heavily toward one purpose or another, and it's easy to say, without any doubt, that the author's *primary* purpose was to inform or to persuade. However, keep in mind that some writing blends information and persuasion. For example, a writer who wants to inform her readers about changes that have taken place in Berlin, Germany, since the Berlin wall† came down also needs to persuade her readers that her account is accurate and trustworthy. Similarly, an author may wish to convince his readers that they should give more money for AIDS research. But to make that position persuasive, he will probably inform them about current funding.

As a reader, you should always try to determine an author's primary, or major, purpose. But you also need to be aware that authors occasionally offer readers a perfect balance of the two, and it's not always possible to claim with absolute certainty that a writer meant to inform *or* persuade. Some writers do both equally.

---

†the Berlin wall: the wall that divided East and West Germany. It was erected by the Communist government to keep East Germans from fleeing to democratic West Germany.

■ **DIGGING DEEPER** Do you agree or disagree that our culture places too much emphasis on being thin? Explain your answer.

■ **WRITING SUGGESTION** Write a paper in which you explain why it is that so many people are perpetually concerned about being overweight and trying to diet off excess pounds.

EXERCISE 2

DIRECTIONS Read each of the following excerpts and circle the letter of the statement that identifies the author's purpose.

EXAMPLE
Navajo Skinwalkers

Among the Navajo of the southwestern United States, it is said that no human being is all good or all evil. In the Navajo view, human beings each have both qualities or, more accurately, the capacity to do both good and evil. According to Witherspoon (1977), the goal of Navajo life is to bring one's impulses under control so that one grows and develops through a complete life in a condition of *hozho*—the state of beauty, harmony, good, and happiness—and then dies naturally of old age and becomes one with the universal beauty, harmony, and happiness that make up the ideal positive environment.

A person's *ch'indi*, or potential for evil, can be controlled by rituals that restore one to a state of *hozho*. Although the state of inward beauty achieved through living in outward harmony with the ideal environment can be disrupted by contact with dangerous (*bahadzid*) things or by the sorcery of others, perhaps leading to illness or to death, such states can be countered by a traditional ritual chant, or "Sing," of which there are over 60. Rituals channel supernatural power by reenacting the Navajo creation myths, which relate the deeds of the gods, both good and evil. (Richley Crapo, *Cultural Anthropology*. Guilford, Conn.: Dushkin Publishing, 1987, p. 211.)

Which statement most effectively describes the author's purpose?
(a.) The primary purpose of this reading is to inform.
b. The primary purpose of this reading is to persuade.
c. The author intended this reading to inform and persuade equally.

EXPLANATION In this case, *a* is the best answer because the author is not presenting his own point of view but rather the opinion of the

Navajo nation. Note that the author doesn't judge or evaluate that opinion in any way. Instead, he limits himself to describing it and avoids the use of connotative language that might encourage readers to view the Navajo belief system either positively or negatively. Note, too, the absence of personal pronouns like *I* or *we*.

1. **Don't Speak to Strangers**

The notion that strangers must be feared is not only lamentable* but also wrong. The media have documented the crimes of psychopathic rapists, kidnappers, child-snatchers, and criminals. Such monsters exist. But the harsh truth is that more people are hurt by those they know than they are by those whom they don't. Women are more likely to be battered by their husbands and lovers than by strangers. They are more likely to be raped by someone they know. Social workers and physicians frequently find that when the elderly are neglected and abused, the perpetrators are spouses and children and not paid caretakers. And when children are abducted, sexually molested, and/or abused, the culprit is most often a parent, a stepparent, or a trusted relative. (Joan Retsinas, "Don't Speak to Strangers," *Newsweek,* October 31, 1988, p. 10.)

Which statement most effectively describes the author's purpose?

a. The primary purpose of this reading is to inform.

b. The primary purpose of this reading is to persuade.

c. The author intended this reading to inform and persuade equally.

2. **Tracing the African-American Literary Tradition**

Whereas the Great Depression and World War II inhibited certain cultural activities, they saw no lessening of artistic achievement by African-Americans in literature. The new poets included Melvin B. Tolson of Wiley College, who published a collection, *Rendezvous with America* (1944), which included his most famous piece, "Dark Symphony"; and Robert Hayden of the University of Michigan, whose first volume was *Heart-Shape in the Dust* (1940). Commentator* Arna Bontemps produced *God Sends Sunday* (1931) and two historical novels, *Black Thunder* (1936) and *Drums at Dusk* (1939), before collaborating with Jack Conroy on *They Seek a City* (1945), an enthralling account of the urbanization of

---

*lamentable: depressing, causing grief or sadness.
*commentator: broadcaster.

African-Americans. George W. Lee described Memphis life in *Beale Street* (1934) and then brought out *River George* (1936), while Waters Turpin concentrated on the upper south of Maryland in *These Low Grounds* (1937) and *O Canaan* (1939). Sculptor Augusta Savage's *Lift Every Voice and Sing* was exhibited at the New York World's Fair of 1939. Chester Himes (b. 1909) described racial tension and friction in a wartime industrial community in *If He Hollers, Let Him Go* (1945), which vividly evokes the confusion and bitterness felt by African-Americans who had recently moved to industrial towns. (Sean Dennis Cashman, *African-Americans and the Quest for Civil Rights.* New York: New York University Press, 1991, pp. 66–67.)

Which statement most effectively describes the author's purpose?

a. The primary purpose of this reading is to inform.

b. The primary purpose of this reading is to persuade.

c. The author intended this reading to inform and persuade equally.

3. Buddhism was founded in India in the sixth century B.C. by Gautama, who is known as the Buddha ("enlightened one"). According to Buddhism, there is no independent, unchanging "self" and no physical world—both are illusions. Belief in their reality, attachment to them, and craving for human pleasures are, according to Buddhism, the source of human misery. To escape this misery is to attain Nirvana (salvation). It requires meditation—freeing one's mind from all worldly desires and ideas—and right thinking, right speech, right action, and the right mode of living. (Adapted from Alex Thio, *Sociology.* New York: HarperCollins, 1992, p. 384.)

Which statement most effectively describes the author's purpose?

a. The primary purpose of this reading is to inform.

b. The primary purpose of this reading is to persuade.

c. The author intended this reading to inform and persuade equally.

4. No modern society can hope to become a just society without a high level of universal literacy.* Putting aside for the moment the practical arguments about the economic uses of literacy, we can contemplate the even more basic principle that underlies our national system of education in the first place—that people in a democracy can be entrusted to decide all important matters for themselves because

---

*literacy: the ability to read and write.

they can deliberate and communicate with one another. Universal literacy is inseparable from democracy and is the canvas for Martin Luther King Jr.'s picture as well as for Thomas Jefferson's. (E. D. Hirsch, *Cultural Literacy*. Boston: Houghton Mifflin, 1987, p. 12.)

Which statement most effectively describes the author's purpose?

a. The primary purpose of this reading is to inform.

b. The primary purpose of this reading is to persuade.

c. The author intended this reading to inform and persuade equally.

Responding to Tone in Persuasive Writing

As a critical reader, you need to be particularly conscious of tone when the author is intent on persuasion. For example, you don't want to let a folksy, down-to-earth tone like the following lull you into accepting an opinion you may not really share.

> We all know that daycare is no substitute for a full-time mom who loves being at home with her kids.

Confronted with a statement like this one, critical readers would respond by asking themselves if they did, in fact, share the author's point of view, as the pronoun *we* suggests.

Similarly, critical readers would not let themselves be intimidated by a tone so confident that it allows no room for disagreement.

> Over the years, it has become obvious to all concerned that pouring more money into our schools is not going to improve our system of education. More money is *not* the answer.

In this passage, the writer's tone is so confident and so sure that what she thinks is right, you might be tempted to agree without considering whether that opinion is justified. As a critical reader, however, you need to challenge that confident tone by asking some hard questions: Exactly what schools have received this outpouring of money that the author mentions? And, is it really true that the schools didn't benefit as a result? Critical readers know that *an overly confident tone suggesting that no sensible person would disagree often masks an unjustified opinion.* Thus, readers would be quick to demand some relevant facts before they made the author's opinion their own.

EXERCISE 3

DIRECTIONS In each passage, the author tries to persuade readers to feel, think, or behave in a particular way. After reading the passage, identify the author's purpose and circle the letter that best describes the author's tone.

EXAMPLE Any person with no steady job and no children naturally finds time to sit around and think a lot. For instance, me—I've developed a theory about crows. It goes like this: Crows are bored. They suffer from being too intelligent for their station in life. They are dissatisfied with the narrow goals and horizons of that tired old Darwinian struggle† and on the lookout for a new challenge. See them there, lined up conspiratorially along a fence rail or a high wire, shoulder to shoulder, alert, self-contained, missing nothing, feeling discreetly thwarted, waiting, like an ambitious understudy, for their break. Dolphins and whales and chimpanzees get all the fawning publicity, great fuss over their near-human intelligence. But don't be fooled. Crows are not stupid. Far from it. They are merely underachievers. (Adapted from David Quammen, *Natural Acts*, New York: Dell Publishing, 1985, p. 30.)

1. In this passage, the author wants to convince readers that

    crows are really very smart.

2. To accomplish this purpose, the author assumes which of the following tones?
    a. passionate and concerned
    b. friendly and folksy
    c. emotionally neutral

EXPLANATION In this example, the author tries to convince his readers that crows are intelligent creatures. To achieve this goal, he uses a friendly and folksy tone. He creates that tone by referring to his personal life, speaking directly to his audience, and talking about crows as if they were actors waiting to go on stage.

1. You probably don't realize how important a role the sense of smell plays in your affairs. Like most of us, you value your ability to see and hear, but you completely ignore your sense of smell. Yet the ability to smell is as important as the ability to see or hear. Those

---

†Darwinian struggle: refers to the way animals adapt to nature and thereby survive as a species.

of you who doubt the importance of smell should try downing a piece of pizza or chocolate cake while holding your nose. Chances are, you won't even know what you're eating.

1. In this passage, the author wants to convince readers that ____

   Smelling is as important as hearing and seeing

2. To accomplish this purpose, the author assumes which of the following tones?

   (a) friendly and informal

   b. solemnly serious

   c. emotionally neutral

2. In his book *An Anthropologist on Mars,* the renowned neurologist Dr. Oliver Sacks gives readers an important and insightful perspective on injuries and disorders of the brain. According to Dr. Sacks, some injuries and disorders result in greater creativity and achievement. With compassion and insight, Dr. Sacks describes, for example, a painter who becomes color blind through a car accident. Initially in despair, the painter eventually starts painting stunning black and white canvases that win him more critical acclaim than ever before.

As he has in his previous work, Dr. Sacks gives readers an unexpected perspective on disease and injury. In *An Anthropologist on Mars,* he once again makes us rethink what we believe to be true. His book should be required reading for anyone interested in the power of human beings to adapt to and ultimately overcome loss.

1. In this passage, the author wants to persuade readers to _____

   read the book

2. To accomplish this purpose, the author assumes which of the following tones?

   a. comical

   (b) admiring

   c. emotionally neutral

3. The mind is often too full of opinions and "facts" about the way things *were* to accurately evaluate the way things *are.* For many people, the mind's job is to prove that what it already knows is enough, and there's no need to learn anything new.

As John Kenneth Galbraith† pointed out, "Faced with the choice between changing one's mind and proving there is no need to do so, almost everyone gets busy on the proof."

Firmness of mind, to a point, is a good thing. It keeps us from being wishy-washy, swayed by every new bit of information that comes our way. Carried beyond a certain point, however, the mind becomes closed to any new information from any source. The closed mind is, obviously, not open to learning. (John Roger, *Life 101.* Los Angeles: Prelude Press, 1991, p. 31.)

1. In this passage, the author wants to persuade readers to _____

   _____

2. To accomplish this purpose, the author assumes which of the following tones?

   a. anxious and worried

   b. friendly but serious

   c. emotionally neutral

4. It's possible to gather a great deal of knowledge about a person's emotional state simply from observing his or her physical behavior. Such observation can reveal contradictory messages that the subject might not verbally acknowledge. One need only think of the guest lecturer who speaks with authority while nervously pulling his tie or adjusting his glasses. Gestures of this sort clearly reveal an underlying tension and anxiety not verbally expressed. Similarly, the corporate executive who claims not to feel the pressure of her occupation may reveal her fears by an inordinately erect posture and a stiff facial expression.

1. In this passage, the author wants to convince readers that ____

   _____

2. To accomplish this purpose, the author assumes which of the following tones?

   a. passionate and angry

   b. down to earth and folksy

   c. emotionally neutral

†John Kenneth Galbraith: a famous economist and writer of numerous influential books.

Recognizing Irony in an Author's Tone

Authors who use an ironic tone say the opposite of what they actually mean and expect their readers to infer a point or message that contradicts their actual words. This might sound confusing at first. But, like most of us, you've probably assumed an ironic tone more than once in your life. Have you, for example, ever had a really horrible day and said to someone, "Boy, what a great day this was!" Or, seeing a friend wearing a sad expression, maybe you said, "Gee, you look happy."

If either of these examples sounds familiar, then you know more about irony than you think you do, and you're prepared for writers who assume an ironic tone like the one used in the following example:

> The school board has decided to reduce the school budget once again. But why take half measures? Why not eliminate the budget altogether and close our schools? After all, a little learning is a dangerous thing, or so they say. Better to keep our children totally ignorant and out of harm's way.

The author of this paragraph doesn't want his readers to take what he says *literally*. He definitely does not want them to further reduce the school budget. However, instead of saying that directly, he makes an outrageous suggestion designed to draw attention to where the cuts could lead. When writers present what seems to be an outrageous or impossible opinion as if it were obvious common sense, critical readers assume the writer is using irony to make a point, and they respond by inferring a message directly opposed to the author's actual words.

As you might expect, an ironic tone is a dead giveaway to purpose, and writers who use it are almost always intent on persuasion.

EXERCISE 4

DIRECTIONS Read each passage and circle the letter that best identifies the author's tone.

EXAMPLE Killing animals for their fur is wrong. Consider the cute mink, the cuddly raccoon, the loveable harp seal. These animals haven't hurt us, so why should we savagely murder these adorable creatures? Think of a puppy. Picture its soulful, trusting eyes. Would you want to wear Spot's hide on your back? The answer, from any thoughtful individual, must be a resounding "No!"

Tone (a.) furious

    b. ironic

    c. emotionally neutral

EXPLANATION In this example, *a* is the best answer. The author clearly doesn't want you to infer the opposite of what he says; so answer *b* is inappropriate. Likewise, *c* would never apply to a passage so filled with connotative language.

1. When people talk about how difficult it is to change a behavior they don't like, they often resort to an explanation: "Well, that's just my nature." Often what's implied by this statement is "And because it's my nature, don't expect me to change." Perhaps none of us can do much about human nature, especially our individual natures. It could be that we're pretty much stuck with them. Yet the "it's just human nature" school of thought robs us of the opportunity to change. There's another perspective we can take—one that opens up far more possibilities for the quality of our lives. Instead of talking about human nature, we can talk about habits. We can speak of our ability to control habits. We can change habits by eliminating unwanted ones and adding new ones. People stop smoking, drinking, and overeating. People also start to exercise, fasten seat belts, and develop scores of other effective habits. (Dave Ellis, *Becoming a Master Student.* Boston: Houghton Mifflin, 1994, p. 14.)

Tone a. relaxed and friendly

    b. formal and distant

    c. angry and passionate

2. This month in Belgrade, the United Nations Educational, Scientific and Cultural Organization will meet to blather about the report of its commission on "the news media." That report suggests, among other outrages, that the press ought to promote, and perhaps ought to be *required* to promote, the "social, cultural, economic and political goals set by governments." We're not the least bit surprised. That's exactly the kind of idea you can expect from an outfit calling itself "educational." (Richard Mitchell, *The Leaning Tower of Babel.* Boston: Little, Brown, 1984, p. 243.)

Tone a. comical

    b. disgusted

    c. ironic

3. When the voters of Michigan sent Charles Diggs, Jr., to the United States House of Representatives in 1954, he became the first black congressman in the state's history. He was not, however, the first black congressman in the United States. During the period of Reconstruction, from 1865 to 1877, the United States government tried to rebuild the South after the political and economic devastation of the Civil War. Black citizens held prominent government positions throughout the nation, including the posts of mayor, governor, lieutenant governor, state supreme court justice, U.S. senator, and U.S. congressman. (Juan Williams, *Eyes on the Prize.* New York: Penguin, 1987, p. 49.)

Tone a. outraged

    b. lighthearted

    c. emotionally neutral

4. It is refreshing to note that many right-thinking citizens are calling for a ban on the celebration of Halloween because the holiday encourages devil worship. Hallelujah? It doesn't take the intellect of a TV evangelist to see that the wearing of "Casper the Friendly Ghost" costumes leads children to the wanton embrace of Beelzebub.† And it is a known fact that candy corn is the first step toward addiction. Only the devil (or an underemployed dentist) would knowingly offer popcorn balls to innocent children. But why stop at Halloween? Many other holidays conceal wickedness behind a vicious veil of greeting cards and Bob Hope TV specials. (Steve Ruebal, "Toss Out Halloween? Let's not Stop There," *USA Today,* October 29, 1991, p. 11A.)

Tone a. confident

    b. enthusiastic

    c. ironic

5. I prefer the scruffy feel of the dog to the putting-green smoothness of the cat, a tail that wags happily to a tail that curls and uncurls like a cobra, an exuberant* bark to a maddeningly complacent* purr—"the most hideous of all the sounds in the world," according to the English man of letters Hilaire Belloc. Dogs lick you as if you were an ice cream cone, with grateful, life-affirming slurps; cats perform exploratory, clinical swabs with their tiny, pink, emery-board tongues. Before choosing a pet, consider a few chapter titles from Desmond Morris's book *Dogwatching*: "Why Does a Dog Wag Its Tail?" "Do Dogs Show Remorse?" and "Why Do Male Dogs Like Having Their Chests Scratched?" Now compare those with a few from

---

†Beelzebub: another name for the devil.
*exuberant: excited, happy.
*complacent: self-satisfied.

Morris's *Catwatching*: "Why Does a Tomcat Tear at the Fabric of Your Favorite Chair?" "Why Does a Cat Spray Urine on the Garden Wall?" (George Howe Colt, "Why We Love Dogs," *Life*, October, 1994, p. 80.)

Tone a. humorous

b. disgusted

c. emotionally neutral

DIGGING DEEPER What point does the author make through his allusions to two different books by Desmond Morris?

▨ Summing Up

Listed below are the most important points in Chapter 8. Put a check mark in the box if you think the point is clear in your mind. Leave the box blank if you need to review the material one more time. The page numbers in parentheses tell you where to look in order to review each point on the list.

☐ **1.** Like a person's speaking voice, a writer's style can reveal a particular tone or attitude. Tone in writing can vary with the writer's audience, purpose, or subject matter. (pp. 231–232)

☐ **2.** Sometimes authors purposely assume an emotionally neutral tone, one that conceals their personal feelings. (pp. 232–233)

☐ **3.** To evaluate how effectively an author has supported or explained a main idea, you need to identify an author's purpose. You should decide if the author is writing primarily to inform or to persuade. Remember, it's also possible that the author is trying to do both equally. (pp. 237–241)

☐ **4.** Tone is an important tool of persuasion, and critical readers don't let an author's tone lull them into accepting opinions they haven't thoroughly considered. (p. 245)

☐ **5.** An ironic tone is a common device of writers who want to persuade. (p. 249)

Working with Words

Here are some of the words defined in Chapter 8. Use the following exercises to gain more practice with these words and to learn more about their history and meaning.

EXERCISE 5

DIRECTIONS Fill in the blanks with one of the following words. *Note:* You will have to use some words more than once.

lucid: clear

maxims: sayings that reveal a lesson about life

erroneously: mistakenly

burgeoning: growing, increasing

lamentable: depressing, causing grief or sadness

enthralling: fascinating

exuberant: excited, happy

complacent: self-satisfied

1. Once the scientist forgot her shyness, she gave a remarkably ____lucid____ account of her theories, and everyone in the room thoroughly understood the purpose of her research.

2. It is ____Maxims____ that many Americans no longer feel secure about the future.

3. My uncle is always reciting the _____ he claims have guided his life. "Neither a borrower nor a lender be" is one of his favorites.

4. If the lead actor had been better prepared, the play would have been _____.

5. The actor's early death is _____; he had a great future ahead of him.

6. She had been on top for so long, she had become ____Complacent____ about her performance, and she no longer worked to perfect it.

7. The child's _____ laughter infected everyone else in the room, and the atmosphere went from tense to lighthearted and happy.

8. The newspaper had _____ reported that the strike was over; in fact, it was still going strong.

9. At the time, no one fully realized what the _____ civil rights movement would accomplish.

10. Many people try to make their writing impressive by using big words, but they would be better off making sure their writing was

    _____ enough to communicate their ideas.

■ **EXERCISE 6**

DIRECTIONS To answer the following questions, use a hardbound dictionary.

1. At the root of the word *egregious* is the Latin word *greg*, mean-

   ing _____.

2. At the root of the word *enthralling* is the Middle English word *thrall*,

   meaning _____.

3. The word *burgeon* comes from the French word *burjon*, mean-

   ing _____.

4. Used in the context of speech or writing, *lucid* means "clear" or "easily understood." However, if you say that a person is "lucid," you

   mean that he or she is _____.

⚡ Chapter 8: Review Test

Read each selection and identify the author's tone and purpose by circling the letters identifying the correct answer.

1. Religions that most need protection seem to receive it least. Contemporary America is not likely to enact legislation aimed at curbing the mainstream Protestant, Roman Catholic, or Jewish faiths. But Native Americans, having once been hounded from their lands, are now hounded from their religions, with the complicity of a Supreme Court untroubled when sacred lands are taken for road building or when Native Americans under a religious compulsion to use peyote† in their rituals are punished under state antidrug regulations. (Imagine if New York City were to try to take St. Patrick's Cathedral by eminent domain† to build a new convention center, or if Kansas, a dry state, were to outlaw the religious use of wine.) And airports, backed by the Supreme Court, are happy to restrict solicitation by devotees of Krishna Consciousness, which travelers, including this one, find irritating. (Picture the response should the airports try to regulate the wearing of crucifixes or yarmulkes on similar grounds of irritation.) (Adapted from Stephen Carter, *The Culture of Disbelief.* New York: Basic Books, 1993, p. 8.)

Tone  a. serious

b. relaxed

c. humorous

Purpose a. The author's primary purpose is to inform readers about the way some religious groups have been treated.

b. The author's primary purpose is to convince readers that all religions need the same degree of protection.

2. The relationship of trust and respect that Susan Butcher shares with her dogs is one of the things that has made Butcher the finest long-distance sled dog racer of all times. Fighting sub-zero temperatures and razor-sharp winds in the grueling sled dog race known as the Iditarod, Butcher has had nothing else to rely on except her wits and her dogs. Both have served her well. A four-time winner of the Iditarod, her record is equalled only by sled dog racer Rick Swenson.

---

†peyote: a hallucinatory drug derived from a form of cactus.
†eminent domain: refers to the right of the government to take over land needed for public works.

Tone a. ironic

       b. admiring

       c. critical

Purpose a. The author's primary purpose is to inform readers about the harshness of the Iditarod.

        b. The author's primary purpose is to convince readers that Susan Butcher is one of the finest sled dog racers alive today.

3. The fact that more women are lawfully arming themselves should be good news for everyone concerned with violence against women.

Since the publication of Betty Friedan's "The Feminine Mystique," feminists have been urging women to be independent and self-sufficient. What better evidence that women have "arrived" than that they no longer have to rely exclusively on police (still mostly male) for protection?

Feminists should applaud every woman who is skilled in handgun use. (Talk about controlling your own body.) Liberation from fear when walking on a dark street, driving on a country road late at night or withdrawing cash from a bank machine is more important on a daily basis to most women than smashing any glass ceiling in the workplace. (Laura Ingraham, "Armed and Empowered," *Pittsburgh Post-Gazette.* May 19, 1996, p. E-3.)

Tone a. ironic

       b. confident

       c. relaxed and friendly

Purpose a. The author's primary purpose is to inform readers about a growing trend—the ownership of handguns among women.

        b. The author's primary purpose is to convince readers that the ownership of handguns among women is a positive step forward.

4. The attraction to babylike creatures appears to be so strong that it is even triggered by the young of other species. Place a puppy or a kitten on someone's lap and nine times out of ten you will provoke a stock emotional reaction: The person will tend to caress and fondle the animal, bring it close to his or her face, look into its eyes, cuddle it, and accompany all these actions with a chorus of verbal endearments. If the animal yelps or mews or shows other signs of distress, the person will display concern and do his or her utmost to comfort it. In other words, just the sight of a baby animal seems to be enough to override normal behavior and replace it with something closely resembling the sorts of actions and activities that human parents generally direct toward their own infants. Biologists have coined the phrase "cute response" to describe this reaction. (Adapted from James Serpell, *In the Company of Animals.* Oxford, England: Basil Blackwell, Ltd., 1986, p. 61.)

Tone a. comical

      b. sad

      (c.) emotionally neutral

Purpose (a.) The author's primary purpose is to inform readers about the nature of the "cute response" in human beings.

      b. The author's primary purpose is to convince readers that the "cute response" is a ridiculous form of behavior.

5. Alfred Nobel, born in 1833, was the inventor of dynamite. However, he was also a committed promoter of peace. When a newspaper erroneously printed the Swedish businessman's obituary, calling him a "merchant of death," Nobel grew obsessed with leaving behind a peaceful legacy. When he died in 1896, his relatives were outraged by his will: Ninety-four percent of his vast fortune was to be used for an annual award to a handful of people around the globe whose work—in physics, chemistry, medicine, literature, and peacemaking (the economics category was added in 1969)—had "conferred the greatest benefit on mankind." The will's wording was so vague, however, that its executors spent five years quarreling over what it meant. Thus, the first Nobel Prizes were not bestowed until the fifth anniversary of Nobel's death.

Tone a. annoyed

      b. lighthearted

      (c.) emotionally neutral

Purpose a. The author's primary purpose is to tell readers how the Nobel Peace Prize came into being.

      b. The author's primary purpose is to convince readers that Alfred Nobel was a great man.

C H A P T E R   9

Recognizing and Evaluating Bias

 In this chapter, you'll learn

- **how to evaluate bias in persuasive writing.**
- **how to recognize bias in informative writing.**

As the title suggests, Chapter 9 returns to the subject of *bias*. In this chapter, you'll learn more about the ways in which an author's personal leaning or perspective can intrude itself into a text, even when an author tries hard to remain completely neutral.

Bias Isn't All Bad

DAVID: I think the Democratic plan for creating a jobs program is a good one.

TISHA: A jobs program! Have you lost your mind? With the deficit eating away at America's future, we can't afford to lavish money on another Democratic pipe dream. Where is your head these days?

DAVID: I never should have started this discussion. When it comes to the Democrats, you're so biased, you can't listen to reason. Anything they do is going to be wrong where you're concerned.

As this dialogue illustrates, the word *bias* has a bad reputation. We frequently use it to suggest that someone has a closed mind and cannot or will not listen to opposing points of view.

But expressing a bias isn't necessarily bad. Because of our background, experience, and training, most of us have personal opinions, or leanings, that influence how we see and interpret the world around us. Thus, how critical readers react to or evaluate an expression of bias depends a good deal on the context in which that bias appears and the degree, or strength, of the bias expressed.

For example, unless they are writing for the editorial page, newspaper reporters are expected to report events as objectively as possible. If reporters describe those events in highly connotative or emotionally charged language that reveals their personal point of view, they are doing readers a disservice, and their bias is inappropriate to the context.

In contrast, editorials in newspapers are expected to express a bias. In fact, that's one of the reasons we read them. We want, for example, to get columnists Maureen Dowd's or William Safire's perspective on some current issue. However, even writers determined to persuade should offer readers a fair and reasonable argument. If a writer is so committed to one point of view that he or she can't be logical or fair, then the degree of bias is excessive, and we need to be wary of accepting that writer's point of view.

All writers have biases, and there's nothing wrong with revealing them in the appropriate context. What's important is that writers not let bias interfere with their ability to be logical and fair.

Evaluating Bias in Persuasive Writing

In writing that is meant to persuade, authors are likely to announce how they feel about the subject or issue under discussion. The following passage offers an example of an author who's not shy about expressing his point of view.

> After reading about courses in television literacy,† I must say I am appalled by the sheer idiocy that abounds on so many college campuses today. Why, what should instructors do if they discover that students have trouble reading their textbooks because they have spent too much time watching television? What else? Give those same students more television to watch. That way, teachers can avoid making demands on students *and* avoid doing their job. All they need to do is flip on the television set and call themselves "media specialists."

This author is strongly biased against courses in television literacy, and he openly admits it: "After reading about courses in television literacy, I must say I am appalled by the sheer idiocy that abounds on so many college campuses today."

In response, critical readers would ask themselves if the author's personal leanings are so strong that they interfere with his ability to give an accurate assessment of how useful such courses might or might not be. In this case, the answer would probably be yes. The author's tone of outraged irony suggests that he is too biased to even consider an opposing perspective. Although there might be some good reasons for taking a course in television viewing, readers are not likely to learn about those reasons from this author.

Read the following example. Despite her admission of bias, the author is still capable of keeping an open mind.

> I must admit to being troubled by courses that make commercials and soap operas the focus of study. Although I agree that television programming plays a powerful role in most people's lives and that its influence over our minds and imaginations should be subjected to critical examination, I'm not sure courses in television literacy are the answer. A better alternative would be to make television viewing a small portion of a course on critical reading and thinking. Then students could apply their critical skills to both television scripts and images. This approach would eliminate what seems to be a legitimate objection to courses in television literacy—that they encourage students to do more of what they already do: watch too much TV.

Like the previous author, the writer of this passage openly admits a bias: She is not wildly enthusiastic about courses in television literacy. Nevertheless, her controlled and direct tone suggests she can recognize that such courses might have merit. Although she has a personal bias, that bias has not prevented her from evaluating the

---

†courses in television literacy: courses that teach students how to watch television with a more critical eye.

subject more logically and fairly than the writer of the previous passage.

■

DIGGING What do you think about courses in television literacy? Do you
DEEPER think they should or should not be part of the college curriculum?
Explain. *No Because the viewer can be distracted or become Self absorb.*

Recognizing Bias in Informative Writing

Writers whose primary goal is to inform rather than persuade usually work hard to keep their biases to themselves. For example, the author of a textbook on modern American history might be a longtime Republican who considers Democrat Lyndon Baines Johnson the worst president ever to have lived. Yet, in writing a chapter that covered Johnson's presidency, he would probably control his inclination to criticize Johnson's record. Like writers of reference works, authors of textbooks are expected to provide an impersonal and objective account of events and allow students to form their own opinions.

Still, writers are only human. Try as they might, they can't always eliminate every shred of personal bias from their writing. Although the overall tone of a passage may be emotionally neutral, the connotations of individual words or phrases can still suggest a personal bias or leaning. Note, for example, the italicized words in the following paragraph. These words have negative connotations and suggest that the authors do not admire the way former president Harry Truman handled foreign policy.

President Truman . . . had a personality that tended to increase international tensions. Whereas Roosevelt had been *ingratiating,** patient, and evasive, Truman was *brash,** *impatient,* and direct. *He seldom displayed the appreciation of subtleties so essential to successful diplomacy.* In his first meeting with V. M. Molotov, the Soviet commissar of foreign affairs, Truman sharply *berated** the Soviet Union† for violating the Yalta accords,† a charge Molotov

---

*ingratiating: eager to please.
*brash: hasty and unthinking.
*berated: criticized harshly.
†Soviet Union: the former name of fifteen separate republics governed by the communist party, also called "Soviet Russia."
†Yalta accords: agreements made at the end of World War II in the city of Yalta located near the Black Sea.

denied. When Truman *shot back* that the Soviets should honor their agreements, Molotov stormed out of the room. The president was pleased with his "tough method": "I give it to him straight 'one-two to the jaw.'" This *simplistic display of toughness* became a trademark of American Cold War† diplomacy.* (Norton et al., *A People and a Nation,* p. 488.)

The authors of this textbook passage are probably not fans of Harry Truman. But would you say the same about the author of the next passage?

On his first day in office, Harry Truman remarked to a newspaperman, "Did you ever have a bull or a load of hay fall on you? If you ever did, you know how I felt last night." Yet President Truman's *native intelligence enabled him to grasp quickly the situation into which he was so suddenly thrown,* and on which he had not been briefed by Roosevelt. He had to have a few boon* companions from Missouri around the White House for relaxation, but *he won the friendship and respect of gentlemen in politics* such as Dean Acheson, soldiers such as General Marshall, and foreign statesmen such as Clement Attlee. He made good cabinet, judicial, and ambassadorial appointments; *he kept a firm hand* on the new Department of Defense and the foreign service; and, *with more fateful decisions than almost any president in our time, he made the fewest mistakes.* Truman was always folksy, always the politician, *but nobody can reasonably deny that he attained the stature of a statesman.* (Samuel Eliot Morrison, *The Oxford History of the American People.* New York: Oxford University Press, 1965, p. 1051.)

In contrast to the authors of the previous passage, the author of this passage admires Harry Truman's record as president, and his choice of words encourages readers to do the same.

When they recognize bias in writing meant to inform, critical readers don't throw up their hands in horror and refuse to read further. Instead, they try to identify the author's particular leaning and make sure that they don't absorb it right along with the author's description of events or ideas. Readers of either passage about Truman, for example, would have to know a good deal more before deciding if Truman was a gifted or an incompetent president.

---

†Cold War: a period of hostile rivalry between the United States and Communist Russia.
*diplomacy: the conduct by government officials of relations between nations.
*boon: in this context, good-natured, jolly.

Recognizing and Evaluating an Author's Bias

1. Look carefully at the language used. Pay special attention to words with strong negative or positive connotations.

2. Consider whether the author's tone reveals some degree of bias in favor of one position or another.

3. Look for references to contradictory points of view. An author who wants to be perceived as unbiased or emotionally neutral is likely to include opposing points of view. An author who is deeply biased, however, is likely to emphasize one perspective and ignore any opposition.

4. Read closely any passages in which the author explains contradictory positions. An author who ridicules or distorts the opposition is usually overly biased in favor of one position.

5. Study the author's selection of details. An author who has selected only those details that praise or criticize a particular point of view may be expressing a subtle bias. In some cases, *what is left out can be as important as what is included.*

6. Look for hasty generalizations and circular arguments. The presence of unjustified opinions usually indicate a bias so strong it clouds the author's ability to reason effectively.

■ **EXERCISE 1**

DIRECTIONS Read each selection and identify the author's tone and purpose. Then indicate whether you think the author reveals any personal bias or inclination toward one side or another.

EXAMPLE Here at Glassboro State, we have no language requirements. Nor do we have any *foreign* language requirements. This may seem strange to someone out in the world, but most of us think it is a very good and proper thing. In fact, to suggest the possibility of a language requirement around here is like asking for a bacon sandwich at a bar mitzvah† in Brooklyn.

---

†bar mitzvah: ceremony in Jewish religion in which a boy officially becomes a man. For orthodox Jews, eating pork is forbidden, and a bacon sandwich would be utterly inappropriate at a bar mitzvah.

There are—let's face it—certain subjects that are just not suitable for study in the schools, and one of them is foreign language. The study of *any* foreign language is an egregiously* unhumanistic enterprise in which even *good* students can actually make an . . . *error!* That's humiliating and undemocratic. . . . (Mitchell, *The Leaning Tower of Babel*, p. 6.)

Tone (a.) ironic

    b. confident

    c. emotionally neutral

Purpose a. The author's primary goal is to inform.

    (b.) The author's primary goal is to persuade.

Bias (a.) The author is in favor of teaching foreign languages in college.

    b. The author is not in favor of teaching foreign languages in college.

    c. It's impossible to determine the author's personal feelings.

EXPLANATION In this reading, the author's tone is heavy with irony as he argues that foreign languages are not appropriate for study in school. Because irony always suggests the opposite of what's actually said, we can assume that the author is personally in favor of teaching foreign languages to college students, and his purpose is to make readers share his point of view.

1. Every year, the city council makes the same ridiculous proposal: special laws governing the owners of pit bulls, along with strict leash and muzzle laws for the dogs themselves. Here's an idea. Why don't we just round up all the dogs and shoot them? This will get rid of the problem once and for all and pit bull owners like me won't have to be exposed to the yearly round of horror stories about pit bull attacks. Over the period of a year, there might be ten dog attacks on people, but which one gets the most publicity? Guaranteed, it's the one involving the pit bull.

Tone a. ironic

    b. enthusiastic

    c. emotionally neutral

---

*egregiously: horribly, terribly.

Purpose a. The author's primary goal is to inform.

      b. The author's primary goal is to persuade.

Bias a. The author is a supporter of special laws for pit bulls and their owners.

      b. The author does not support special laws for pit bulls and their owners.

      c. It's impossible to determine the author's personal feelings.

2. It is naive to believe that chemical and biological weapons can be wished away by positive thinking or paper treaties. Simplistic editorialists, grandstanding* politicians, and deluded liberals are dangerously wrong in advocating that the USA abandon or even lower its defenses against chemical or biological warfare.

Although "civilized" nations signed protocols* against the use of chemical and biological weapons as early as 1925 and as recently as three years ago, chemical warfare particularly is, regrettably, a growth industry. Because these barbaric weapons are cheap to manufacture (their ingredients are easy to obtain and difficult to track), intelligence agencies estimate between 22 and 38 nations have or will have the capability to produce chemical weapons. (Peter Gemma, "No Treaty Can Control Chemical Weapons," *USA Today*, February 22, 1991, p. 7A.)

Tone a. ironic

      b. confident and impatient

      c. emotionally neutral

Purpose a. The author's primary goal is to inform.

      b. The author's primary goal is to persuade.

Bias a. The author favors treaties banning the use of chemical and biological weapons.

      b. The author does not favor treaties banning the use of chemical and biological weapons.

      c. It's impossible to determine the author's personal feelings.

3. In January 1943, a young French naval engineer named Jacques-Yves Cousteau and his partner, Emile Gagnan, toted a contraption†

---

*grandstanding: attention-getting.
*protocols: treaties.
†contraption: device.

consisting of little more than a regulator (modified from a gadget Gagnan had designed to allow wartime cars to run on cooking gas) and two tanks of compressed air to the Marne River outside Paris. They were testing a device inventors had tried to build for a century: a backpack-like apparatus that would deliver air to a diver automatically, without clumsy hoses to the surface.

Cousteau's wife snapped photographs as he slipped into the frigid water. A minute later, he resurfaced, cursing. The Aqua-Lung (as its creators call it) had failed. But later that day, after making minor readjustments, Cousteau strapped it on again, dived into an indoor tank, and breathed comfortably while performing subsurface somersaults. (Lorraine Glennon, ed., *Our Times.* Atlanta: Turner Publishing, 1995, p. 322.)

Tone a. ironic

b. serious and concerned

c. emotionally neutral

Purpose a. The author's primary goal is to inform.

b. The author's primary goal is to persuade.

Bias a. The author personally believes that Cousteau was a genius.

b. The author is personally not very impressed by Cousteau's achievement.

c. It's impossible to determine the author's personal feelings.

4. Most rules about writing should not be expressed (in textbooks), stored (in our minds), or enacted (on the page) as . . . mathematical, unvarying directives.* True, a few rules apply in virtually all situations (for example, certain formatting rules or capitalization rules). But most rules do not. Writing rules, like any rules about language, have a history and have a time and place. They are highly context-bound.

Should you always, as some textbooks suggest, place your thesis sentence at the beginning of your first paragraph, or, as others suggest, work up to it and place it at the end of the paragraph? Well, the answer is that both injunctions* are right . . . and wrong. Students writing essay exams would be well-advised to demonstrate their knowledge and direct the reader's attention as soon as possible. But the writer who wants to evoke a mood might offer a series

---

*directives: rules.
*injunctions: commands, rules.

of facts and events that gradually leads up to a thesis sentence. The writing situation, the rhetorical* purpose, and the nature of the material one is working with will provide the answer. A single-edged rule cannot. (Mike Rose, "Writing Around Rules," *About Language.* Boston: Houghton Mifflin, 1995, p. 25.)

Tone a. friendly and funny

b. confident

c. emotionally neutral

Purpose a. The author's primary goal is to inform.

b. The author's primary goal is to persuade.

Bias a. The author knows that other people don't believe in writing according to the rules, but he himself considers rules essential.

b. The author personally believes that writers don't always write according to a fixed set of rules.

c. It's impossible to determine the author's personal feelings.

 5. A trial is often compared to a boxing match. Both are contests between *adversaries*, persons who oppose or fight one another. In a trial, the adversaries are called **litigants** and, rather than hitting each other, they challenge each other's evidence and testimony. For this reason, an American trial is often labeled an **adversary proceeding.** The judge acts as a referee and interprets the rules of the "match."

The person who files suit in a civil case is called the **plaintiff.** In a criminal trial, the prosecution brings the charges. The United States Attorney is the prosecutor in federal cases. In state trials, the prosecutor may be known as the state's attorney, county prosecutor, or district attorney. The person being sued or charged with the crime is the defendant.

Every trial has two purposes: to establish the facts of the case, and to find the law that applies. The role of the jury is to decide questions of fact. (Adapted from Richard J. Hardy, *Government in America.* Boston: Houghton Mifflin, 1993, p. 502.)

Tone a. casual and friendly

b. serious and sad

c. emotionally neutral

---

*rhetorical: related to the effective use of language.

Purpose   a. The author's primary goal is to inform.

        b. The author's primary goal is to persuade.

Bias   a. The author is describing the elements of a trial and clearly favors our legal system.

        b. The author is describing the elements of a trial and is clearly critical of our legal system.

        c. It's impossible to determine the author's personal feelings.

■ EXERCISE 2

DIRECTIONS Read each of the following textbook selections. See if you can determine the authors' personal bias.

1. The Presidency of John F. Kennedy

John F. Kennedy's ambitious social program, the New Frontier, promised more than Kennedy could deliver: an end to racial discrimination, federal aid to education, medical care for the elderly, and government action to halt the recession* the country was suffering. Only eight months into his first year, it was evident that Kennedy lacked the ability to move Congress, which was dominated by conservative Republicans and southern Democrats. Long-time members of Congress saw him and his administration as publicity hungry. Some feared the president would seek federal aid to parochial schools. The result was the defeat of federal aid to education and of a Kennedy-sponsored boost in the minimum wage.

Still struggling to appease conservative members of Congress, the new president pursued civil rights with a notable lack of vigor. Kennedy did establish the President's Committee on Equal Employment Opportunity to eliminate racial discrimination in government hiring. But he waited until late 1962 before honoring a 1960 campaign pledge to issue an executive order forbidding segregation in federally subsidized housing. Meanwhile, he appointed five die-hard segregationists to the federal bench in the Deep South. The struggle for racial equality was the most important domestic issue of the time, and Kennedy's performance disheartened* civil rights advocates. (Adapted from Norton et al., *A People and a Nation*, p. 991.)

---

*disheartened: discouraged.
*recession: an extended economic decline.

a. The authors are admirers of John F. Kennedy.

b. The authors are critical of John F. Kennedy.

c. It's impossible to determine the authors' bias.

2. **Reaganism**

Ronald Reagan brought to the White House two distinct advantages over Nixon, Ford, and Carter. He had a clear and simple vision of the type of America he wanted and an unusual ability to convey that image to the American public. Called the "Great Communicator" by the press, Reagan and his staff expertly used imagery and the media. Reagan presented images and visions, but he did not create the policies to bring them about. Secretary of Treasury Donald Regan once commented, "The President's mind is not cluttered with facts." A hands-off president, Reagan delegated authority to the cabinet and executive staff and made little effort to initiate, direct, or control policy. He set the grand agenda. His lieutenants assumed the blame when policies failed or could not overcome opposition.

Budget Director David Stockman was a believer in **supply-side economics**—the idea that lowering taxes will increase revenue from taxation by increasing the amount of money available for investments. Stockman fashioned a tax package and budget that reduced income and corporate taxes and slashed federal spending on social programs. The **Economic Recovery Tax Act,** passed in 1981, cut income and most business taxes by an average of 25 percent; upper income levels received the largest tax reduction. Stockman later admitted that "none of us really understand what's going on" or what to expect and that the tax act was really a "Trojan Horse"† to help the rich. Conservative Democrats in the House joined with Republicans to cut $25 billion from social programs, including food stamps, Aid to Families with Dependent Children, and jobs and housing programs. Reagan also ended Nixon's federal revenue-sharing programs and reduced the amount of federal monies paid to the states for Medicare and Medicaid programs. To halt inflation, Federal Reserve chairman Paul Volker pushed interest rates upward, reducing the money supply.

The impact of smaller appropriations* and higher qualifications for welfare reduced the number of people on federal welfare rolls, and the number living in poverty increased. Reduced federal

---

†Trojan Horse: According to a Greek historian, the Greeks gained entry to the enemy city of Troy by hiding themselves in a huge wooden horse. The allusion suggests the tax act concealed hidden gifts for the rich.
*appropriations: public funds set aside for specific purposes.

support for a variety of state and local social and economic programs forced state and local governments to eliminate or limit programs and to raise taxes. By the end of Reagan's first term, the reduction in the number of poor brought about by President Johnson's War on Poverty had vanished. Their numbers swelled by reductions in federal housing programs, the homeless became symbols of an economy that liberals called unfair. (Adapted from Berkin et al., *Making America*, pp. 981–982.)

a. The authors are admirers of Ronald Reagan.

b. The authors are critical of Ronald Reagan.

c. It's impossible to determine the authors' bias.

Summing Up

Listed below are the most important points in Chapter 9. Put a check mark in the box if you think the point is clear in your mind. Leave the box blank if you need to review the material one more time. The page numbers in parentheses tell you where to look in order to review each point on the list.

☐ **1.** Although the word *bias* has negative connotations, expressing bias in writing is not necessarily bad. In fact, it's extremely difficult to write without revealing any personal bias. How critical readers react to or evaluate bias depends on the context in which a bias appears and the degree or strength of the bias expressed. (p. 259)

☐ **2.** In writing meant to persuade, authors are likely to announce their personal bias. In response, critical readers know that they have to determine whether the author's bias interferes with his or her ability to offer a logical argument or present an accurate picture of the opposition. (pp. 259–261)

☐ **3.** Writers whose primary goal is to inform usually work hard to keep bias out of their writing. However, completely suppressing personal bias is not easy, because an author's word choice or selection of details often unintentionally reveals a bias. Even with writing meant to inform, critical readers need to be alert to the way an author's choice of words or selection of details can reveal an author's personal feelings about the subject at hand. (pp. 261–262)

Working with Words

Here are some of the words defined in Chapter 9. Use the following exercises to gain more practice with these words and to learn more about their history and meaning.

EXERCISE 3

DIRECTIONS Use the following words to fill in the blanks.

ingratiating: eager to please

brash: hasty and un-thinking

berated: criticized harshly

egregiously: horribly, terribly

grandstanding: attention-getting

protocols: treaties

injunctions: commands, rules

rhetorical: related to the effective use of language

disheartened: discouraged

appropriations: public funds set aside for a specific purpose

1. The reporter's questions were so _____ and rude, the president refused to answer them.

2. Now that the presidential campaign is upon us, we can expect to hear from more than one _____ politician who claims to have all the answers for the country's ills.

3. The poor waiter was so _____, it was embarrassing.

4. The coach _____ the team members for not giving the game their best effort.

5. Alone in his office, the president read through the _____ _____ for nuclear disarmament.

6. The young actors were _____ by the small size of the audience.

7. Most writers don't believe that the same _____ rules apply to every writing context.

8. The new senator wanted to cut all _____ set aside for low income housing, but he was having trouble getting support for such drastic measures.

9. The religion had many _____ that applied solely to the behavior of women.

10. The wedding cake was so _____ decorated, the bride and groom didn't want it in their wedding pictures.

■

■ EXERCISE 4

DIRECTIONS To answer the following questions, you'll need a hard-bound dictionary.

1. Which one of the words listed in the previous exercise is a synonym for the word *directive*? _____

2. The word *diplomacy* can apply to international relations, but it can also apply to dealings between _____.

3. In computer science, a *protocol* is _____ _____.

4. If used in the context of a church service, the word *recession* refers to _____.

5. The adjective *brash* can be applied to people or to _____ _____.

📐 Chapter 9: Review Test

Part A   Read each selection and identify the author's purpose and tone. Then indicate whether you think the author reveals any personal bias toward one side or the other.

1. It's rude out there. Rude all over the place. In the country that invented "Have a Nice Day," citizens now wear sweatshirts that scream "Back Off," or worse. On the football field and on the basketball court, the old ideal of sportsmanlike conduct has degenerated into a fiesta of trash talk and aggressive taunting.

   Since the 1940s, the Salvation Army has put out drop-off bins so that kindhearted citizens could donate old clothes and furniture. Last month, it announced that it would retire the bins in eight Midwestern states because people were using them as Dumpsters. There's a problem here. (William Grimes, "Have a Nice Day," *New York Times*, October 17, 1993, p. 2.)

Tone
   - (a.) ironic
   - b. casual but concerned
   - c. emotionally neutral

Purpose
   - (a.) The author's primary goal is to inform readers about the increase in rudeness throughout American society.
   - b. The author's primary goal is to convince readers that strong measures must be taken to make people be more polite.

Bias
   - a. The author is recounting other people's opinions about rudeness in American society; he himself is not concerned.
   - (b.) The author personally believes that rudeness is on the rise.
   - c. It's impossible to determine the author's personal feelings.

2. What, precisely, is the mind, the elusive entity where intelligence, decision making, perception, awareness, and sense of self reside? Where is it located? How does it work? Does it arise from purely physical processes—pulses of electricity zapping from brain cell to brain cell, helped along their way by complex chemicals? Or is it something beyond the merely physical—something that might be close to the spiritual concept of the soul?

   Great thinkers have had no shortage of ideas on the subject. Plato† was convinced that the mind must be located inside the

   ---
   †Plato: Greek philosopher (427–347 B.C.)

head, because the head is shaped more or less like a sphere, his idea of the highest geometrical form. Aristotle† insisted that the mind was in the heart. His reasoning: warmth implies vitality; the blood is warm; the heart pumps the blood. By the Middle Ages, though, pretty much everyone agreed that the mind arose from the brain—but still had no clear idea how it arose. (Michael D. Lemonick, "Glimpses of the Mind," *Time*, July 17, 1995, p. 46.)

Tone
    a. emotionally neutral

    b. enthusiastic and excited

    c. casual and comical

Purpose
    a. The author's primary goal is to inform readers about two different theories of the mind.

    b. The author's primary goal is to persuade readers that Plato's theory of the mind was more accurate than Aristotle's.

Bias
    a. The author personally believes that questions about the location and working of the mind are silly.

    b. The author himself is fascinated by questions about the location and working of the mind.

    c. It's impossible to determine the author's personal feelings.

3. For established Westerners, everything is fundamentally changing—and fast, as thousands of newcomers consume the available property. The West's traditional industries—mining, ranching, and logging—are clear losers in the new order. That old economy, based on "extracting"† wealth from rocks, grass, and trees, is dying, pushed aside by market forces (it's a lot cheaper to raise cows on feedlots in Florida than on poor pasture in Wyoming), replaced by high-skilled workers in high-tech companies. There are only 3,000 miners left in all of Idaho—fewer than one lone company, Micron Technology Inc., employs in two counties near Boise. Currently, the region's most rapidly expanding employers are museums, amusement parks, and fitness clubs. The steepest declines are in the traditional extractive jobs. So cowpats and coal mining are out; cappuccino and cilantro† are in. On Yankie Street in the New Mexico mining

---

†extracting: taking or pulling out.
†cilantro: an herb associated with fancy or fashionable recipes.
†Aristotle: Greek philosopher (384–322 B.C.)

town of Silver City, the A.I.R. Espresso Bar and Gallery says it all: "A.I.R." stands for "artist in residence." (Michael Elliott, et al., "The West at War," *Newsweek,* July 17, 1995, p. 24.)

Tone   a. emotionally neutral

b. angry and outraged

c. relaxed and humorous

Purpose   a. The author's primary goal is to tell readers how the West is changing.

b. The author's primary goal is to convince readers that steps must be taken if the old West is to be preserved.

Bias   a. The author hates the changes taking place in the West.

b. The author loves the changes taking place in the West.

c. It's impossible to determine the author's personal feelings.

4. Since we now know that, in order to become literate, young children must gain a store of traditional information at an early age, it is time to reconsider the use of phrases like "memorization" (better to say "learning by heart") and "piling up facts" as though they were insult terms. Many "higher-order skills" of literacy are gained *only* by piling up information. No study of language learning, for instance, has challenged the notion that children learn the names of objects by repeatedly being told those names until they remember them. Thus, at the very root of learning a language we find memorization. Later on, in earliest training, children must learn the alphabet by heart. I cannot conceive how a child could acquire the alphabet other than by memorization. The same applies to the multiplication table, the days of the week, and the months of the year. There's no other way of acquiring those skills. (Adapted from E. D. Hirsch, "Restoring Cultural Literacy in the Early Grades," *Educational Leadership,* vol. 45, no. 4 [December 1987/January 1988], p. 10.)

Tone   a. emotionally neutral

b. serious and concerned

c. lighthearted and humorous

Purpose   a. The author's primary goal is to inform readers about the way the term *memorization* is usually treated.

(b.) The author's primary goal is to persuade readers to have greater respect for memorization.

Bias   a. The author explains how other people view memorization, but he himself is critical of the practice.

(b.) The author personally believes that memorizing facts is an important part of education.

c. It's impossible to determine the author's personal feelings.

Part B In each of the following passages, the author's purpose is to persuade. You have to (1) identify the opinion or point of view the author wants you to hold and (2) indicate whether the author's bias affects his or her ability to be convincing.

5. Life in the hospital is a trial. Patients find their normal conceptions of life shattered, and ordinary rights and abilities once taken for granted vanish like smoke. Patients, so long used to the rights to life, liberty, and happiness, find the latter two abused at the expense of the former. They find themselves at the bottom of a vast and complex hierarchy that includes not only doctors, nurses, and orderlies, but also faceless drones working for insurance companies, whose goal is to produce as much red tape as is humanly possible.

a. The author wants to convince readers that _life in the hospital is a trial_.

b. (1.) Despite an obvious bias, the author is quite convincing.

    2. The author is so biased, it's hard to take his opinion seriously.

6. The United States has to speed up the process of nuclear disarmament. It is vital that we lead the world in this process because getting rid of nuclear weapons is an absolute necessity. If we do not get rid of nuclear weapons now, they will remain with us until we die. Without disarmament, the threat posed by these weapons will stay with us.

a. The author wants to convince readers that _United States has to speed up the process of nuclear disarmament_.

b. 1. Despite an obvious bias, the author is quite convincing.

2. The author is so biased, it's hard to take her opinion seriously.

7. Baseball great Art Shires had a violent temper. Shires was known for beating up members of opposing teams, but he had a special fondness for beating up his manager, Len Blackburne. During the 1929 spring training, Blackburne told Shires he could be captain of the Chicago White Sox if he behaved himself. To celebrate, Shires went out and broke all the training rules. To penalize Shires, Blackburne took away his offer of the captaincy. Shires responded by giving him a black eye. On another occasion, Blackburne made Shires remove his favorite red hat during batting practice, and the two got into an argument on the field. Shires later ambushed Blackburne in the clubhouse and beat him up.

a. The author wants to convince readers that _Baseball great Art Shires had a Violent temper._

b. (1.) Despite an obvious bias, the author is quite convincing.

   2. The author is so biased, it's hard to take his opinion seriously.

Part C Read each textbook selection. Then circle the appropriate letter to indicate the presence or absence of bias.

8. President Wilson's† third attorney general, A. Mitchell Palmer, was a Pennsylvania politician with a presidential bee in his bonnet. Appointed alien property custodian in 1917, he sequestered† some $600 million worth of German and Austrian property in the United States, and saw to it that his friends got some of the bargains when this property was sold. As attorney general, Palmer decided (like Joseph McCarthy† more than thirty years later) that the way to fame and power was to crack down on the "Reds." Wilson, at the first cabinet meeting since his breakdown, in April 1920, said, "Palmer, do not let this country see red!" But Palmer had been doing just that for five months. He instigated a series of lawless raids on homes and labor head-

---

†President Wilson: Woodrow Wilson, the twenty-second President of the United States.
†sequestered: took possession of.
†Joseph McCarthy: U.S. Senator who accused countless people of being communists and destroyed their lives in the process.

quarters, on a single night of January 1920, arresting more than 4000 alleged communists in 33 different cities. (Samuel Eliot, *The Oxford History of the American* People. New York: Oxford University Press, 1965, p. 883.)

The author of this selection is

a. an admirer of A. Mitchell Palmer.

b. critical of A. Mitchell Palmer.

c. unwilling to express a bias.

9. Hillary Rodham Clinton is not the first First Lady to play a prominent political role in her husband's administration. Eleanor Roosevelt was a visible and tireless advocate for causes she believed in. (Republicans were critical of her, some calling the liberal First Lady "Lenin† in skirts.") But just as Rosie the Riveter† returned to the kitchen after World War II, the First Ladies who followed Mrs. Roosevelt, Bess Truman and Mamie Eisenhower, were content to stand in the background and play the role of dutiful wife and mother. (Janda et al., *The Challenge of Democracy*, p. 416.)

The authors of this selection are

a. admirers of Eleanor Roosevelt.

b. critical of Eleanor Roosevelt.

c. unwilling to express a bias.

10. Plath, Sylvia (1932–1963) American poet. She left America in 1956 when she married Ted Hughes. She had a history of mental illness and had attempted suicide in 1953. Some time after her marriage to Ted Hughes had broken up, she killed herself. The failure of a prescription to arrive was a factor mentioned at the inquest.

The poetry in her first volume, *The Colossus* (1960), did not attract much attention; it consists of fairly quiet poetry about objects, and contains only hints of the later, violent style found in *Ariel* (1965), which was written in a last burst of mad energy before her death. The poems in *Ariel* have been overrated, but they are very impressive and horrifyingly fascinating. Plath is

---

†Lenin: Vladimir Ilich Lenin (1870–1924), leader of the Russian Revolution in 1917.
†Rosie the Riveter: magazine illustration used to inspire women to help out in the war effort for World War II (for more on Rosie, see pages 441–445).

undeniably powerful. Yet, she has, as I have remarked, been overrated (the reverent tone of such intelligent though overgenerous critics as Richard Howard or M. L. Rosenthal is not, alas, deserved): she was sick, and finally she fails to transcend her sickness (as a major poet must). (Adapted from Martin Seymour Smith, *Who's Who in Twentieth Century Literature*. New York: McGraw-Hill, 1976, p. 283.)

The author of this selection is

a. an admirer of Sylvia Plath.

b. critical of Sylvia Plath.

c. unwilling to express a bias.

C H A P T E R   1 0

Analyzing and Evaluating Longer Arguments

 In this chapter, you'll learn

- **how to analyze longer, more detailed arguments.**

- **how to decide if an author's argument is effective or ineffective.**

- **how to recognize common errors in reasoning that undermine an author's ability to effectively argue an opinion.**

Chapter 10 returns to the subject of arguments. This chapter, however, focuses on arguments that extend beyond a paragraph. It also looks more closely at arguments that rely heavily on reasons. Once you finish Chapter 10, you'll know how to determine which arguments are worthy

of serious consideration and which arguments only appear to be.

◰▰◕ Analyzing Longer Arguments

Critical readers know that authors who want to persuade frequently offer reasons why their readers should share or at least seriously consider a particular point of view. In response, critical readers are quick to analyze the author's argument and reduce it to its bare bones. They try to identify the opinion or conclusion the author wants readers to share and to search out the author's reasons for believing that his or her opinion should be shared by others.

In the following passage, for example, the author hopes to convince her readers that war is a curse and no cause for joy, no matter who wins or loses. In support of that opinion, she offers three reasons: (1) War brings with it death and destruction; (2) war destroys feelings like compassion and understanding; and (3) war encourages aggression and brutality.

> How is it that anyone can be jubilant or joyous during wartime, no matter who wins or who loses? For both winners and losers, war is a curse. It brings with it death and destruction. It destroys feelings of compassion and understanding and it encourages aggression and brutality. Horrified by a human being who takes the life of another during peacetime, we pin medals on those who do it during wartime.
>
> To those who argue that war is not a curse but a reasonable and rational way to defend property and prestige, I can only shake my head in sorrow. Losing control of overseas markets, maintaining face before the rest of the world—these are not adequate reasons for war and all its attendant evils. Nothing but the necessity of self-defense is an adequate justification for this, the most terrible of human tragedies.

Notice here that, in addition to providing reasons for her conclusion, the author also answers those readers she imagines might disagree with her and claim that war is not a curse but a reasonable and necessary defense of government interests. She responds to the opposition by insisting that, because war brings with it such horrors, self-defense is the only possible justification. No other reason is acceptable, at least from her point of view.

Responding to potential disagreement is a common element in arguments extending beyond a paragraph. Of course, not all writers take the time to respond to the opposition, but many do. They know that readers are more likely to be persuaded by authors who can counter, or effectively answer, potential criticism or disagreement.

To truly understand an author's argument, you need to analyze it, by breaking the argument down into its essential elements:

Read here

1. The opinion or conclusion offered for consideration
2. The reasons meant to convince
3. The author's description of potential objections or criticism
4. The author's response to those objections

Reduced to its bare bones, the above argument would look something like this:

Opinion No matter what the outcome, war is cause for sorrow.

Reasons 1. It causes death and destruction.
2. It discourages feelings like compassion and understanding.
3. It encourages feelings of brutality and aggression.

Potential Objection Sometimes we need to make war to protect property and maintain prestige.

Response Given the horrors of war, those are not adequate reasons.

Critical readers know that if they can outline the essential elements in an argument, they are in a better position to evaluate it.

◄■ EXERCISE 1

DIRECTIONS Read each argument. Then answer the questions that follow. *Note:* Not every argument contains a response to potential objections.

EXAMPLE
Grading Teachers

Unfortunately, many students believe they cannot control the quality of instruction they receive at their university. They think that their only option is to complain privately but say nothing in public. There is, however, an alternative to being silently miserable and dissatisfied. Students would have a lot more control over the quality of their instruction if they would consider using a public rating system for their professors. With such a system, teachers would be rated on everything from willingness to hold office hours to clarity of lectures, and the results would be published and distributed schoolwide.

On an immediate level, such a rating system could serve to guide students in the selection of courses. For the most part, students, particularly new students, have no idea who does the most effective job teaching a particular subject. They do not know, for example, that Professor X does not keep office hours or return papers, and they register for his course. Equally important, they do not know that Professor Y, who teaches the same subject, returns every paper and regularly meets with students. If they did, they would probably have the good sense to choose Professor Y's course instead of Professor X's.

Such a system of public rating would have long-term effects as well. Professors who could not infer from their decreasing enrollment that their methods were inadequate would still have to face the results of the public rating. Given consistently negative evaluations, the majority of instructors would seek to change their style of instruction. It is hard to imagine an instructor who would receive low ratings year after year and still continue to do exactly the same thing he or she did before.

Admittedly, such a rating system for instructors could be abused, and some students might use it to retaliate against instructors who had given them low grades. But that problem could easily be solved by analyzing all the responses and breaking them down into percentages, to give each instructor a rating like the following: "Encourages students' questions: 75 percent very satisfied, 20 percent satisfied, and 5 percent not satisfied." With this method, the few students wishing to use the rating system for retaliation could do little harm, because it would be clear that they were in the minority.

Far too often, students in college feel that the only way they can respond to inadequate instruction is to withdraw from the course and lose the credits. But, in the end, that does not solve the problem of inadequate or incompetent instruction. The teacher does not learn anything—and neither does the student. A better solution is for students to speak out. By adopting the method of rating and evaluation described here, students can do just that.

a. What opinion does the author want you to consider?

Students should use a public rating system to grade their instructors, and the ratings should be published.

b. In an effort to convince readers, what two reasons does the author offer?

1. *The rating system could guide students in the selection of their courses.*

2. *Professors with poor ratings would work to improve their performance.*

c. What possible objection to the conclusion does the author describe?

The public grading of teachers could be abused: Some students might use it to retaliate against instructors who gave them low grades.

d. How does the author respond to that objection?

All of the responses could be broken down into percentages, making it clear which opinions were in the minority.

EXPLANATION Having identified the author's opinions, reasons for holding that opinion, and his response to possible objections, we have all the essential elements of his argument.

1. Do We Really Benefit from the Lottery?

On the editorial page of this newspaper, an argument recently was put forth in favor of a state-run lottery. According to the article, there are many benefits to a state-run lottery and apparently no drawbacks. The writer of that article may honestly believe that a lottery would be a boon to everyone in the state, but I would like to suggest that legalized gambling is a disaster waiting to happen.

As you might expect, legalized gambling tends to create a large population of people ready and willing to throw away their hard-earned money on the chance of winning a jackpot. To the gambler, it doesn't matter if that money is needed to pay the mortgage. The dream of winning overcomes all common sense. In fact, a number of studies have shown that receipts in grocery stores decline when lottery stakes are high, evidence that people are using money they do not have in order to gamble.

Legalized gambling also blurs an important moral distinction, the distinction between money that has been honestly earned and "ill-gotten" gains. Money through gambling is ill-gotten because it is not connected with any honest labor that benefits society. When we approve of legalized gambling, we approve of bestowing wealth on people who have not worked for it.

To those who claim that a state-run lottery cannot possibly harm anyone, let me point out that it is not the rich who buy lottery tickets. Generally, the majority of people who play the lottery are those who can least afford it. Inspired by the dream of getting rich, the hard-working poor buy lottery tickets and hope to solve their financial problems. Most of the time, their dreams are not realized, and they are that much poorer. They are the real victims of a state-run lottery.

a. What opinion does the author want you to consider?

_____

_____

b. In an effort to persuade readers, what two reasons does the author offer?

   1. _____

      _____

   2. _____

      _____

c. What possible objection does the author describe?

_____

_____

d. How does the author respond to that objection?

_____

_____

2. Banning Bathing Suits

After far too many years, critical attention has finally been paid to the portion of the Miss America pageant known as the swimsuit competition. Thankfully, people are beginning to complain about this event. In 1995, a telephone poll was conducted on the night of the pageant to determine if the swimsuit competition should remain. Unfortunately, the majority of callers voted to retain it. Let's hope, however, that in the next pageant we finally see an end to the swimsuit competition.

After all, it should be clear to everyone that there are women whose appearance and intellect make them likely candidates for the crown. Yet these same women might well be eliminated from the competition for some minor physical flaw, like bulging thighs. A woman who has the appropriate appearance and intellect should not be eliminated because she bulges in a bathing suit. Beauty and brains are infinitely more important criteria for choosing Miss America than are ten extra pounds of body fat.

Many who insist on retaining the swimsuit competition will argue that it is a tradition. Yet, as any fool knows, traditions change with the times, and the times are ripe for a change. Women of the nineties do not deserve to be judged by their love handles.

a. What opinion does the author want to you to consider?

_____

_____

b. In an effort to persuade readers, what reason does the author offer?

_____

_____

c. What possible objection does the author describe?

_____

_____

d. How does the author respond to that objection?

_____

_____

3. China, a Most Favored Nation?

The president has again granted the People's Republic of China most-favored-nation trading status. May I respectfully say that this is a mistake of almost catastrophic proportions.

The Chinese government has in no way earned the political approval that comes with most-favored-nation status. On the contrary, reports out of China suggest that the political repression instituted immediately following the 1989 massacre in Tiananmen Square† continues. Any and all dissent against government policy is met with severe reprisals. People are thrown into jail without being charged. They are isolated, starved, and tortured. Can we honestly say we approve of such a regime?

In support of the president's decision, some claim we must encourage good relations with the People's Republic in order to maintain a degree of influence over those in power. Yet China had most-favored-nation status for a full two years following the tragedy of Tiananmen Square. During that time, the Chinese government in no way modified its policy of silencing all political dissent. It moved no closer to a democracy. If we have exerted no influence over the government in the past, it seems ridiculous to assume that we will be able to influence it in the future. What we have done, in effect, is to publicly approve a government that openly exists by rule of force.

a. What opinion does the author want to you to consider?

_____

_____

b. In an effort to persuade readers, what reason does the author offer?

_____

_____

c. What possible objection does the author describe?

_____

_____

---

†Tiananmen Square: place where men and women demonstrating for democratic reforms were beaten, killed, and imprisoned.

d. How does the author respond to that objection?

_____

_____

4. Restricting Pesticide Use

No one can deny that pesticides have improved the ability of farmers to bring their crops to market. Thanks to pesticides, farmers no longer have to worry that they will lose an entire crop to an army of cut worms or fruit flies. As a result, Americans can rely on a large and varied food supply.

However, we Americans need to become more informed about the effects of those pesticides on our food. More specifically, we need to think about what new legislation is necessary to protect ourselves from a diet too rich in pesticide residue.* If we don't demand greater restrictions on pesticide use, we may be surprised, dismayed, and ultimately horrified by the consequence of its use.

On the most obvious level, farm workers who continue to use the pesticides at their present rate will be stricken with serious diseases. It's no coincidence that farmers exposed to herbicides have a six times greater risk of getting cancer. In addition, children who live in homes where pesticides are used have an increased chance of getting childhood leukemia.[1]

But the farmers are not the only ones at risk. Consumers may also suffer serious side effects from daily consumption of foods tainted by pesticides. Although scientists have yet to prove the link conclusively, they are concerned that pesticide use may be one reason for the startling increase in various forms of cancer like breast and colon cancers.

We need new legislation that adopts stricter standards governing pesticide residues in food. Much of the current legislation is based on ignorance. Simply put, we allow high levels of carcinogens in our food because we don't know for sure that they do cause cancer in humans. Yet, why should we take the risk? If there's a chance that a pesticide causes cancer, then it should be banned from use.

a. What opinion does the author want to you to consider?

_____

_____

---

*residue: remains, leftovers.
[1]Al Meyerhoff, "No More Pesticides for Dinner," _New York Times_, September 19 1993, p. 20.

b. In an effort to persuade readers, what two reasons does the author offer?

1. _____

_____

2. _____

_____

c. What possible objection does the author describe?

_____

_____

d. How does the author respond to that objection?

_____

_____

■ **DIGGING DEEPER** What's your position on the swimsuit competition in the Miss America pageant? Should it stay or go? Explain your answer.

■ **WRITING SUGGESTION** Write a paper in which you argue that beauty pageants are or are not a good way for a woman to achieve fame and fortune.

Evaluating Arguments

Once you have broken down an author's argument into its essential elements, you need to take the next step and evaluate the argument as a whole. You need, that is, to determine how effectively an author has argued his or her position.

Less effective arguments are likely to supply reasons that are irrelevant or not directly related to the author's conclusion. They also tend to be short on facts and long on emotionally charged language designed to stir the reader's emotions and short-circuit the reader's ability to think clearly. Unfortunately, circular reasoning is another characteristic of ineffective arguments, and you will occasionally encounter reasons that simply repeat the author's opinion in different words.

To understand the differences between effective and ineffective arguments, compare the essential elements of the following two arguments, both of which propose an end to boxing:

Argument 1

Opinion Boxing should be abolished.

Reason It is an extremely dangerous sport.

Factual Support Research by the leading figure in brain injury, Dr. Harold T. Maitland, has shown that even a light blow to the head causes the brain to move back and forth, causing damage to the brain tissue.

Argument 2

Opinion Boxing should be abolished.

Reason Only inhumane fools would support such a brutal sport.

Factual Support None.

Both arguments offer the same opinion, but they differ widely in the reasons they give for the reader to share that opinion. The first author claims that boxing should be abolished *because* it is physically dangerous. The evidence to support that conclusion is research showing that even a light blow to the head can damage brain tissue.

Now look at the second argument. The author of this argument does not explain *why* boxing should be abolished. Instead, the writer insults anyone who would support the sport. While it may be emotionally satisfying to call someone who disagrees with you an inhumane fool, *name calling* is not a sound basis for an argument. Critical readers would not be persuaded.

◾ EXERCISE 2

DIRECTIONS Read each argument, then label it with an *E* to indicate that it's an effective argument or an *I* to indicate that it's ineffective.

EXAMPLE I am opposed to the death penalty, and current efforts to reinstate it in places like New York† and Connecticut sadden and anger me. When will we finally admit that the death penalty is mor-

---

†The death penalty has, in fact, been reinstated in New York State.

ally reprehensible* and, for that matter, not even an effective deterrent* to murder?

When we support the death penalty we support the very act we claim to abhor*—the taking of human life. We stoop to the level of the killers we intend to punish and make it even harder for them to understand why what they have done was morally wrong. If, as a society, we truly believe in the value of human life, then the taking of it—whether justified by law or not—is an immoral act.

Then, too, does anyone really believe that the death penalty acts as a deterrent? According to criminologist William Bowers of Northwestern University, it does not. When Bowers analyzed the murder rate in New York state from 1907 to 1973, he found that the number of murders rose by an average of two following an execution. Bowers believes that executions only encourage acts of murder by legitimizing violence. His research results and his conclusions have been reaffirmed by similar studies in Utah and California. After more than a century of international research, the American Civil Liberties Union has also come to the conclusion that the death penalty does not act as a deterrent to murder.

E
_____

EXPLANATION Although you may or may not agree with the author's position, you would have to agree that it's effectively argued. After insisting that the death penalty is morally reprehensible, the author offers two reasons in support of her opinion: (1) The death penalty contradicts the notion that life is precious and, therefore, should not be taken by another human being. (2) The death penalty does not deter crime. The author also supplies relevant facts that help make her reasons convincing.

1. Protecting the Sharks

Millions of sharks are killed each year by humans, and much of this killing is sparked by fear of these mysterious creatures. The number of humans killed annually by sharks number in the single digits; your chances are greater of being killed by falling airplane wreckage or by bee stings than by a shark.

Instead of hunting these marvelous creatures, we should protect them. Because sharks kill weak, wounded, or diseased fish (all of which would be too slow to evade a shark), they func-

_____
*reprehensible: deserving of criticism.
*deterrent: something that inhibits action.
*abhor: hate, despise.

tion as a "clean-up crew" for the oceans. They help keep fish populations down, just as land predators such as wolves help regulate the deer population, preventing the land from becoming overrun by deer. In hunting sharks to the brink of extinction (as we have already done with several species), humans are tampering with the natural system of checks and balances in the ocean.

Sharks may also help scientists tackle one of the worst diseases known: cancer. Sharks do not get cancer. Scientists know that this is partly because sharks have no bones in their bodies but they do not fully understand the reason for sharks' immunity to this terrible disease. In studying sharks, a cure for cancer may be found, but this will become more difficult as the shark populations dwindle.

Many refuse to see the important roles that sharks play in the world and fall back on the fear of these creatures that has been fueled by movies like *Jaws*. The fear and ignorance that encourage the widespread hunting of sharks has been seen before throughout history, from the killing of the last Dodo bird to the massacre of the American buffalo. If the killing of sharks does not stop, the result will be the same: extinction.

――――

2. And They Call This Mercy

The word *euthanasia* means "good death" or "mercy killing." But the name does not fit with the act. When one person assumes the right to take the life of another, there is no goodness or mercy involved. No one has the right to decide when a life should end.

Life is our most precious gift and we cannot just fling that gift away when it suits us. Refusing to accept assistance from machinery that maintains respiration is one thing, but asking to die is another. That's why the book *Final Exit* is such a disgrace to the publishing industry. The book suggests that we as individuals have the right to plan our own death; to decide, in effect, that we are tired of living. Yet that decision—to decide when life ends— lies in God's hands, not in ours.

Jack Kevorkian, the man who has championed an individual's right to take his or her own life, has not done the public a service by making headlines aiding and abetting suicide. Instead, he has encouraged others to believe that they, too, can choose when to die. That choice, however, is not ours to make.

――――

Recognizing Faulty Reasoning in Arguments

Critical readers do not assume that every argument that makes its way into print is sound. In fact, the more they sense an author is determined to persuade, the more carefully critical readers analyze and evaluate the argument, looking for faulty or unsound arguments like those outlined in the following pages.

Attacking the Person

Be wary of an author who substitutes character attacks for relevant reasons. In the following passage, for example, the author doesn't give any reasons why the funds for *Dolphin 54* should be denied. Instead, he attacks the character of the man who has testified in support of funding.

> General Thomas has testified that the navy's expensive *Dolphin 54* should be funded because of its superior underwater performance. But let me say openly that this project does not deserve to be funded because General Thomas has a personal interest in the project. In a few months, he will retire to become a vice president in the very company that makes this same submarine.

What's the conclusion of the author's argument? *Dolphin 54* should not be funded. Why shouldn't it be funded? Because General Thomas may personally benefit from its production. Unfortunately, the "why" of the author's argument is not relevant, or related, to the conclusion.

True, the general's potential for benefit from the project raises the distinct possibility of conflict of interest. It suggests that his arguments should be thoroughly examined before being accepted. But, *by itself*, the general's ability to profit from the submarine's production is not adequate support for the author's conclusion. To be logically convincing, the author would have to give evidence that the submarine does *not* perform well. That reason would be relevant to his conclusion. Without other supporting evidence, the attack on the general's character or motives cannot be considered adequate evidence.

Missing Facts

Even when an author does give you a good reason for an opinion, you still have to ask yourself if that reason needs to be backed by some factual evidence. Take, for example, the following passage:

Pornography must be more strictly censored. It does, in fact, offer a clear and present danger to the lives of women. Studies have shown again and again that pornography is directly related to the number of rapes and assaults on women. As if that weren't enough, by repeatedly presenting women as sexual objects, pornography encourages sexual discrimination.

What's the author's conclusion? Pornography should be strictly censored. Why should it be censored? Two reasons are offered: Pornography encourages rape, and it encourages sexual discrimination. Those reasons are certainly relevant, but, unfortunately, they are unsupported by facts. No specific information is given about the studies that might prove a relationship between pornography and sexual assaults. There is also no indication of how the author arrived at his opinion about sexual discrimination and pornography. This is clearly a case in which an author was so caught up in his point of view that he couldn't imagine an audience that didn't share his position. Thus, he neglected to supply any factual support for his claims.

Circular Arguments

As you know, when authors use circular arguments, they offer an opinion and a reason that make the same claim. Look carefully, for example, at how the author of the following argument defends her claim that the high school curriculum is in need of change.

Opinion We have to make radical* changes in our high school curriculum.
Reason We cannot continue with the way things are.

The author's conclusion tells us that we need to make some crucial changes in the high school curriculum. So far so good, but the key question now is, Why must we make these changes? Unfortunately, that question remains unanswered. (Perhaps that's why this particular error in reasoning is often called "begging the question.") The author might have said that the curriculum has to change *because* there is not enough emphasis on mathematics or science. But, instead of supplying a reason, she repeats her conclusion as if repetition alone were enough to convince. Critical readers, however, would not be satisfied.

---

*radical: deep-rooted, dramatic.

Careless Comparisons

Authors sometimes use comparisons to make a point. Yet, all too often the things compared are more different than similar. Although authors who offer comparisons as reasons tend to ignore the differences between the things they compare, critical readers don't make the same mistake. Instead, they ask themselves if the two things being compared are as similar as the author maintains. Here, for example, an author makes a comparison between the sports of boxing and football in order to prove boxing should remain legal.

Opinion Boxing should not be outlawed.

Reason Boxing is just like football, another sport that involves danger; but nobody talks about abolishing football.

Consider now just these two differences between boxing and football:

- Football players wear a lot of protective clothing and headgear. Boxers wear very little.
- In football, teammates offer a degree of physical protection. In boxing, a man goes into the ring alone. No one else protects a boxer from injury.

Although football can be physically dangerous, it's not appropriate to claim that boxing is "just like" football. There are significant differences between the sports.

Appealing to Emotions

A writer who has a weak argument to begin with may try to sidestep logic and appeal to readers' emotions. Here, for example, is a passage by an author who tries to do precisely that:

> On this very page, an argument was recently made against hunting. Reading it, I couldn't imagine how anyone could take the author seriously. Why this country survived because hunters were willing to brave the wilderness and bring home meat to their hungry families. Hunting is what made this country great.

This author might have solid reasons for telling her readers not to take the argument against hunting seriously. But she doesn't tell us what they are. Instead, she tries to evoke her readers' feelings of patriotism and to stir up so much emotion that they forget the weakness of her argument. Critical readers, however, would not be fooled. They would not be sidetracked into letting their emotions take over. Instead, they would be even more intent on discovering whether the author could actually support her claim.

Doubtful Authority

Authors frequently cite the opinion of experts to support their claims. This is an excellent strategy as long as the person cited is truly an *expert* in the field discussed, someone whose training and experience qualify him or her to offer an informed judgment. Occasionally, however, an author may attempt to support an argument by citing a famous person who does not really qualify as an expert, as in the following passage:

> We should abolish NATO, leave the United Nations, and end foreign aid. After all, didn't George Washington tell us to avoid entangling ourselves in the affairs of other nations? Even today, we should let his wisdom be our guide and steer clear of foreign entanglements that drain our energy and our resources.[2]

In the eighteenth century, George Washington may well have qualified as an expert in foreign affairs. But to cite him as an authority on modern problems is a mistake. It is doubtful that Washington could have imagined America's current status as an international power. Because his opinion could not be considered adequately informed, critical readers would not be impressed by references to his name and authority.

Questionable Cause and Effect

When an author describes a cause and effect relationship to prove a point, critical readers are quick to ask if the two events described truly share a cause and effect relationship, or if they simply happen close together in time. That question is crucial to evaluating the argument in the following passage:

> Our city council needs to have a more conservative leadership. During the term of liberal council members, we have seen crime increase on our city streets. This is a direct result of poor decisions

---

[2]Adapted from James D. Carney and Richard K. Scheer, *Fundamentals of Logic.* New York: Macmillan Company, 1964, p. 27.

based more on liberal dreams than on a realistic appraisal of the situation in our city.

This author wants his readers to support a more conservative city council. In answer to the question "Why?" he implies a cause and effect relationship: Because liberals were on the council (*cause*), there is more crime in the streets (*effect*). To accept this argument, critical readers would need more evidence. They would not automatically assume that two events happening close together in time guarantee a cause and effect relationship. If that were true, we might as well assume that a rooster's crowing at dawn causes the sun to rise.

EXERCISE 3

DIRECTIONS Read each passage and label each one *E* for effective argument or *I* for ineffective argument. If you write *I* in the blank, circle the letter indicating the type of error in reasoning you think makes the author's argument unsound.

EXAMPLE It has been argued that Joan Crawford, a movie star popular in the forties and fifties, played liberated women on screen and thereby encouraged American women to think more highly of themselves and their abilities. But this argument could not be more misguided. Joan Crawford could never have had a positive influence on American women. Married several times, she was known to be a difficult and demanding woman who consistently abused her adopted children.

_*I*_

(a.) attacking the person

b. circular argument

c. careless comparisons

EXPLANATION Joan Crawford's personal life may have been a disaster, but that is not relevant to the author's opinion, which claims that Crawford's screen presence encouraged women's ambitions. That's the conclusion that has to be addressed, but the author sidesteps it with an attack on the star's personal character.

1. Parents worried about a decline in their children's reading scores should consider whether they want a television in their home. At the same time that reading scores have been declining, the number of hours children watch television has been increasing. Television is clearly the culprit.

_____

    a. circular argument

    b. careless comparisons

    c. questionable cause and effect

2. Feminists in the area have been demanding the right to join Harry's, a private men's club. The feminists claim that they should be allowed entry because Harry's is a place where important business is transacted. This position is ridiculous. Women should not have the right to enter a private men's club. These clubs are only for men. Why can't women accept the logic of that argument?

_____

    a. attacking the person

    b. missing facts

    c. circular argument

3. Scientists are still trying to find a cure for the common cold. But those of us versed in nutrition have already found it—huge doses of vitamin C taken at two-hour intervals. Those who doubt the effectiveness of this cure and are too timid to test it themselves should read the work of Ladislaw Gottlieb, a world-famous astronomer who supports the use of vitamin C as a treatment for the common cold.

_____

    a. attacking the person

    b. appeal to emotions

    c. doubtful authority

4. Animal rights activists are constantly complaining about the unnecessary suffering of laboratory animals. But their complaints make no sense. How can they worry about the fate of animals when all over the world helpless little children are suffering from terrible diseases?

_____

    a. careless comparisons

    b. doubtful authority

    c. appeal to emotions

5. Several women who were imprisoned for murdering their husbands were pardoned recently because it was shown that for years they had been abused by those very same husbands. Now there appears to be a widespread movement to reconsider the fate of other women who have been similarly imprisoned. To let these women go free or receive a lesser sentence is an outrageous proposal. A woman who kills her husband because he abused her is like any other murderer. She should be tried, convicted, and sent to jail for the rest of her life.

_____

a. doubtful authority

b. questionable cause and effect

c. careless comparisons

6. History classes in high school and college should pay more attention to the many groups and cultures that shaped America's past. History curriculums that take a multicultural approach would better prepare students to live in a diverse world. If children learn about different cultures early in life, they might be less likely as adults to put negative labels on those who are different. In addition, there is some evidence that teaching students more about their own history can improve their self-esteem. In one study, conducted in 1991 by the science and education foundation, students at North Carolina State University improved their grade point average after being enrolled in an Afro-centric educational program. Analysis of the test results suggests a definite cause and effect relationship between the improved grades and the changed curriculum.

_____

a. doubtful authority

b. circular argument

c. careless comparisons

7. A number of widely respected artists have publicly condemned any attempts to censor musical lyrics, even if those lyrics celebrate violence and hatred. While respecting the talent these people possess, one cannot help but criticize their logic. Musical lyrics that seem to approve the mistreatment of women and violence against the police should be censored. It has been proved again and again that musical lyrics, like images in films, can stimulate aggressive behavior. How can anyone who knows the facts claim to condemn the lyrics but refuse to support their being censored?

_____

    a. attacking the person

    b. missing facts

    c. careless comparisons

8. Once again, David DeGrecco, columnist for the *New Jersey Sun*, has presented his annual case for gun control. As usual, DeGrecco argues that gun control laws can help eliminate some of the violence plaguing the city streets across the country. Outspoken as always, DeGrecco is curiously silent about his own recent bout with criminal behavior. Less than two weeks ago, he and several others were arrested at a demonstration against the opening of a nuclear power plant. For one so determined to bring law and order to our streets, DeGrecco does not seem to mind breaking a few laws himself.

    ———

    a. attacking the person

    b. careless comparisons

    c. doubtful authority

9. Health care workers, from hospital technicians to doctors, should be forced to undergo AIDS testing, and the results should be published. Although there has been much talk about this subject, too little has been done, and the public has suffered because of it. We need to institute a program of mandatory testing as soon as possible.

    ———

    a. circular argument

    b. careless comparisons

    c. questionable cause and effect

10. The issue of cameras in the courtroom has become the subject of argument recently. Some hold that courtrooms should not be open to television crews, while others see no problem in allowing TV cameras access to courtroom proceedings. The truth of the matter is that the presence of these cameras can in no way help and will sometimes hurt the legal system. The Nazis filmed the atrocities they committed in concentration camps during World War II. They claimed it was for the purpose of record keeping, just as we claim that court TV is for the record. By putting our courtrooms on television, we are no better than the Nazis.

    ———

a. careless comparisons

b. questionable cause and effect

c. attacking the person

◪ Summing Up

Listed below are the most important points in Chapter 10. Put a check mark in the box if you think the point is clear in your mind. Leave the box blank if you need to review the material one more time. The page numbers in parentheses tell you where to look in order to review each point on the list.

☐ **1.** To truly understand an argument, you need to analyze, or break it down, into its essential elements: (1) the opinion or conclusion the author wants you to consider, (2) the author's reasons for holding that opinion or arriving at that conclusion, and (3) any response the author makes to potential objections. Remember, however, that not all authors respond to potential objections. (pp. 281–282)

☐ **2.** Critical readers don't just analyze an argument. They also evaluate it, deciding how effectively an author has argued his or her position. Sound or effective arguments should provide readers with relevant reasons for the author's conclusion. Sound arguments also supply any facts that might be necessary to support either the author's conclusion or reasons. (pp. 289–290)

☐ **3.** Critical readers study arguments carefully in an attempt to discover faulty reasoning like (1) attacks on the person, (2) inadequate evidence, (3) circular reasoning, (4) careless comparisons, (5) emotional appeals, (6) doubtful authority, and (7) questionable cause and effect. (pp. 293–297)

Working with Words

Here are some of the words defined in Chapter 10. Use the following exercises to gain practice with these words and to learn more about their history and meaning.

EXERCISE 4

DIRECTIONS Use the following words to fill in the blanks.

residue: remains, leftovers

reprehensible: deserving of criticism

deterrent: something that inhibits action

abhor: hate, despise

radical: deep-rooted, dramatic

1. If punishment does not control or modify behavior, it is not an effective _____.

2. At the bottom of the glass, was a gray _____ that could have been arsenic.

3. The farmers are demanding _____ changes in the government's agricultural policies.

4. The behavior of the owner was so _____, he was not allowed in his own restaurant.

5. It was all too easy to _____ her behavior, but what they really needed to do was control their disgust and discover the reason for her actions.

EXERCISE 5

DIRECTIONS To answer the following questions, use a hardbound dictionary.

1. _____ is a synonym for *reprehensible.*

2. The adjective form of the word *deterrent* is _____.

3. In the context of law, *residue* is _____

   _____.

4. In botany, the word *radical* means _____.

5. At the root of the word *abhor* is the Latin word *abhorrēre* meaning _____.

◤ Chapter 10: Review Test

Part A   Read the following argument. Then analyze it by answering the questions that appear at the end.

1. Opening Adoption Files

In some states, people who have been adopted are not allowed to have access to their files. They have no idea who their real parents are or why they were put up for adoption, and all their attempts to discover this information are met with firm bureaucratic resistance. In short, adoption officials will tell them nothing.

However, in the past decade, many adoptees have publicly protested this situation, and many states have changed their policies. What I want to argue here is that this change in adoption policy should take place nationwide. Adopted children need to know about both their parents and their past, and those who do not care can simply refuse access to their files.

What people do not realize is that restrictions against opening adoption files do not necessarily deter those adoptees who want to discover who their biological parents are. Those men and women who want to find their biological parents will, if they can afford it, hire a detective to find out what they want to know. If they cannot afford it, some are willing to devote all their time and energy to learning more about their origins. What this shows is just how important it is for adoptees to recover their past.

Adoptees frequently feel guilty because they were put up for adoption. They tend to assume that they did something wrong, something that made them unlovable, and forced their parents to give them up. To counteract such feelings, these men and women need to know the real causes for their adoption. It helps the adoptee to know, for example, that his mother gave him up for adoption because she was too young to support him, not because she didn't love him. This knowledge helps relieve the painful burden of guilt some adoptees carry around all their lives.

There are also physical—rather than psychological—reasons why adoptees need access to their files. To take proper care of their health, they need to know what diseases they might be prone to inheriting. In more extreme cases, knowledge about the biological parents can make the difference between life and death. Sometimes adoptees need to have an organ that comes from a natural relative, but if all their relatives are unknown, they are at a terrible disadvantage—one that could cost them their life.

Beverly

Many parents who have given up their children for adoption resent the idea of opening up adoption files. They feel that their right to privacy will be threatened. Yet this objection is based on the assumption that adopted children want to hunt down their parents and intrude on their lives. But, at most, what adoptees want is to know who their biological parents are. In some cases, they may even want to meet them, but they do not want to push their way into the lives of people who will not accept them. Giving the adopted person access to files does not mean that the parent or parents forsake all rights to privacy. It only means that the adopted child can attempt to make contact if he or she wishes, and the parents can refuse or accept.

a. What opinion does the author want you to consider or share?

Adopted children need to know about both their parents an their past.

b. What three reasons does the author offer to support that conclusion?

1. _They need to take proper care of their health._

2. _Need to know what diseases they might be prone to inheriting_

3. _Knowledge about the biological parents can make the difference between life and death._

c. Does the author describe any potential objections to her argument? If your answer is yes, identify the objections.

They feel that their right to privacy will be threatened.

d. How does the author respond to those objections? (Leave blank if your answer to question c was no.)

adopted children want to hunt down their parent and intrude on their lives.

Part B   Identify the type of faulty reasoning that weakens each of the following arguments.

2. Many people doubt the authenticity of astrologers' predictions. While it is true that astrology is not an exact science, many fields of study that people accept are by no means grounded in hard fact. Psychology is not an exact science, yet it is taught in accredited institutions all over the world. Astrology is much the same as psychology, yet it is unfairly met with unwarranted public skepticism.

   a. attacking the person
   b. missing facts
   c. careless comparisons

3. Ginseng, an herbal extract from ginseng root, is the only substance you need to take to prolong your youth. Ginseng prevents hair loss and unwanted weight gain. It has also been proven to increase sexual potency while actually making the user more desirable to the opposite sex. Ginseng makes the user feel more energetic and revitalizes the immune system, preventing sickness and cancer.

   a. attacking the person
   b. missing facts
   c. doubtful authority

4. Every building in the United States must be accessible to the physically handicapped. It is a disgrace that so many buildings in this country are not built to accommodate people in wheelchairs. Old buildings must be revamped to provide access for the handicapped, and every new building must provide entrances that are easily negotiated by those in wheelchairs.

   a. circular argument
   b. careless comparisons
   c. questionable cause and effect

5. The sale of guns to private citizens must stop. By ignoring the fact that these items are present at almost any professional robbery, the government turns a blind eye to one of the major contributors to crime in our country. The robberies are direct results of the criminals' ability to obtain guns. Cut off the gun supplies and the robberies will stop.

Beverly

    a. careless comparisons

    b. doubtful authority

    c. questionable cause and effect

6. During the past half century, many overenthusiastic activists have filled our law books with laws preventing the supposed cruelty to animals. Such laws, unfortunately, interfere with progress, and, in some cases, prevent animals from being used as experimental subjects. Let us not forget that René Descartes, the great French philosopher and scientist, was a proponent of using animals in scientific research. Descartes defended the practice of vivisection,† reporting that animals had no souls, no thoughts, and no feelings. His words are still relevant.

    a. attacking the person

    b. doubtful authority

    c. questionable cause and effect

7. For many years, there has been a determined effort to limit or, in some cases, ban certain books from school libraries. This is no different from the bans on books that took place in Nazi Germany. Most would agree that the Nazi ideals were a disgrace. To avoid becoming like the Nazis, we should not put limitations on personal freedom.

    a. careless comparisons

    b. doubtful authority

    c. questionable cause and effect

---

†vivisection: the act of cutting into living animals for the purpose of scientific research.

PART 3

Additional Readings

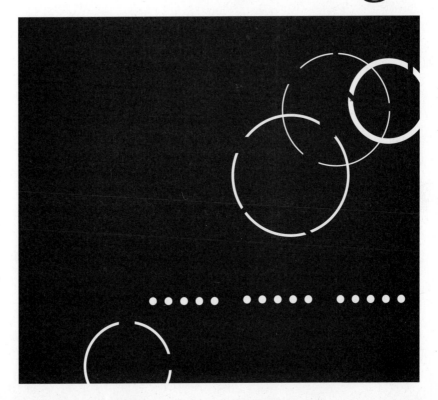

Male and Female, Masculine and Feminine

 The following four readings concentrate on the role of men and women in American society. As you read, think about whether you've ever been stereotyped on the basis of your sex. Consider, too, if you've ever been guilty of stereotyping. If you have, what do you plan to do about it?

Learning Gender Roles in Childhood

Men's Liberation

Women in Management

Talk to Me!

■ **READING 1**

LEARNING GENDER ROLES IN CHILDHOOD

LOOKING AHEAD   In this reading, drawn from a popular psychology text, the authors describe how children learn to form gender roles. They learn what behavior is considered appropriate for each sex.

DEVELOPING A FOCUS   Read the section titled "Word Watch." Then read the first paragraph, all of the headings, illustrations, marginal notations, and the last paragraph of the selection. Based on your survey, make one or two predictions. What point or points do you expect the author to make?

gender role of sex v

In addition to making predictions, jot down one or two questions you'll try to answer as you read.

STRATEGIES FOR IN-DEPTH LEARNING   As you read, think back to your own childhood and ask yourself if you ever refrained from an activity because you were worried about being unfeminine or unmasculine.

Consider, too, the authors' descriptions of each sex's gender role. Do you think gender roles have changed since you were a child? Or are they pretty much the same even today?

yes their is change

WORD WATCH   Because context does not always provide enough clues, some of the more difficult words in the reading are defined below. In the reading, these words are marked with an asterisk.

assertive: able to express oneself firmly

nurturant: providing care and affection

conceptions: ideas

vehemently: heatedly

cognitive: related to thinking

simulated: imitated, made as a substitute for

demure: shy

demeanor: behavior

egalitarian: favoring equality

aspirations: desires, dreams

1 EACH OF US OCCUPIES MANY SOCIAL POSITIONS IN LIFE—AS a daughter, friend, teacher, and tennis player, for example. The social expectations about how someone should act in each position form a social *role*. Social expectations about what men and women should do or be like form **gender roles** (or sex roles). Gender roles are widely held rules about the way men and women ought to be. Each of us learns these rules as we grow up, and they can have a major impact on our personalities and behavior.

2 Even before a child is born, the parents-to-be have notions of what they want their sons and daughters to be like, and they proceed to communicate those expectations to their children, beginning in infancy. Andrée Pomerleau and her associates at the University of Quebec in Canada found that the environments of girls and boys in the first two years of life are often very different (Pomerleau and others, 1990). Little girls are likely to be dressed in pink, to wear jewelry, and to have bedrooms that are pink or yellow. Little boys are more likely to be dressed in blue or red and to have rooms decorated in blue. Although both boys and girls are given stuffed animals, books, rattles, and construction toys, girls more often have dolls and toy furniture, and boys more often have trucks and cars.

3 Throughout childhood, parents continue to encourage what they consider to be "sex-appropriate" activities and interests (Lytton and Romney, 1991). Messages about the meaning of masculinity and femininity also come from teachers, the media, and many other sources. In general, boys are taught to "get ahead" and "stay cool" (Pleck and Sawyer, 1974). They are encouraged to be ambitious and assertive* and are discouraged from expressing their weaknesses or their tender feelings. Girls, in contrast, learn to play a more submissive and dependent role. They are taught to cooperate, be polite, and act as if they have no aggressive impulses at all. Girls are also expected to be tender and nurturant,* whether with their dolls or with baby sisters and brothers.

4 Gender-role learning is not a passive process on the part of the child (Kohlberg, 1966). To the contrary, once the child learns his or her sex—which virtually all children do by age 3—the child invariably wants to demonstrate that he or she can behave like a member in good standing of that sex. This desire reflects every child's motivation to be a competent and consistent human being. As a result, the child actively seeks clues about how a "boy" or a "girl" should behave by observing the same-sex parent and other same-sex models. This desire to behave "consistently" with one's sex helps to explain why young children's conceptions* of gender

Mom the Hunter

Many anthropologists assumed that in non-industrial societies where food is provided by hunting animals and gathering edible plants, women are kept from hunting by the biological necessities of motherhood. Wrong, says a team of researchers who spent three years studying the hunting practices of the Agta Negrito people of northern Luzon in the Philippines (Goodman and others, 1985). Here, women hunt successfully and effectively both individually and in groups. Mothers typically take nursing babies with them on the hunt but leave weaned toddlers at home with relatives. According to careful counts by the researchers, women brought back nearly a third of the large game animals captured. These anthropologists concluded that motherhood is not necessarily incompatible with hunting.

gender role Social expectations about what men and women should do and what they should be like.

Parents usually have definite notions about the appropriate gender roles.

are often so difficult to change. When I (Anne) was a preschooler, I vehemently* insisted that I would never wear blue jeans because "only boys wear pants." Neither my family nor my teacher, who herself wore slacks to school, could dissuade me. Only later, as my cognitive* skills developed, was I able to overcome this rigid idea.

5   Children's gender roles are also influenced by peers—friends, classmates, and siblings (Carter, 1987). One of the most striking features of childhood is the tendency for children to segregate themselves into all-boy and all-girl groups and, often, to avoid persons of the other sex. On a preschool playground, Jake and Danny are on the big swing together. When Laura excitedly asks if she can join them on the swing, the boys emphatically say, "No!" Jake adds, "We don't want you on here. We only want boys on here" (Rubin, 1980, p. 102). This pattern of same-sex play first appears in preschool and continues through early adolescence. As John enters the seventh-grade classroom and heads for a seat in an empty section of the room, Harry quickly warns him, "Don't sit there, that's where all the girls sit." John hastily retreats to the "boys'" section of the room (Schofield, 1981, p. 62).

sexism Prejudice and discrimination based on gender.

6   Is children's preference for companions of the same sex simply an early example of **sexism**—prejudice and discrimination based on gender? In a way, it is. But there are other reasons as well. Children of the same sex may share an interest in the same toys and games: Girls may favor Barbie dolls or make-up kits, and boys may prefer football or video games. Beyond that, Eleanor Maccoby (1990a) has suggested that each sex develops a distinctive style of interaction that makes same-sex playmates more compatible. Research shows that boys usually enjoy a rough-and-tumble style of play that emphasizes physical contact, competition, and dominance. Girls, in contrast, engage in less physical contact, try to minimize conflict, and so may find boys' play style aversive. Maccoby explained that "on wheeled vehicles boys (3 to 5) play ramming games while girls ride around and try *not* to bump into each other" (1990b, p. 5). Consequently, the preferred play styles of boys and girls are not compatible. In this case, initially small sex differences in activity level or in rough-and-tumble play lead children to segregate themselves by sex. This in turn leads to the creation of same-sex "cultures" with different play activities and styles of interacting.

Living Gender Roles in Adulthood

7 As adults, people continue to alter their behavior to conform to the social demands of daily life. In fact, most adult men and women have the potential to behave in a broad range of ways—more or less assertively, more or less sensitively, and so on. But we usually show the parts of ourselves that we consider most appropriate for a particular social setting or for the role we are performing (Deaux and Major, 1990). A woman psychotherapist may reveal virtually no personal information to her clients, believing that professional distance should be maintained in her therapist role. Outside the office, however, she talks freely about her life with close friends. A colleague who was recently appointed dean at a large university provides another example of roles shaping behavior. Gone are his old casual jeans and shirts, replaced by dark suits and new ties deemed more fitting for his new role.

8   When we interact with another person, we often try to figure out what he or she expects of us and how we should behave for the interaction to run smoothly. This point is illustrated in a study of college women taking part in a simulated* job interview with a male interviewer (Von Baeyer, Sherk, and Zanna, 1981). Before the interview, half the women were led to think that the interviewer was a rather traditional man who believed working

"You Just Don't Understand!"

When Sarah told her boyfriend about her troubles with her parents, Scott helpfully suggested: "If they upset you, stop seeing them so often." Rather than appreciating Scott's advice, Sarah was irritated. What went wrong in this communication? Linguist Deborah Tannen (1990) believes that women usually talk about problems in order to feel understood. What Sarah really wanted Scott to say was, "I know, my parents bug me sometimes, too." But men tend to see a problem as a "challenge" to be fixed, so Scott was mystified that Sarah would rather talk about her problem than solve it. Tannen hopes that awareness of sex differences in communication can help us to avoid, or at least better understand, such conflicts.

women should be unassertive, gentle, and demure.* The other half of the women were led to believe that the interviewer had a more egalitarian* view of working women—that he thought they should be independent and assertive. These expectations affected the women's behavior in subtle but revealing ways. Women who expected the traditional male interviewer presented themselves in a more traditionally feminine way—they wore more make-up and fashion accessories. In addition, as compared to the women who expected to meet the egalitarian interviewer, these women talked less during the interview and were less likely to look directly at the interviewer while they were talking. Their behavior, in other words, reflected precisely the sort of feminine demeanor* that they believed the interviewer expected.

9   In the past, adult women and men had very different major roles in life. Once they were married, women typically worked at home taking care of children and housework, and men held paid jobs that enabled them to be the financial "provider" for the family. These traditional roles had a profound impact on how men and women spent their days, the skills they developed, and the topics that concerned them. For example, regardless of her personal interests or temperament, the traditional wife was expected to develop expertise in cooking and childcare and to defer to her husband's wishes. Today, much has changed. Both economic necessity and women's desire for self-development have led more and more women to take paid jobs. In the 1990s, almost 70 percent of adult women between the ages of 18 and 64 are in the paid labor force, including a majority of married women and mothers (Hyde, 1991).

10   It is interesting to note that when researchers compare men and women who occupy the same occupational roles, few psychological differences between the sexes are found. In a study of blue-collar workers in the steel industry, for example, Kay Deaux and Joseph Ullman (1983) found almost no evidence of sex differences: Men and women were similar in their self-evaluations, aspirations,* and likes and dislikes about their work. Studies of managers in organizations also show great similarity among the managerial styles of women and men in similar job positions (Eagly and Johnson, 1990). It may be that similar sorts of people, regardless of their sex, tend to choose particular occupational roles. It is also likely, however, that the role itself shapes the person who occupies it.

Zick Rubin, Letitia Anne Peplar, and Peter Salovey,
Psychology. Boston: Houghton Mifflin, 1990,
pp. 301–304.

_____

_____

_____

■   **WRITING**   Write a paper in which you explain why, as a parent, you would or
     SUGGESTION   would not try to teach your child about the behavior appropriate to
                    his or her gender role.

Profound
_____

Read—322 (handwritten)

■ **READING 2**

MEN'S LIBERATION

LOOKING AHEAD In this reading from a sociology text, Alex Thio explores the issue of men's liberation. Created in response to the women's movement, the men's movement has its own set of specific goals.

DEVELOPING A FOCUS Read the section titled "Word Watch." Then read the first and last paragraphs of the selection. Based on your survey, make one or two predictions. What points do you expect the author to make?

Men are expected to be tough, aggressive, and competitive, also increasing participation of educated women in labor force will lead to great ev— (handwritten)

gender equality (handwritten)

In addition to making predictions, jot down one or two questions you will try to answer as you read.

Why shouldn't men and woman have equal oppertunity in the work force. (handwritten)

STRATEGIES FOR IN-DEPTH LEARNING As you read, jot down the goals of the men's movement and think about how they are similar to or different from those of the women's movement.

WORD WATCH Because context does not always provide enough clues, some of the more difficult words in the reading are defined below. In the reading, these words are marked with an asterisk.

imperatives: commands **mitigate:** undercut, soften

affluent: wealthy

1 A QUIET REVOLUTION HAS BEEN GOING ON AMONG SOME MEN who want to free themselves from the demands of the traditional male role (Goldberg, 1976). Men are expected to be tough, aggressive, and competitive. They are supposed to suppress their emotions even if they feel like crying when they are sad. The social expectation that they be superior to women makes some men doubt their adequacy as providers or lovers. This is particularly the case when the men's wives do not conform to the traditional notion of femininity—by demanding as much sexual enjoyment as men or making more money than their husbands. The men likely to suffer from these kinds of problems are obviously incapable of fulfilling the male-role demands.

MAKING CONNECTIONS BETWEEN READINGS According to the previous reading, "Learning Gender Roles in Childhood," children learn about gender roles early on. What do you think parents might teach little boys that would encourage them to become what the author of this reading calls "tough men"? How might parents discourage a little boy from thinking he has to be a Rambo-type male?

_____

_____

_____

WRITING SUGGESTIONS
1. Write an essay in which you argue that men do or do not need a men's movement.

2. Write an essay arguing that the old stereotype of the Rambo-like male was more positive than many people believe.

Reading #3 —

■ **READING 3**

WOMEN IN MANAGEMENT

LOOKING AHEAD In this reading, the authors of a business text point out that women have made a good deal of progress in the business world. They also suggest, however, that women in management have a long way to go.

DEVELOPING A FOCUS Read the section titled "Word Watch." Then read the first and last paragraphs of the selection and all of the headings. Look at the charts on p. 332. Based on your survey, make one or two predictions. What point or points do you expect the author to make?

_____

_____

In addition to making predictions, jot down one or two questions you'll try to answer as you read.

_____

_____

STRATEGIES FOR IN-DEPTH LEARNING As you read, try to formulate at least two essay questions that could test a reader's understanding of the material. Formulate as well two or three short answer questions that could test a reader's understanding of the facts and figures mentioned in the reading.

WORD WATCH Because context does not always provide enough clues, some of the more difficult words in the reading are defined below. In the reading, these words are marked with an asterisk.

hierarchically: ordered according to status or ability

counterparts: people who closely resemble each other

autonomy: independence

patriarchical: ruled or controlled by men

discriminatory: tending to favor one group over another

1 THE MOST PRESTIGIOUS AND HIGHEST-PAID JOBS IN A corporation are in top management. Because corporations are organized hierarchically,* top management jobs are few in number.

For that reason, only a minority of either men or women can hope to reach the upper levels of management. Men have traditionally filled most of these desirable spots. Business's challenge now is to broaden these high-level leadership opportunities for women.

Where Women Manage

2   Over 5 million U.S. women were managers by the late 1980s, doubling their numbers in one decade. In 1988, four out of every ten managers were women, and every tenth working woman was a manager. Clearly women had broken into the management ranks. Women are more likely to be managers, though, in occupational areas where women are more numerous at lower levels, including medicine and health care, personnel, labor relations, and education. They also are concentrated in service industries and in finance, insurance, real estate, and retail businesses.

3   Where women managers are scarce is in the executive suites of large corporations. Rarely do they represent more than 1 to 3 percent of these top jobs. Occasional exceptions do occur, as in Avon Products, where women hold 81 percent of managerial positions.[1]

4   Access to management jobs is restricted in most areas of the world, according to a study of women managers in several nations.

> In country after country, the proportion of women holding managerial positions falls short of that of men. Corporations, it appears, have systematically ignored women as a potential resource. In all countries, the higher the rank within the organization, the fewer the women found there. In some countries, the percentages, though small, have increased over the last decade; but in none have they approached equality. This pattern prevails in oriental and occidental cultures, communist, socialist, and capitalist systems, and [in] both economically developed and developing countries.[2]

Do Women and Men Managers Manage Differently?

5   When women do become managers, do they bring a different style and different skills to the job? Are they better, or worse, managers than men? Are women more highly motivated and committed than male managers? Are they accepted by those they manage, or do customary ways of thinking cause both men and women to react negatively to having female managers?

6   The research evidence strongly favors the no-difference point of

---

[1]"Best Employers for Women and Parents," *Wall Street Journal*, Nov. 30, 1987, p. 21.
[2]Adler and Izraeli, op. cit., pp. 7–8.

Figure 1 Where women manage.

Source: Women's Bureau, U.S. Department of Labor, "Facts on Working Women," December 1989.

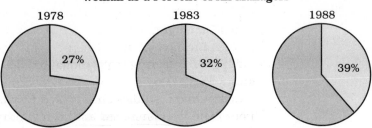

Woman as a Percent of All Managers

1978   27%

1983   32%

1988   39%

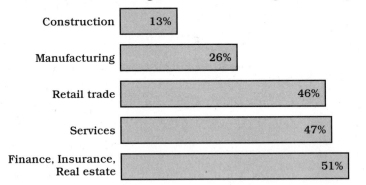

Percent of Women Managers in Selected Management Categories

Construction — 13%

Manufacturing — 26%

Retail trade — 46%

Services — 47%

Finance, Insurance, Real estate — 51%

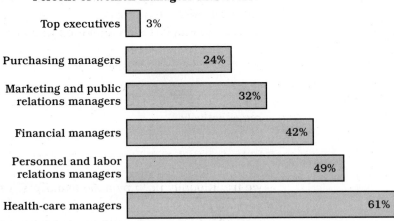

Percent of Women Managers in Selected Industrial Sectors

Top executives — 3%

Purchasing managers — 24%

Marketing and public relations managers — 32%

Financial managers — 42%

Personnel and labor relations managers — 49%

Health-care managers — 61%

view. According to this research, managers of both sexes do not seem to differ in any significant way in performing their tasks. Women managers do not appear to be more people-oriented than men, nor do they tackle task-oriented jobs less effectively than their male counterparts.* Men managers and women managers score about the same on motivation tests, but one study of 2,000 managers, cited by Gary N. Powell, seemed to demonstrate that "female managers were more concerned with opportunities for growth, autonomy,* and challenge" and exhibited a "more mature and higher-achieving motivational profile" than the men in the study.

7   Commitment studies show mixed results, with women sometimes more job-committed and men at other times registering stronger commitment. For both sexes, commitment is always stronger when people have satisfying jobs, believe their work is meaningful, and when their skills are used and appreciated. On-the-job sex discrimination can contribute to lowered job commitment by making the workplace less attractive for women. The amount of time and commitment that anyone brings to a job and career is also affected by the amount of home-based support one receives. Women who bear a disproportionately large share of household tasks and family care may be unable to make as full a commitment to job and career as they would prefer.

8   Reaction of subordinates to women managers varies, but "once subordinates have worked for both female and male managers, the effects of [traditional sex-role] stereotypes disappear and managers are treated as individuals rather than representatives of their sex."[3]

9   Some research supports the idea that women bring different attitudes and skills to management jobs, such as greater cooperativeness, an emphasis on affiliation and attachment, nurturance, and a willingness to bring emotional factors to bear in making workplace decisions. These differences are seen to carry advantages for companies, because they expand the range of techniques that can be used to help the company manage its workforce effectively.[4]

10   A study commissioned by the International Women's Forum discovered a management style used by some women managers (and also by some men) that differs from the command-and-control style traditionally used by male managers. Using this "interactive leadership" approach, "women encourage participation, share power and information, enhance other people's self-worth, and get others excited about their work. All these things reflect their

[3]Gary N. Powell, "One More Time: Do Female and Male Managers Differ?" *Academy of Management Executive,* August 1990, pp. 68–75. For a discussion of similarities and differences among men and women managers, see Powell's book *Women and Men in Management,* Newbury Park, CA: Sage, 1988; and Morrison et al., op. cit., pp. 48–54.
[4]Jan Grant, "Women as Managers: What They Can Offer to Organizations," *Organizational Dynamics,* Winter 1988, pp. 56–63.

belief that allowing employees to contribute and to feel powerful and important is a win-win situation—good for the employees and the organization." The study's director predicted that "interactive leadership may emerge as the management style of choice for many organizations."[5]

The Glass Ceiling

11 Although women are as competent as men in managing people and organizations, they still do not attain the highest positions in corporations. Their ascent seems to be blocked by an invisible barrier. At some point, they bump into what is called "the glass ceiling."

12 Failure to attain the topmost jobs in some cases is due to lack of experience or inadequate education. Because gender bias has kept women out of management until recent years, they have not had time to acquire the years of experience that are typical of most high-ranking executives. Also in earlier years, women were discouraged from entering graduate schools of engineering, science, business, and law which have been pathways to corporate management. Even as those barriers have been lowered, though, women remain underrepresented at executive levels. As a group, they have not yet broken through the glass ceiling to become chief executive officers, presidents, or board chairpersons. Something continues to hold them back.

13 In one authoritative study, women executives identified three kinds of pressures that complicated their professional advancement: (a) the day-to-day, year-in-year-out demands and hectic pace of executive work (which men also feel); (b) their pioneering role as "first woman executive" and the special need to prove themselves to others; and (c) the strain of meeting family obligations.[6] In other words, these women managers faced all of the normal demands of executive work that men experience plus two additional requirements traceable to their customary roles in society. Having proven managerial talent was not enough. Psychologically, they had to prove themselves the equal of men (or even better). Socially, they found themselves carrying a disproportionate share of family obligations and homemaking responsibilities. These psychological and social brakes can hold back the most skilled and dedicated manager, even in companies where gender bias is at a minimum.

14 The glass ceiling blocks the rise of women managers, not be-

---

[5]Judy B. Rosener, "Ways Women Lead," *Harvard Business Review*, November–December 1990, pp. 120, 125.
[6]Morrison et al., op. cit., pp. 15–20.

Beverly

_____

_____

_____

10. How would you describe the authors' primary purpose?

    a. The authors want to convince readers that women need more leadership opportunities in business.

    b. The authors want to describe for readers the discrimination in business that women have suffered.

Explain how you arrived at your answer.

_____

_____

_____

_____

_____

THINKING FOR YOURSELF The authors say that "once subordinates have worked for both female and male managers, the effects of traditional stereotypes disappear." Why do you think that happens?

_____

_____

_____

_____

Do you believe that there is a glass ceiling for women in business? Why or why not?

_____

_____

_____

_____

MAKING CONNECTIONS BETWEEN READINGS In the reading "Men's Liberation," the author describes men who are uncomfortable in the role of the traditional "tough" male. Do you think these men would support women who wanted to break through the "glass ceiling"? Explain your answer.

_____

_____

_____

_____

_____

■ **WRITING SUGGESTION** Write a paper in which you first explain what the "glass ceiling" is. Then describe at least two ways businesses can make sure the glass ceiling disappears. Be as specific as possible in your suggestions. If possible, draw on your own personal experience.

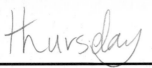
■ **READING 4**

TALK TO ME!

LOOKING AHEAD In this reading, Deborah Tannen argues that men and women don't always agree on the importance of personal communication. In Tannen's view, women are often saying "talk to me" and men are often saying "no."

DEVELOPING A FOCUS Read the section titled "Word Watch." Then read the first and last paragraph. Based on your survey, make one or two predictions. What points do you expect the author to make?

_____

_____

In addition to making predictions, jot down one or two questions you will try to answer as you read.

_____

_____

STRATEGIES FOR IN-DEPTH LEARNING As you read, consider whether the author's description of how men and women feel about talking fits your own experience. Consider, too, your own position. Do you agree or disagree with the author's point of view?

WORD WATCH Because context does not always provide enough clues, some of the more difficult words in the reading are defined below. In the reading, these words are marked with an asterisk.

stock: standard, typical   **utterance:** expression

disgruntled: annoyed   **ruminations:** thoughts

incredulous: disbelieving   **antidote:** remedy

taciturnity: unwillingness to talk   **forums:** places open for discussion

1   WOMEN'S DISSATISFACTION WITH MEN'S SILENCE AT HOME IS captured in the stock* cartoon setting of a breakfast table at which a husband and wife are sitting: He's reading a newspaper; she's glaring at the back of the newspaper. In a Dagwood strip, Blondie complains, "Every morning all he sees is the newspaper!

I'll bet you don't even know I'm here!" Dagwood reassures her, "Of course I know you're here. You're my wonderful wife and I love you very much." With this, he unseeingly pats the paw of the family dog, which the wife has put in her place before leaving the room. The cartoon strip shows that Blondie is justified in feeling like the woman who wrote to Ann Landers: invisible.†

2 Another cartoon shows a husband opening a newspaper and asking his wife, "Is there anything you would like to say to me before I begin reading the newspaper?" The reader knows that there isn't—but that as soon as he begins reading the paper, she will think of something. The cartoon highlights the difference in what women and men think talk is for: To him, talk is for information. So when his wife interrupts his reading, it must be to inform him of something that he needs to know. This being the case, she might as well tell him what she thinks he needs to know before he starts reading. But to her, talk is for interaction. Telling things is a way to show involvement, and listening is a way to show interest and caring. It is not an odd coincidence that she always thinks of things to tell him when he is reading. She feels the need for verbal interaction most keenly when he is (unaccountably, from her point of view) buried in the newspaper instead of talking to her.

3 Yet another cartoon shows a wedding cake that has, on top, in place of the plastic statues of bride and groom in tuxedo and gown, a breakfast scene in which an unshaven husband reads a newspaper across the table from his disgruntled* wife. The cartoon reflects the enormous gulf between the romantic expectations of marriage represented by the plastic couple in traditional wedding costume, and the often disappointing reality represented by the two sides of the newspaper at the breakfast table—the front, which he is reading, and the back, at which she is glaring.

4 These cartoons, and many others on the same theme, are funny because people recognize their own experience in them. What's not funny is that many women are deeply hurt when men don't talk to them at home, and many men are deeply frustrated by feeling they have disappointed their partners, without understanding how they failed or how else they could have behaved.

5 Some men are further frustrated because, as one put it, "When in the world am I supposed to read the morning paper?" If many women are incredulous* that many men do not exchange personal information with their friends, this man is incredulous that

---

†In another section of her book, the author describes a letter to columnist Ann Landers. In the letter, a woman complained about being ignored by her husband.

many women do not bother to read the morning paper. To him, reading the paper is an essential part of his morning ritual, and his whole day is awry if he doesn't get to read it. In his words, reading the newspaper in the morning is as important to him as putting on makeup in the morning is to many women he knows. Yet many women, he observed, either don't subscribe to a paper or don't read it until they get home in the evening. "I find this very puzzling," he said. "I can't tell you how often I have picked up a woman's morning newspaper from her front door in the evening and handed it to her when she opened the door for me."

6   To this man (and I am sure many others), a woman who objects to his reading the morning paper is trying to keep him from doing something essential and harmless. It's a violation of his independence—his freedom of action. But when a woman who expects her partner to talk to her is disappointed that he doesn't, she perceives his behavior as a failure of intimacy: He's keeping things from her; he's lost interest in her; he's pulling away. A woman I will call Rebecca, who is generally quite happily married, told me that this is the one source of serious dissatisfaction with her husband, Stuart. Her term for his taciturnity* is *stinginess of spirit.* She tells him what she is thinking, and he listens silently. She asks him what he is thinking, and he takes a long time to answer, "I don't know." In frustration she challenges, "Is there nothing on your mind?"

7   For Rebecca, who is accustomed to expressing her fleeting thoughts and opinions as they come to her, *saying* nothing means *thinking* nothing. But Stuart does not assume that his passing thoughts are worthy of utterance.* He is not in the habit of uttering his fleeting ruminations,* so, just as Rebecca "naturally" speaks her thoughts, he "naturally" dismisses his as soon as they occur to him. Speaking them would give them more weight and significance than he feels they merit. All her life she has had practice in verbalizing her thoughts and feelings in private conversations with people she is close to; all his life he has had practice in dismissing his and keeping them to himself.

What to Do with Doubts

8   In the above example, Rebecca was not talking about any particular kind of thoughts or feelings, just whatever Stuart might have had in mind. But the matter of giving voice to thoughts and feelings becomes particularly significant in the case of negative feelings or doubts about a relationship. This difference was highlighted for me when a fifty-year-old divorced man told me about his experiences in forming new relationships with women. On this

matter, he was clear: "I do not value my fleeting thoughts, and I do not value the fleeting thoughts of others." He felt that the relationship he was currently in had been endangered, even permanently weakened, by the woman's practice of tossing out her passing thoughts, because, early in their courtship, many of her thoughts were fears about their relationship. Not surprisingly, since they did not yet know each other well, she worried about whether she could trust him, whether their relationship would destroy her independence, whether this relationship was really right for her. He felt she should have kept these fears and doubts to herself and waited to see how things turned out.

9   As it happens, things turned out well. The woman decided that the relationship was right for her, she could trust him, and she did not have to give up her independence. But he felt, at the time that he told me of this, that he had still not recovered from the wear and tear of coping with her earlier doubts. As he put it, he was still dizzy from having been bounced around like a yo-yo tied to the string of her stream of consciousness.

10   In contrast, this man admitted, he himself goes to the other extreme: He never expresses his fears and misgivings about their relationship at all. If he's unhappy but doesn't say anything about it, his unhappiness expresses itself in a kind of distancing coldness. This response is just what women fear most, and just the reason they prefer to express dissatisfactions and doubts—as an antidote* to the isolation and distance that would result from keeping them to themselves.

11   The different perspectives on expressing or concealing dissatisfactions and doubts may reflect a difference in men's and women's awareness of the power of their words to affect others. In repeatedly telling him what she feared about their relationship, this woman spoke as though she assumed he was invulnerable and could not be hurt by what she said; perhaps she was underestimating the power of her words to affect him. For his part, when he refrains from expressing negative thoughts or feelings, he seems to be overestimating the power of his words to hurt her, when, ironically, she is more likely to be hurt by his silence than his words.

12   These women and men are talking in ways they learned as children and reinforced as young adults and then adults, in their same-gender friendships. For girls, talk is the glue that holds relationships together. Boys' relationships are held together primarily by activities: doing things together, or talking about activities such as sports or, later, politics. The forums* in which men are

_____

_____

_____

MAKING CONNECTIONS BETWEEN READINGS In reading 1, the authors discussed the ways children learn the social behaviors considered appropriate to their sex. Do you think Deborah Tannen would agree or disagree with this point of view? Explain your answer.

_____

_____

_____

■ **WRITING SUGGESTIONS** Choose one of the following:

1. Write a paper in which your thesis statement indicates your agreement with the author of "Talk to Me!" Then provide at least three additional examples of how men and women differ in their use of, or attitude toward, speech.

2. Write a paper in which your thesis statement indicates your disagreement with the author of "Talk to Me!" Then provide at least two examples of situations in which men and women do not differ in their use of language.

Living with the Animals

 In the past two decades, the issue of animal rights has become a heated source of controversy. Reading the following articles should give you some insight into that controversy and help you form or sharpen your own opinion.

The Animal-Rights Debate

Deciding the Fate of Laboratory Animals

A Scientist: I Am the Enemy

The Sadness of the Hunter

■ READING 5

THE ANIMAL-RIGHTS DEBATE

LOOKING AHEAD Drawn from a psychology textbook, this article outlines both sides of the debate over animal rights. As you read the selection, ask yourself which side of the debate you think you're on.

DEVELOPING A FOCUS Read the section titled "Word Watch." Then read the first and last paragraph of the selection along with the headings and marginal notes. Look at the illustration and read the caption. Based on your survey, make one or two predictions. What points do you think the authors will make?

_____

_____

In addition to making predictions, jot down one or two questions you will try to answer while you read.

_____

_____

STRATEGIES FOR IN-DEPTH LEARNING As you read, annotate the text by outlining the two sides in the animal-rights debate. When you finish reading, try to sum up each side's argument without looking back at your notes. Consider, too, what you already know about animal-rights protests. Have you seen pictures of them on television? Have you ever participated in one?

WORD WATCH Because context does not always provide enough clues, some of the more difficult words in the reading are defined below. In the reading, these words are marked with an asterisk.

countered: responded

fervor: passion

sadists: people who enjoy inflicting pain

domain: field, area

unethical: immoral

sanitized: cleaned or censored to eliminate anything unpleasant

polarized: split

1 IN APRIL 1991, ABOUT FIFTY PROTESTERS MARCHED OUTSIDE the home of scientist Sharon Juliano, who uses cats in her research on how the brain reorganizes nerve signals after a trauma. The picketers were dressed as the ghosts of cats and carried post-

ers showing photographs of bloody body parts. The march was part of a nationwide demonstration at scientists' laboratories and homes to mark what animal-rights advocates called Lab Animal Liberation week (Royte, 1992).

2   Despite the central importance of animal research in medicine and psychology, in recent years an increasing number of critics have charged that such research is immoral and have made concerted efforts to make it more humane and, in some instances, to stop it. Many scientists have countered* that animal research is essential to conquer physical and mental illnesses and to save or enhance human lives. In this selection, we examine the stormy debate about animal rights and animal research.

> Some say it would be immoral to abandon research that can reduce human suffering.

The Animal-Rights Movement

3   Opposition to animal research has a long history, going back at least as far as the antivivisectionist movement† of the nineteenth century. In recent years, the growth of the animal-rights movement was spurred by a book called *Animal Liberation* (1975), by Australian philosopher Peter Singer. Singer argued that many uses of animals by humans—for food, for clothing, and as captive research subjects—reflected "speciesism": the exploitation of certain species (nonhuman animals) for the benefit of another (humans). Because animals, like humans, can feel pain, Singer argued, they are entitled to just as much consideration as humans are.

4   In Singer's view, speciesism is a form of discrimination that is just as evil as racism and sexism. "Would the experimenter be prepared to perform his experiment on a human infant?" Singer asks. "If not, then his readiness to use nonhumans is simple discrimination" (Singer, 1976, p. 156).

5   Many animal-rights supporters have advanced their views in books and articles and have worked for laws and regulations that would ensure the humane treatment of animals. Others have resorted to acts of terrorism in the name of animal rights (Jasper and Nelkin, 1992). Some activists have invaded animal laboratories, destroyed equipment, stolen data, and let the animals out of their cages. Animal-rights activists have also staged dramatic demonstrations, such as the one outside Sharon Juliano's home, in an attempt to convince the public of what they see as the cruelty of animal research.

---

†In the nineteenth century, antivivisectionists fought against the use of live animals in medical research.

Animal rights activists protest against the use of monkeys in research on drug addiction.

6   The animal-rights movement has been accused by researchers of painting a distorted picture of animal research. In fact, most animal research is neither cruel nor painful, and the large majority of animal researchers are concerned about animal welfare (Novak, 1991). When researchers employ surgical procedures with animals, they almost always use anesthesia to eliminate pain. Many animal-rights supporters acknowledge such humane practices but believe that animal research remains unnecessarily cruel. But the moral fervor* of other animal-rights advocates has led them to engage in misleading portrayals of scientists as sadists* and laboratories as torture chambers.

The Importance of Animal Research

7 Virtually every important medical advance of the past century, from the polio vaccine to the development of life-saving techniques of organ transplantation and open-heart surgery—owes its existence to animal research (Loeb and others, 1989). In the domain* of psychology, much of our knowledge of the biological foundations of behavior—including the structure and functions of the brain—comes from studies of nonhuman animals. The applications of such research range from the development of drug treatments for depression to the use of behavioral techniques for teaching retarded children.

8 Animal research is necessary for several reasons. Because humans and their animal relatives have a similar psychological make-up, animals can be used to study basic principles of biological functioning. For example, Sharon Juliano's research with cats has shed light on the functions of acetylcholine, a neurotransmitter† that is deficient in people suffering from Alzheimer's disease. Because animals can be selectively bred and reared under controlled laboratory conditions, more highly controlled experiments can be conducted with animals than with humans. And because some research requires procedures that may be painful or harmful, conducting it with humans is considered unethical.*

9 Despite the claims of animal-rights advocates, there is often no alternative to research with animals. Although some valuable research can be done by using tissue cultures, much medical and psychological research must be done on functioning organisms. And although computer modeling can sometimes give rise to valuable insights, such models must then be tested in experiments. "To think of using a computer to replace an animal," says the Nobel Prize–winning neuroscientist† David Hubel (1991, p. 7), "is, today, a little like planning a visit to Neptune."

10 Is it ethical to subject animals to pain or discomfort in the hope of enhancing human lives? Most scientists would say yes. Although the scientists agree that animals deserve consideration, they take sharp issue with the view of some animal-rights advocates that all animals—from rats to humans—deserve *equal* consideration. What would really be immoral, the researchers suggest, would be to abandon research that can help to alleviate human pain and suffering.

Raising Consciousness

11 One valuable contribution of the animal-rights movement has been to raise people's consciousness about the treatment of animals in research. In a famous series of experiments, psychologist Harry Harlow (1959) studied mother-infant attachment by separating infant rhesus monkeys from their mothers and observing the consequences. These infants experienced great distress and lasting maladjustment. Harlow's research helped to advance our understanding of social and personality development. But when this research is presented and discussed, surprisingly little attention is typically paid to the suffering of Harlow's subjects.

---

†neurotransmitter: a chemical substance that carries nerve impulses.
†neuroscientist: someone who deals with the nervous system.

12   Most introductory psychology textbooks discuss Harlow's research in a sanitized* way that plays down or ignores the animals' plight. Instead, the texts focus on experimental conditions
in which the infant monkeys, deprived of their own mothers, became attached to cloth-covered constructions that served as
"mother substitutes." As Peter Field notes, "The cute photos of
baby monkeys clinging to a cloth mother-substitute do not convey
much real feeling of emotional pain" (1989, p. 14). Whether we ultimately conclude that Harlow's research—or any other study—
was ethically justified, we should not fail to take an unblinking
look at the pain it may have inflicted on its animal subjects.

13   Peter Field is research director of a group called Psychologists
for the Ethical Treatment of Animals (or "PsyETA"). Although Psy-
ETA shares many of the concerns of animal-rights groups, it does
not advocate the elimination of all animal research. Instead, Psy-
ETA has encouraged psychologists to replace painful or stressful
laboratory research with observational studies, preferably in the
animal's natural environment (Shapiro and Field, 1987).

> PsyETA has forcefully
> called upon research-
> ers to treat animals
> with empathy and
> respect.

14   PsyETA has forcefully called upon researchers to treat animals
with empathy and respect (Shapiro, 1991). These psychologists
are especially concerned about researchers' treatment of our
"sibling species," the chimpanzee. Although about 90 percent
of animal research subjects are rodents, usually rats or mice
(Greenough, 1991), some studies of chimpanzees and other pri-
mates are conducted. Because chimpanzees are so closely related
to humans, PsyETA suggests that researchers should discontinue
all invasive or injurious studies of chimpanzees (Psychologists for
the Ethical Treatment of Animals, 1985).

The Future of Animal Research

15 The debate between animal-rights advocates and the defenders of
animal research has become so sharply polarized* that it is difficult to imagine any possible reconciliation. For many animal-
rights advocates, for example, the notion of injecting a monkey
with a deadly virus is so cruel as to be unthinkable. But in the
view of many researchers, *not* doing such research would be
immoral. "It is very difficult to [infect a monkey] knowing that it
will cause its demise," admits one AIDS researcher. "But there
are HIV patients who call the center every day and ask how we
are progressing with the vaccines. My heart goes out to the monkeys, but even more to the patients who call" (quoted by Segal,
1992).

16   Some researchers believe that the animal-rights movement has

had a positive impact in spurring the enactment of federal regulations that set strict standards for the care and treatment of laboratory animals. But other researchers believe that these regulations have become much too strict and are impeding the progress of research (Royte, 1992). And the researchers express concern that animal rights activism may be steering some young people away from careers in the biomedical sciences. "The poor kid interested in science today," complains one leading researcher, "has to fight not only the image of the nerd but of the sadist as well" (quoted by Royte, 1992).

17   In the years to come, the debate about animal rights and animal research will continue and may even escalate. In forming your own conclusions, beware of the misstatements and the propaganda. Instead, try to learn more about how a study was actually conducted, about its potential benefits, and about the short-term and long-term costs to the animal subjects. Only then will you be able to arrive at your own informed view about whether the research was justified.

Adapted from Zick Rubin, Letitia Anne Peplau,
and Peter Salovey, Psychology. Boston:
Houghton Mifflin, 1993, pp. 68–76.

TEST YOUR UNDERSTANDING   Circle the letter of the correct answer.

1. Which of the following more effectively paraphrases the thesis statement?

   a. Although we tend to think that the animal-rights movement has existed for only a short time, the movement actually has a long history that reaches back into the nineteenth century.

   b. Recently, animal-rights activists have begun to sharply attack the use of animals in scientific research as cruel and immoral. Scientists have responded to those attacks by insisting that without the use of animals, they cannot alleviate suffering or save human lives.

2. According to the reading, the animal-rights movement was spurred into action by

   a. A Canadian exposé of the horrible conditions under which animals must live.

   b. Peter Singer's book *Animal Liberation.*

   c. A series of articles in the *New York Times* on the subject of experimental animals.

3. According to the philosopher Peter Singer, speciesism is

   a. equal to racism and sexism.

   b. much worse than racism or sexism.

   c. not in the same league as racism or sexism.

4. Which sentence more effectively paraphrases the topic sentence in paragraph 7?

   a. Most of the medical progress in the past hundred years has relied on the use of animals in research.

   b. Without the use of animals, research in psychology would currently be at a standstill.

5. Which sentence more effectively paraphrases the topic sentence in paragraph 8?

   a. Conducting research on people rather than animals is not an acceptable alternative.

   b. There are a number of reasons why we need to continue using animals in research.

6. In paragraph 8, which of the following is *not* an essential detail?

   a. "Because humans and their animal relatives have a similar physiological make-up, animals can be used to study basic principles of biological functioning."

   b. "Because animals can be selectively bred and reared under controlled laboratory conditions, more highly controlled experiments can be conducted with animals than with humans."

   c. "Sharon Juliano's research with cats has shed light on the functions of acetylcholine, a neurotransmitter that is deficient in people suffering from Alzheimer's disease."

7. According to the authors, one valuable contribution of the animal-rights movement has been

   a. to improve the living conditions of animals used in research.

   b. to increase people's understanding of how animals are treated in research.

   c. to decrease the number of animals used in research.

8. According to the authors,

   a. there are no alternatives to research with animals.

   b. sometimes there are no alternatives to using animals in research.

   c. research on animals could be replaced by computer modeling.

9. What's the implied main idea of paragraph 16?

   a. Researchers do not necessarily agree on the impact of the animal-rights movement.

   b. Researchers are convinced that the animal-rights movement is doing more harm than good.

10. At the end of this reading, the authors tell readers to

    a. become involved in the animal-rights movement.

    b. be critical and form their own conclusions in the animal-rights debate.

    c. support the use of animals in research.

SHARPEN YOUR CRITICAL SKILLS Answer the following questions.

1. What does the thesis statement suggest about the authors' purpose in writing?

   a. The authors want to convince readers that members of the animal-rights movement are mistaken.

   b. The authors want to inform readers about the issues involved in the animal rights movement.

2. According to the authors, what reason does Peter Singer give for his claim that animals are entitled to just as much consideration as humans are?

   Animals, like humans
   can feel pain

   _____

3. In paragraph 5, the authors say that some animal-rights activists "have resorted to acts of terrorism in the name of animal rights." What connotations does the word *terrorism* have, positive or negative? _Negative_ What associations do most people have when they hear the word *terrorism*?

   Some one of violent behavior attack
   with force, which include some
   kind of political reason

4. In paragraph 6, the authors tell us that "most animal research is neither cruel nor painful, and the large majority of animal research-

ers are concerned about animal welfare." How do the authors argue this opinion?

By showing that when researcher
employ surgical procedures with animals
they almost always use anesthesia to
eliminate pain.

5. What questions might critical readers pose about the authors' evidence?

What kind of survey was done
to support this evidence, and
who done the research

6. Reread paragraphs 5 and 6, and decide which one of the following statements is accurate.

a. The authors are inclined to be critical of animal-rights supporters.

b. The authors are inclined to favor animal-rights supporters.

c. It's impossible to determine the authors' personal bias.

Explain how you arrived at your answer.

7. What opinion do the authors argue in paragraph 8?

Conducting research with
humans is considered unethical

What reasons do the authors offer in support of that opinion?

it is ethical to subject animals
to pain or discomfort in the hope
of enhancing humans life.

_____

_____

8. In paragraph 10, the authors tell readers that most scientists believe it's acceptable for animals to suffer if that suffering enhances human life. What questions might critical readers pose in response to that statement?

Why should the animal suffer?
What proof does the scientists have
to show.

9. How would you describe the authors' tone?

  a. emotionally neutral

  b. passionate and serious

  c. friendly and relaxed

10. In paragraph 9, the authors use expert opinion to support their claim that computer modeling cannot replace the use of animals in research. Based on what you have learned about the use of experts,

are you satisfied with the authors' use of an expert's opinion? _No_ Explain your answer.

The experts opinion was the
authors own personal point of
view, the survey was insufficent

THINKING FOR YOURSELF

1. Do you think animals should or should not be used in research? Why or why not? If you discovered that a medicine you were using had been developed at the expense of animals' suffering, would you stop using it? Explain.

_____

_____

_____

2. Currently, research is being done to see whether pigs can be raised in sterile conditions and used as the source of organs for people who need transplants. Do you support the use of animals as a source of transplants? Why or why not?

_____

_____

_____

■   **WRITING**   Write a paper explaining why injecting chimpanzees with the AIDS
SUGGESTION virus in order to find a cure for the disease is or is not morally acceptable from your point of view.

■ **READING 6**

DECIDING THE FATE OF LABORATORY ANIMALS

LOOKING AHEAD In this reading, the author describes some of the experiments that have deeply disturbed members of the animal-rights movement. She also outlines some of the movement's goals and achievements.

DEVELOPING A FOCUS Read the section titled "Word Watch." Then read all the headings along with the first and last paragraphs. Based on your survey, make one or two predictions. What points do you expect the author to make?

_____

_____

_____

In addition to making predictions, jot down one or two questions you will try to answer as you read.

_____

_____

_____

STRATEGIES FOR IN-DEPTH LEARNING Each time you finish a section of the reading, try to answer the question posed in the heading. In addition, annotate the margins by making up possible short-answer test questions, like "Who was Harry Harlow?" When you finish reading, go back to find out how well you answered your own questions.

WORD WATCH Because context does not always provide enough clues, some of the more difficult words in the reading are defined below. In the reading, these words are marked with an asterisk.

conviction: belief

landmark: historically important

redundant: repetitive

nurturing: caretaking

toxicity: the quality or condition of being poisonous

ingest: eat

objectivity: lack of bias

implemented: put into practice

1 STATISTICS INDICATE THAT AMERICANS SPEND A SMALL fortune on the care of their pets. We are apparently willing to do almost anything to spare them pain and suffering. It seems all the more surprising, then, that until quite recently we ignored the suffering and pain inflicted on laboratory animals.

2 One reason for this lack of attention was undoubtedly the conviction* that the suffering of laboratory animals was justified. It served a worthy cause by lengthening human life and eliminating human pain. For years, it was easy to silence animal-rights activists with a simple slogan: "Your child or your dog." And, to be sure, there was some truth in those words. Research involving animals has helped ease human suffering. The vaccine for hepatitis B was first tested on animals; so were the techniques used in heart surgery and organ transplants. Vaccines developed through animal research have virtually wiped out such diseases as smallpox and polio. Animal testing has helped improve, even save, lives.

3 But as the philosopher Peter Singer has shown in his landmark* book *Animal Liberation,* many experiments cannot readily be justified by claims that they improve the quality of human life: "Among the tens of millions of experiments performed, only a few can possibly be regarded as contributing to important medical research" (40). A significant number of experiments involving animals do little or nothing to improve the quality of human life. In many cases, they appear to be redundant,* even pointless.

Were These Experiments Necessary?

4 High on the list of such experiments were those performed in the sixties by the late Dr. Harry Harlow. To prove that pathological behavior can be traced to a disruption in the mother-child relationship, Harlow and his colleagues raised rhesus monkeys in a variety of deprived environments. Some infant monkeys were kept in barbed-wire cages, others in stainless steel chambers. All experienced profound social isolation. All were separated from their mothers. Not surprisingly, Harlow discovered that prolonged isolation, practically from birth, produced "profound and apparently permanent social deficits" (McNeil, 152). The monkeys were fearful. They tended to huddle and rock, to hunch over and hug their bodies.

5 Harlow's experiments fulfilled their objective. Clearly, a lack of parental nurturing* during infancy has far-reaching psychological effects.

6 However, that insight was already available to researchers in 1951, when the British psychiatrist John Bowlby studied the effects of maternal deprivation on children orphaned by war.

Bowlby had come to the same conclusion that Harlow later reached: "It is submitted that evidence is now such that it leaves no room for doubt. . . . deprivation of the young child of maternal care may have grave and far-reaching effects on his character" (Singer, 32). Given Bowlby's results, the question has to be raised: Were Harlow's experiments really necessary?

7   A similar question should be posed about another experiment, performed on Shetland ponies. In this experiment, the ponies were first deprived of anything to drink. They then were given water bowls that could emit electric shocks. Loudspeakers were placed on either side of their heads. If noise came from the left speaker, the ponies received an electric shock while drinking. They quickly learned not to drink if they heard noise coming from their left side.

8   Not satisfied with these results, researchers placed the speakers closer together. As a result, the ponies had difficulty distinguishing where the noise was coming from, and they could no longer avoid being shocked. Based on similar research with rats, dogs, cats, and monkeys, the researchers concluded that the ponies had difficulty distinguishing the direction of noise (Singer, 49). But it is difficult to see how this conclusion could in any way benefit or improve human life.

9   One wonders, too, about the wisdom behind toxicity* tests used to develop products like shoe polish, oven cleaner, and floor wax. In these tests, animals are force-fed high quantities of normally inedible substances. The objective is to discover at what point the animals show symptoms of being poisoned—trembling, vomiting, diarrhea, and, ultimately, death. Yet it is hard to understand how relevant these tests are to the circumstances in which humans will use the products. Even children who might accidentally eat or drink such products are not going to ingest* the huge quantities force-fed to the animals. The foul taste of substances like oven cleaner and shoe polish would preclude that. In addition, given the way the tests are performed, it's not clear whether the animals are poisoned by the substances themselves or by the quantity they consume.

10   But this point has been made before. After tests on rats suggested that the sugar substitute saccharin could endanger human health, Dr. Elizabeth Whelan, the executive director of the American Council on Science and Health, expressed a certain skepticism. "It doesn't take a Ph.D. in the sciences to grasp the fact that rodent exposure to the saccharin equivalent of 1,800 bottles of soda pop a day doesn't relate well to our daily ingestion of a few glasses of the stuff" (Singer, 57).

11   The list of seemingly pointless experiments like these is long and depressing. It challenges the notion that the suffering and death of animals in research serves a worthy cause. The experiments described here did not ease human suffering. Nor did they preserve human life.

12   There is, however, some cause for optimism. Since the publication of books like Singer's *Animal Liberation* and Andrew Rowan's *Of Mice, Models, and Men: A Critical Evaluation of Animal Research,* the public has changed. It has become more knowledgeable about and more critical of the treatment of animals used in research. That change in consciousness has, in turn, produced changes in the laboratory.

What Progress Has Been Made?

13 For many years, one of the most troubling tests performed on laboratory animals was the Draize irritancy test. In this test, substances such as bleach or shampoo were placed in the eyes of rabbits. The rabbits were prevented from removing the irritating substances. Over time, observers checked the rabbits' eyes to note the degree of infection, swelling, or blindness.

14   Outraged by the Draize tests, animal-rights activists began to organize. On April 15, 1980, the *New York Times* ran a full-page advertisement. The ad posed a disturbing question: "How Many Rabbits Does Revlon Blind for Beauty's Sake?" Animal-rights activists in rabbit costumes also began appearing at Revlon board meetings. It took almost a decade, but by April 1989, Revlon announced that it had completed its long-term plan to eliminate animal testing in all phases of research. Other cosmetic companies have announced similar developments. Avon, Noxell, Mary Kay, and Victoria Jackson all announced they were decreasing or eliminating the use of laboratory animals for research.

15   Prodded by the animal-rights movement, manufacturers of pharmaceuticals and household products have also changed their policies. They have begun to eliminate the LD50 ("lethal dose 50 percent") experiment, in which animals are forced to consume nonedible substances like bleach or ink until 50 percent of them die. For many years, LD50 was a standard method of quality control. But since the late seventies, when books and articles on animal rights began to appear, the use of the LD50 test has declined by 96 percent (Cowley et al., 55).

Where Do We Go From Here?

16 Because of the work done by animal-rights activists, laboratory animals have been spared much needless pain and suffering. As

Science magazine reported in April of 1988, major manufacturers have begun to reduce the number of animals used in toxicity testing. "Alternative methods . . . are increasingly being seen not just as good public relations but as desirable both economically and scientifically" (Holden, 252).

17   That does not mean, however, that all needless suffering of laboratory animals has been eliminated. In the same April issue, *Science* reported that "unnecessary testing is still wasting a lot of animals" (Holden, 252). One reason for the continued testing is that information about previous tests is not easy to obtain. Theodore M. Farber, director of the toxicology branch of the Environmental Protection Agency, has pointed out that files in his agency are not computerized. It's difficult, therefore, to discover whether a test using animals is redundant. As Farber himself claimed, many tests using laboratory animals have been done before: "Many of us in regulatory toxicology see the same studies over and over again" (Holden, 25).

18   It is clear that more needs to be done if laboratory animals are to be spared needless suffering. One thing the United States should do is look to the kind of legislation enacted in other countries. In Britain, for example, every experimental project must be licensed. According to law, that license will not be granted until the secretary of state for home affairs has weighed the "likely adverse effects on the animals concerned against the benefit likely to accrue" (Singer, 77).

19   In Australia, the law requires that all experiments be approved by an animal experimentation ethics committee. The committee must include one person with an interest in animal welfare. To ensure objectivity, that person cannot be employed by the institution conducting the experiment. As in Britain, the goal of the committee is to weigh the scientific or educational value of the experiment against the effects suffered by the animals.

20   In 1985, the U.S. Congress did seem intent on enacting legislation to improve animal welfare. Congress passed a series of amendments to the federal Animal Welfare Act. The amendments called for a national data bank that would list the results of all animal experimentation. Obviously, such a bank would go a long way toward eliminating needless repetition.

21   According to the amendments, all laboratories using live animals would be required to set up animal-care committees. They would also be required to submit to annual inspections. The overall goal of the amendments was threefold. They were designed *to reduce* the number of animals used in experiments, *to refine* the techniques that cause suffering, and, finally, *to replace* live ani-

mals with simulations or cell cultures (Cowley et al., 54). Unfortunately, this praiseworthy attempt to improve animal-welfare legislation has not been implemented. The amendments are still stalled in the federal budget office.

Laraine Flemming

Sources

Caras, Roger, "We Must Find Alternatives to Animal Research," *Newsweek,* December 26, 1988, p. 57.

Cowley, Geoffrey et al. "Of Pain and Progress," *Newsweek,* December 26, 1988, pp. 50–59.

Holden, Constance. "Industry Toxicologists Keen on Reducing Animal Use," *Science* (236), 1987, p. 252.

McNeil, Elton B. *The Psychology of Being Human.* San Francisco: Confield Press, 1974, pp. 151–152.

Singer, Peter. *Animal Liberation.* New York: Random House, 1990.

TEST YOUR UNDERSTANDING Circle the letter of the correct answer.

1. What's the main idea of this selection?

   a. Many of the scientific experiments using animals have not, as some have claimed, been essential to improving the life and health of human beings.

   b. Although a few of the scientific experiments that use animals have been pointless and redundant, most have paved the way for important medical breakthroughs.

2. Which of the following statements in the reading does *not* provide an essential detail?

   a. "Statistics indicate that Americans spend a small fortune on the care of their pets."

   b. "For many years, one of the most troubling tests performed on laboratory animals was the Draize irritancy test."

   c. "One thing the United States should do is look to the kind of legislation enacted in other countries."

3. According to the author, what is one reason why in the past people did not pay attention to the suffering of laboratory animals?

   a. People were crueler in the past.

   b. People didn't know that laboratory animals suffered.

   c. People assumed that the suffering served a worthy cause.

4. According to Peter Singer,

   a. only a very few experiments actually inflict pain on animals.

   b. most scientific experiments on animals are important for the health of human beings.

   c. only a few of the experiments on animals make significant contributions to medical research.

5. From the author's perspective, Harry Harlow's research

   a. offered a new and important insight into the nature of the mother-child relationship.

   b. may have been unnecessary given the earlier findings of John Bowlby.

   c. was crucial because it reaffirmed the findings of John Bowlby's research.

6. According to the author, why is there currently cause for optimism?

   a. Researchers are becoming afraid to use animals in their experiments.

   b. The efforts of animal-rights activists have decreased the number of researchers willing to experiment on animals.

   c. The public has become more knowledgeable and more critical of the ways animals are used in research.

7. Reread paragraph 12. Based on that paragraph, what pattern of organization do you expect will follow?

   a. comparison and contrast

   b. cause and effect

   c. sequence of steps

8. According to the author, what was the test that used to be a standard part of the making of cosmetics?

   a. the Draize irritancy test

   b. LD50

   c. the Harlow experiments

9. Which of the following statements accurately paraphrases the topic sentence in paragraph 15?

   a. Concerned about their public image, pharmaceutical manufacturers have done away with all testing on animals.

    b. Because of efforts made by animal-rights activists, manufacturers of pharmaceuticals and household products have modified their policies on the use of research animals.

10. According to the author, the United States should

    a. devise new standards for experiments involving animals.

    b. look to other countries for ideas about legislation to protect animals used in research.

    c. make illegal the use of animals in medical research.

SHARPEN YOUR CRITICAL SKILLS Answer the following questions.

1. What does the thesis statement suggest to you about the author's purpose in writing?

    a. The author wants to persuade readers to share her opinion that much of the research done on animals is unnecessary.

    b. The author wants to describe for readers some of the most common scientific experiments that use animal subjects.

2. Are the connotations of the word *landmark,* positive or negative?

_____ When the author called Peter Singer's book a "landmark," what does she encourage her readers to do?

_____

_____

_____

3. Label the following statements *F* (fact), *O* (opinion), or *B* (both).

    a. "The vaccine for hepatitis B was first tested on animals." _____

    b. "For many years, LD50 was a standard method of quality control." _____

    c. "It is clear that more needs to be done if laboratory animals are to be spared needless suffering." _____

4. The research of Harry Harlow is cited in support of what opinion?

_____

_____

_____

5. If the author had cited just the Harlow case to support her opinion, would you be satisfied with her argument? _____
Explain your answer.

_____

_____

_____

6. In paragraph 10, the author uses an expert's opinion to support her point of view. Based on what you have learned, do you think the author makes effective use of expert opinion? _____
Explain your answer.

_____

_____

_____

7. Compare this reading to "The Animal Rights Debate." Are the authors' purposes the same or different? _____
Explain your answer.

_____

_____

_____

8. How would you describe the author's tone?
   a. passionate
   b. serious
   c. emotionally neutral

9. The author describes experiments involving dogs, cats, ponies, rabbits, and chimpanzees. However, a large portion of scientific experiments involve rats and mice, and they, too, often suffer needlessly. Why do you think the author chose not to describe experiments involving rats or mice?

_____

_____

_____

10. In paragraph 21, the author reveals her feelings about proposed animal-welfare legislation. What are those feelings, and which word or words reveal those feelings?

_____

_____

_____

THINKING FOR YOURSELF

1. Did the author convince you that the use of animals in research is not always justified? _____ Explain your answer.

_____

_____

_____

2. Some animal-rights activists have argued that illegal means are sometimes necessary to protect animals that are helpless to protect themselves. For this reason, they have invaded research labs and have stolen or set free animals destined to undergo painful experiments. Can you imagine yourself participating in such an action? Why or why not?

_____

_____

_____

MAKING CONNECTIONS BETWEEN READINGS How do the authors of "The Animal-Rights Debate" portray, or describe, members of the animal-rights movement? Is that description similar to or different from the description in the reading you just finished? Do you think the scientists using animals for research are portrayed more favorably in one reading than in the other? Explain your answer.

_____

_____

_____

WRITING SUGGESTION Write a paper in which you explain why you would or would not become a member of the animal-rights movement.

■ **READING 7**

A Scientist: I Am the Enemy

LOOKING AHEAD The author of this reading is deeply involved in medical research that uses animals. As you might expect, he has some strong opinions on the subject.

DEVELOPING A FOCUS Read the section titled "Word Watch." Then read the first paragraph and the last paragraph of the selection. Based on your survey, make one or two predictions. What points do you expect the author to make?

_____

_____

In addition to making predictions, jot down one or two questions that you will try to answer as you read.

_____

_____

STRATEGIES FOR IN-DEPTH LEARNING As you read, try to recall everything you already know about protests for animal rights. Have you ever seen or been in one? Ask yourself if the author's description of the animal-rights movement fits what you already know about that movement. Try, too, to get into the mind of the author. What would you do if your research could lead to a cure for cancer but caused terrible suffering to hundreds of animals?

WORD WATCH Because context does not always provide enough clues, some of the more difficult words in the reading are defined below. In the reading, these words are marked with an asterisk.

vilified: hated, insulted

apathetic: uncaring

unconscionably: not influenced by conscience

initiative: the first step toward action

contend: argue, claim

malevolent: evil

static: unmoving, having no motion

traumatic: causing great pain or shock

insulated: protected, shielded

1 I AM THE ENEMY! ONE OF THOSE VILIFIED,* INHUMANE physician-scientists involved in animal research. How strange, for I have never thought of myself as an evil person. I became a pediatrician because of my love for children and my desire to keep them healthy. During medical school and residency, however, I saw many children die of leukemia, prematurity, and traumatic* injury—circumstances against which medicine has made tremendous progress, but still has far to go. More important, I also saw children, alive and healthy, thanks to advances in medical science such as infant respirators, potent antibiotics, new surgical techniques, and the entire field of organ transplantation. My desire to tip the scales in favor of the healthy, happy children drew me to medical research.

2 My accusers claim that I inflict torture on animals for the sole purpose of career advancement. My experiments supposedly have no relevance to medicine and are easily replaced by computer simulation. Meanwhile, an apathetic* public barely watches, convinced that the issue has no significance, and publicity-conscious politicians increasingly give way to the demands of the activists.

3 We in medical research have also been unconscionably* apathetic. We have allowed the most extreme animal-rights protesters to seize the initiative* and frame the issue as one of "animal fraud." We have been complacent in our belief that a knowledgeable public would sense the importance of animal research to the public health. Perhaps we have been mistaken in not responding to the emotional tone of the argument created by those sad posters of animals by waving equally sad posters of children dying of leukemia or cystic fibrosis.

4 Much is made of the pain inflicted on these animals in the name of medical science. The animal-rights activists contend* that this is evidence of our malevolent* and sadistic nature. A more reasonable argument, however, can be advanced in our defense. Life is often cruel, both to animals and human beings. Teenagers get thrown from the back of a pickup truck and suffer severe head injuries. Toddlers, barely able to walk, find themselves at the bottom of a swimming pool while a parent checks the mail.

5 Physicians hoping to alleviate the pain and suffering these tragedies cause have but three choices: Create an animal model of the injury or disease and use that model to understand the process and test new therapies; experiment on human beings—some experiments will succeed, most will fail—or finally, leave medical

knowledge static,* hoping that accidental discoveries will lead us to the advances.

6   Some animal-rights activists would suggest a fourth choice, claiming that computer models can simulate animal experiments, thus making the actual experiments unnecessary. Computers can simulate, reasonably well, the effects of well-understood principles on complex systems, as in the application of the laws of physics to airplane and automobile design. However, when the principles themselves are in question, as is the case with the complex biological systems under study, computer modeling alone is of little value.

7   One of the terrifying effects of the effort to restrict the use of animals in medical research is that the impact will not be felt for years and decades: Drugs that might have been discovered will not be; surgical techniques that might have been developed will not be; and fundamental biological processes that might have been understood will remain mysteries.

8   Fortunately, most of us enjoy good health, and the trauma of watching one's child die has become a rare experience. Yet our good fortune should not make us unappreciative of the health we enjoy or the advances that make it possible. Vaccines; antibiotics; insulin; and drugs to treat heart disease, hypertension, and stroke are all based on animal research. Most complex surgical procedures, such as coronary-artery bypass and organ transplantation, are initially developed in animals. Presently undergoing animal studies are techniques to insert genes in humans in order to replace the defective ones found to be the cause of so much disease. These studies will effectively end if animal research is severely restricted.

9   In America today, death has become an event isolated from our daily existence—out of the sight and thoughts of most of us. As a doctor who has watched many children die, and their parents grieve, I am particularly angered by people capable of so much compassion for a dog or a cat, but with seemingly so little for a dying human being. These people seem so insulated* from the reality of human life and death and what it means.

10   Make no mistake, however: I am not advocating the needlessly cruel treatment of animals. To the extent that the animal-rights movement has made us more aware of the needs of these animals, and made us search harder for suitable alternatives, they have made a significant contribution. But if the more radical members of this movement are successful in limiting further research, their efforts will bring about a tragedy that will cost many lives.

The real question is whether an apathetic majority can be aroused to protect its future against a vocal, but misdirected, minority.

Ron Kline, "A Scientist: I Am the Enemy,"
Newsweek, December 18, 1991, pp. 77–78.

TEST YOUR UNDERSTANDING Circle the letter of the correct answer.

1. Which statement more effectively sums up the implied main idea of this reading?

   a. Physicians have not made a strong enough effort to inform the public about the limitations of using computer modeling to do medical research.

   b. It's time for physicians to respond to the misinformed claims of animal-rights activists and make their case for using animals in medical research.

2. What drew the author to medical research?

   a. His desire to help people.

   b. His desire to help children.

   c. His love of medicine.

3. According to the author, how does the public feel about the debate over animal rights?

   a. The public doesn't care about it.

   b. The public is furious at those who use animals in medical research.

   c. Most of the public believes animal-rights activists are crazy.

4. Which statement sums up the implied main idea of paragraph 6?

   a. In the future, computer models may be able to replace the use of animals in medical research, but that time is a long way off.

   b. Although computers can be of some use in medical research, they cannot replace the use of animals, as some animal-rights activists have claimed.

5. Which statement sums up the implied main idea of paragraph 8?

   a. In the last century, discoveries about the causes and cures of various diseases have greatly improved the quality of life in the United States.

b. Those of us lucky enough to enjoy good health should not forget that medical research involving animals is responsible for our good fortune.

6. In paragraph 9, the author expects readers to supply which of the following inferences?

a. People who worry so much about the suffering of animals usually don't have children to worry about, so they focus on animals.

b. Because they are not confronted on a daily basis with what it means to die, it becomes all too easy for animal-rights activists to ignore the suffering of human beings.

7. According to the author, what positive effect have animal-rights activists had?

a. They have severely restricted the use of animals in medical research.

b. They have made researchers ashamed to admit that they do experiments on animals.

c. They have made scientists more aware of the needs and rights of research animals.

8. According to the author, what negative effect might some animal-rights activists have in the future?

a. They will destroy the public's faith in doctors who do research.

b. They will cause funding for medical research using animals to dry up and disappear.

c. Useful drugs and surgical techniques will not be available to heal the sick.

9. Which statement more effectively synthesizes the first three readings in this unit?

a. In all three readings, the authors suggest that medical progress will be seriously undermined if research using animals is not fully supported by the American public.

b. In all three readings, the authors suggest that the animal-rights movement has had a powerful effect on medical research, but they strongly disagree on the nature of that effect.

10. Which pattern helps to organize the supporting details in this reading?

a. series of dates and events

b. sequence of steps

    c. comparison and contrast

    d. cause and effect

    e. classification

SHARPEN YOUR CRITICAL SKILLS   Answer the following questions.

1. What tone does the author take in the first two lines of the reading?

    a. ironic

    b. serious

    c. emotionally neutral

    Explain your answer.

    _____

    _____

    _____

2. What tone does the author take at the end of the reading?

    a. ironic

    b. solemn

    c. emotionally neutral

3. Why do you think the author assumes one tone at the beginning and another at the end?

    _____

    _____

    _____

    _____

    _____

4. What does the author tell readers about his personal and professional life? What's his purpose in providing this information?

    _____

    _____

    _____

5. Label the following statements *F* (fact), *O* (opinion), or *B* (both).

    a. "We in medical research have been unconscionably apathetic."

      _____

    b. "I am particularly angered by people capable of so much compassion for a dog or cat, but with seemingly so little for a dying human being." _____

    c. "Presently undergoing animal studies are techniques to insert genes in humans." _____

6. In the phrase *unconscionably apathetic,* do you think the word *unconscionably* has negative or neutral connotations? _____
Explain your answer.

_____

_____

_____

_____

_____

7. In paragraph 2, the author says that "my experiments supposedly have no relevance to medicine." What does the word *supposedly* imply to readers?

_____

_____

_____

8. In paragraph 2, the author tells readers that "publicity-conscious politicians increasingly give way to the demands of the activists." What questions might critical readers pose in response to that statement?

_____

_____

_____

9. Overall, how would you describe the author's tone?

a. passionate

b. relaxed

c. emotionally neutral

10. How would you describe the author's purpose?

a. He wants to inform readers about the benefits derived from using animals in research.

b. He wants to persuade readers to think twice before accepting the claims of animal-rights activists and demanding an end to experiments on animals.

THINKING FOR YOURSELF If you were convinced that as a scientist you could benefit humanity by means of your research, would you experiment on animals, even if you knew the experiments would cause the animals to suffer intense pain?

_____

_____

_____

_____

MAKING CONNECTIONS BETWEEN READINGS **1.** Of the three readings on animal rights, which one most closely expresses your opinions? Explain. With which of the three do you most strongly disagree? Explain the source of your disagreement.

_____

_____

_____

_____

2. Do all three authors agree or disagree on the tactics and goals of the animal-rights movement? Explain your answer.

_____

_____

_____

_____

■   **WRITING** Write a paper in which you explain what role, if any, animals should
SUGGESTION play in medical research. Concentrate on developing a sound argument that gives at least two reasons for your opinion.

■ **READING 8**

THE SADNESS OF THE HUNTER

LOOKING AHEAD   As a young boy, David Stout was an avid hunter. But, over time, his feelings changed. In this reading he explains why.

DEVELOPING A FOCUS   Read the section titled "Word Watch." Then read the first and the last paragraphs of the selection. Based on your survey, make one or two predictions. What points do you expect the author to make?

_____

_____

In addition to making predictions, jot down one or two questions you will try to answer as you read.

_____

_____

STRATEGIES FOR IN-DEPTH LEARNING   Are you a hunter, or do you know someone who is? Ask yourself if the author's description of hunters and their attitude toward hunting fit your own experience. What about the author's description of nonhunters? Does it ring true?

WORD WATCH   Because context does not always provide enough clues, some of the more difficult words in the reading are defined below. In the reading, these words are marked with an asterisk.

paradox: a statement that seems to be a contradiction but is nonetheless true

upscale: related to a high income

camaraderie: friendship

communion: act of sharing

bedrock: solid, strong

articulate: put into words

inexplicable: unexplainable

1   SO MUCH HAS BEEN WRITTEN ABOUT THE JOY OF HUNTING and so little about the sadness, the sadness that fills the silence after the echo of the shot has died away.

2   If the hunter is skilled, or lucky, he has just killed something. In a moment he may feel joy. But first he must pass through another emotion, one akin to grief. He must pull the trigger to get

there. Nothing could be more appropriate, for grief is supposed to be linked to death.

3   Hunting is going on in many places, and with it the conflict in the heart of the hunter. Hunters use the word "harvest" again and again. Hunters speak of harvesting deer or ducks or grouse or rabbits. There is a paradox* at work here, for the hunter knows better than his nonhunting friends that pork chops and drumsticks do not grow on trees.

Why Do It?

4   "I don't know any hunter who hasn't felt a sense of sadness after he's shot a deer," said David C. Foster, editor of *Gray's Sporting Journal*, a decidedly upscale* hunting and fishing magazine, who is himself an enthusiastic hunter.

5   Why do it, then? It is not enough to speak of loving the outdoors, or the camaraderie,* or the challenge. No, there is some kind of blood communion* between the hunter and that which he kills. "It takes courage to kill an animal as beautiful as a deer," another hunter, Ed Van Put of Sullivan County, N.Y., said. Then he mused: Was courage the right word? For him it was. "It takes something extra to pull the trigger," said Mr. Van Put, who monitors fish in lakes and streams for the New York State Department of Environmental Conservation.

6   Many non-hunters find such talk absurd, or horrible. Many of them wouldn't think of killing wild game yet think nothing of buying meat at the supermarket. There are those who don't eat meat but do eat fish, as though sure that the flopping in a net or boat is merely reflex, not desperation, and that the writhing creature's unblinking eye betrays no more emotion than it will later, staring up from a bed of chopped ice.

7   A longtime hunter may be sad at the sight of a giant tree, toppled in its old age by rot or wind or lightning. This is death too. Such thoughts grow with age, as the hunter's own years add to his knowledge about the frailty of life, and they lead in many directions.

8   Even if the hunter has a sound compass—some bedrock* beliefs about his place in the world, in which all time is borrowed—he will wander around and around, returning only to a question: What life is so precious that it should not be taken?

9   I remember hearing in my boyhood talk about whether it was less noble to kill a doe than a buck; whether it was all right to hunt just for trophy heads, antlers, or tusks; or whether a decent hunter always ate what he shot (not that he needed to). I found myself wrestling with those questions too much. So I took timid

retreat, closeting my own 12-gauge shotgun and trying to shut away some emotions, which still emerge from time to time out of some dark forest of memory.

10   It is reassuring to find that men who still hunt are stalked by these emotions too. "There *is* a momentary feeling of sadness that you had to take a life in pursuit of what you're doing," Jack Samson, the retired editor of *Field and Stream* magazine, said the other day from his home in Santa Fe, N.M., as he reflected on a lifetime of hunting big game and small. Nelson Bryant, a retired outdoors columnist for the *New York Times*, said that he had never shot anything "without a sense of sadness, very brief, but it's there . . . whether a duck or deer or whatever, it was something alive." When pressed on just why they hunt if it brings such sadness, hunters fumble with words. Mr. Van Put responded with, "It's something that man has done forever." Mr. Bryant tried to articulate* his thoughts and said finally, "It's inexplicable."*

11   Inexplicable or not, the lure of hunting is also irresistible, at least for some. *Field and Stream* is celebrating its 100th anniversary and has a circulation of about two million, mostly middle class, according to a managing editor, Slaton L. White. The recent survey for the Interior Department's Fish and Wildlife Service showed that about 75 percent of Americans approve of hunting, 22 percent disapprove. Hugh Vickery, an agency spokesman, said the money hunters contribute for conservation efforts is essential and totaled some $700 million in 1994 through license fees and taxes on firearms and ammunition.

12   There were 15.3 million licensed hunters in the United States in 1994, down from the 1982 peak of 16.7 million. Mr. Vickery said the survey found that dwindling open space was the main reason for the decline.

13   But perhaps there are other reasons, at least for a few. Mr. Bryant said he knew of some men who stopped hunting as they got older, not because they grew infirm but because they grew more keenly aware of the finality of all life.

14   And a personal note on why I gave up hunting. I was not squeamish, say, about slitting the belly of a freshly killed rabbit and dumping the steaming guts onto the damp leaves on a chill November day. But I cannot forget the day when I was 13 and shot at a big rusty fox squirrel three times before it came tumbling down from the tree, bouncing off limbs as it fell, then trying to crawl away.

15   And this hunter who would not remain a hunter grabbed the animal by its tail, dragging it to a clearing to finish it off with the gun butt. Then he stood still in the dusk, listening to a chain saw

in the distance and waiting for his sadness to go away. He has been waiting for 40 years.

David Stout, "The Sadness of the Hunter,"
New York Times, December 10, 1995, p. 3.

TEST YOUR UNDERSTANDING Circle the letter of the correct answer.

1. What's the main idea of the selection?

   a. Although hunters may experience joy when they bring down an animal, most also experience some grief or sadness.

   b. Most hunters are embarrassed by the fact that they kill for sport and truly find it difficult to explain why they hunt.

2. According to the author, many hunters feel

   a. a sense of rage at the animals they kill.

   b. a sense of love for the animals they kill.

   c. a sense of blood communion between themselves and the animals they kill.

3. According to a recent survey, how many Americans approve of hunting?

   a. 50 percent

   b. 75 percent

   c. 22 percent

4. How do nonhunters react to the claim that hunting takes courage?

   a. They believe the claim, but they still hate hunting.

   b. They consider the idea absurd.

   c. They insist that hunters are lying to themselves.

5. According to the author, what question haunts the hunter?

   a. Is it wrong to kill for sport?

   b. Why do people who eat meat from the supermarket believe they are more virtuous than those who hunt?

   c. What life is so precious it should not be taken?

6. According to the author, the sadness associated with hunting

   a. increases with age.

   b. decreases with age.

   c. is more typical of the young hunter than the old.

7. Which statement accurately expresses the implied main idea of paragraph 10?

   a. Even men who love to hunt share the author's sense that sadness comes with killing a living creature.

   b. Real hunters do not share the author's notion that sadness always accompanies the kill.

8. Based on paragraph 10, which inference seems appropriate?

   a. Most hunters refuse to explain why they like to hunt.

   b. Hunters find it hard to explain why they need to hunt.

9. To explain why he gave up hunting, the author tells a story about his boyhood. What inference can you draw from that story?

   a. Killing the squirrel made the author too sad to continue hunting.

   b. The squirrel's suffering made the author want to give up hunting.

10. What pattern of organization do you recognize in paragraph 9?

    a. cause and effect

    b. comparison and contrast

    c. classification

SHARPEN YOUR CRITICAL SKILLS   Answer the following questions.

1. The author tells readers that there is "conflict in the heart of the hunter." Does the author treat this information as a fact or an opinion? _____ Explain your answer.

   _____

   _____

   _____

2. How would you label the statement, "There is some kind of blood communion between the hunter and that which he kills," as a fact, an opinion, or a blend of both? _____ Explain your answer.

   _____

   _____

   _____

3. This reading relies heavily on opinions. Do you think it would be a better reading if it made heavier use of facts? _____
Explain your answer.

_____

_____

_____

4. In paragraph 3, the author says "hunters use the word *harvest* again and again." Does the word *harvest* have positive or negative connotations? _____ In this context, *harvest* is a euphemism for what word? _____

5. In paragraph 6, the author says that many nonhunters "wouldn't think of killing wild game," yet think nothing of buying meat at the supermarket. What does the author imply about the attitude of non-hunters?

_____

_____

_____

_____

_____

6. In paragraph 9, the author talks about emotions that still emerge "out of some dark forest of memory." Why does the author compare his memory to a *dark forest?* What does he want to suggest to readers?

_____

_____

_____

_____

7. In paragraph 10, the author speaks of men who are "stalked" by their emotions. Why do you think the author uses the word *stalked?* What associations does he want to evoke in readers?

_____

_____

_____

8. The references to the magazine *Field and Stream* and to the survey by the Interior Department's Fish and Wildlife Services are used to support what opinion?

_____

_____

_____

9. Do you think these facts are relevant to the author's opinion?

_____

_____

_____

10. How would you describe the author's purpose?

   a. He wants to convince readers that hunting is a vicious and disgusting sport.

   b. He wants to describe the sadness of hunting, a feeling that hasn't been talked about very much.

Explain your answer.

_____

_____

_____

_____

THINKING FOR YOURSELF   **1.** Are you a hunter? If not, can you imagine yourself becoming one? Why or why not?

_____

_____

_____

2. In paragraph 5, Ed Van Put says that it takes courage to "kill an animal as beautiful as a deer." What do you think he means? Why would it take courage?

_____

_____

_____

3. Why do you think many hunters use the word *harvest* instead of *kill?*

_____

_____

_____

MAKING CONNECTIONS BETWEEN READINGS Do you think the author would or would not support the animal-rights movement? Explain your answer.

_____

_____

_____

■ **WRITING SUGGESTION** Write a paper that explains how you feel about hunting. Do you like or dislike the idea of hunting animals for sport? Whichever side you take, explain why you feel that way.

Searching for Heroes

In Bertolt Brecht's play *Galileo,* one of the characters insists that "it is an unhappy country that has no heroes." That statement raises some interesting questions; for instance, what exactly is a hero? And even if we agree on a definition, does that mean everyone has the same heroes, or is it possible that one person's hero is another person's villain?

To think more deeply about heroes—who they are and what they represent—read the following selections.

Is a Hero Really Nothing but a Sandwich?

Creative Achievement and the Heroic Ideal

Dian Fossey: Lone Woman in the Mists

Raoul Wallenberg: A Lost Hero

■ READING 9

Is a Hero† Really Nothing but a Sandwich?

LOOKING AHEAD   In this selection, Ted Tollefson, a Unitarian minister, tries to answer the question "What is a hero?" From Tollefson's perspective, a hero has some very specific traits or characteristics.

DEVELOPING A FOCUS   Read the section titled "Word Watch." Then read the first paragraph and all of the italicized statements. Based on your survey, make one or two predictions. What points do you expect the author to develop?

_____

_____

_____

In addition to making predictions, jot down one or two questions you will try to answer as you read.

_____

_____

_____

STRATEGIES FOR IN-DEPTH LEARNING   As you read, keep asking yourself how you would define a hero if you were to write an essay similar to this one. List some key traits of a hero in the margins of the reading. Think, too, about people who do or do not match Tollefson's description.

WORD WATCH   Because context does not always provide enough clues, some of the more difficult words in the reading are defined below. In the reading, these words are marked with an asterisk.

orator: speaker

transformers: devices used to transform electricity from one circuit to another

zest: excitement, enthusiasm

abundant: rich, full, varied

catalyst: someone or something that causes another event

charismatic: possessed of personal magnetism

_____

†In some parts of the country, a hero is another name for a submarine sandwich.

universal: common to all people

tutelage: teaching, education

disdained: disliked, disregarded

unbridled: uncontrolled

purveyors: people who hand out or give out something

grandiose: grand, great

1   FOR SEVERAL YEARS, A PICTURE OF WARREN SPAHN OF THE Milwaukee Braves hung on my closet door, one leg poised in mid-air before he delivered a smoking fastball. Time passed and Spahn's picture gave way to others: Elvis, John F. Kennedy, Carl Jung, Joseph Campbell, Ben Hogan. These heroic images have reflected back to me what I hoped to become: a man with good moves, a sex symbol, an electrifying orator,* a plumber of depths, a teller of tales, a graceful golfer. Like serpents, we keep shedding the skins of our heroes as we move toward new phases in our lives.

2   Like many of my generation, I have a weakness for hero worship. At some point, however, we all begin to question our heroes and our need for them. This leads us to ask: What is a hero?

3   Despite immense differences in cultures, heroes around the world generally share a number of traits that instruct and inspire people.

4   *A hero does something worth talking about.* A hero has a story of adventure to tell and a community who will listen. But a hero goes beyond mere fame or celebrity.

5   *Heroes serve powers or principles larger than themselves.* Like high-voltage transformers,* heroes take the energy of higher powers and step it down so that it can be used by ordinary mortals.

6   *The hero lives a life worthy of imitation.* Those who imitate a genuine hero experience life with new depth, zest,* and meaning. A sure test for would-be heroes is what or whom do they serve? What are they willing to live and die for? If the answer or evidence suggests they serve only their own fame, they may be celebrities but not heroes. Madonna and Michael Jackson are famous, but who would claim that their adoring fans find life more abundant?*

7   *Heroes are catalysts* for change.* They have a vision from the mountaintop. They have the skill and the charm to move the masses. They create new possibilities. Without Gandhi,† India

---

†Mahatma Gandhi: Indian leader who used nonviolent disobedience to gain India's independence from Great Britain.

might still be part of the British Empire. Without Rosa Parks†
and Martin Luther King, Jr., we might still have segregated
buses, restaurants, and parks. It may be possible for large-scale
change to occur without charismatic* leaders, but the pace of
change would be glacial, the vision uncertain, and the committee meetings endless.

8   Though heroes aspire to universal* values, most are bound to
the culture from which they came. The heroes of the Homeric
Greeks wept loudly for their lost comrades and exhibited their
grief publicly. A later generation of Greeks under the tutelage* of
Plato disdained* this display of grief as "unmanly."

9   Though the heroic tradition of white Americans is barely 300
years old, it already shows some unique and unnerving features.
While most traditional heroes leave home, have an adventure,
and return home to tell the story, American heroes are often
homeless. They come out of nowhere, right what is wrong, and
then disappear into the wilderness. Throughout most of the
world, it is acknowledged that heroes need a community as much
as a community needs them.

10   And most Americans seem to prefer their heroes flawless, innocent, forever wearing a white hat or airbrushed features. Character flaws—unbridled* lust, political incorrectness—are held as
proof that our heroes aren't really heroes. Several heroes on my
own list have provided easy targets for the purveyors* of heroic
perfectionism.

11   The ancient Greeks and Hebrews were wiser on this count.
They chose for their heroes men and women with visible, tragic
flaws. Oedipus'† fierce curiosity raised him to be king but also
lured him to his mother's bed. King David's unbounded passion
made him dance naked before the Ark *and* led him to betray
Uriah so he could take Bathsheba for his wife.

12   American heroes lack a sense of home that might limit and
ground their grandiose* ambitions. American heroes avoid ac-
knowledging their own vices, which makes them more likely to
look for somebody else to blame when things go wrong. Our national heroes seem to be stuck somewhere between Billy Budd†
and the Lone Ranger: pious, armed cowboys who are full of energy, hope, and dangerous naïveté.

---

†Rosa Parks: when, in 1955, African-American Rosa Parks refused to give up her
bus seat to a white man, she helped ignite the civil rights movement.
†Oedipus: the hero of a Greek tragedy who was determined to know the secret of
his birth. When he found it out, he was so horrified, he blinded himself.
†Billy Budd: a character from a short story by Herman Melville. Billy is so innocent he arouses the hatred of his ship's captain.

13 Here are some exercises to give you insights into your own ideas about heroes and villains:

1. Draw a time line with markings every five years in your life. For each era, name an important hero (male or female). Identify three core qualities each stands for. Look at the overall list for recurring qualities. Who or what do your heroes serve?

2. Make a list of enemies, the people who really push your buttons. For each, specify three qualities that make your blood boil. Now look for recurring qualities. What emerges is your "shadow," parts of yourself that you fear, loathe, and therefore loan to others. What does your shadow know that you don't?

3. Make a collage of your heroes, leaving room for their tragic flaws and holy vices. Hang it opposite a large mirror.

Ted Tollefson, "Is A Hero
Really Nothing but a Sandwich?"
Utne Reader, May/June 1993, pp. 102–103.

TEST YOUR
UNDERSTANDING

Circle the letter of the correct answer.

1. Which paragraph introduces the thesis statement?

   a. paragraph 1

   b. paragraph 2

   c. paragraph 3

2. Which of the following accurately paraphrases the thesis statement?

   a. In different stages of our lives, we need different heroes on which to model ourselves.

   b. It doesn't matter where they come from; heroes are likely to share similar traits that are admired and imitated by others.

3. Based on the reading, which of the following is *not* a characteristic of a hero?

   a. Heroes bring about change.

   b. Heroes do something worth talking about.

   c. Heroes are worthy of being imitated.

   d. Heroes have more self-confidence than ordinary people do.

4. According to the author, what is the question that helps identify heroes?

   a. How much fame do they have?

    b. How many people imitate them?

    c. What are they willing to live or die for?

5. Based on what the author says in paragraph 6, which inference is appropriate?

    a. He thinks heroes and celebrities are two words that mean the same thing.

    b. He thinks heroes should not be confused with celebrities.

6. In paragraph 6, which of the following sentences does *not* provide an essential detail?

    a. "Those who imitate a genuine hero experience life with new depth, zest, and meaning."

    b. "Madonna and Michael Jackson are famous, but who would claim that their adoring fans find life more abundant?"

7. Gandhi, Rosa Parks, and Martin Luther King, Jr., are illustrations of which main idea?

    a. Heroes always suffer for their beliefs.

    b. Heroes bring about change in the world.

8. According to the author, heroes are influenced by

    a. the disapproval of others.

    b. the culture in which they live.

    c. the heroic behavior of previous generations.

9. According to the author, heroes in American culture are likely to be

    a. fearless.

    b. violent.

    c. homeless.

10. Which pattern do you recognize in paragraphs 10 and 11?

    a. sequence of steps

    b. comparison and contrast

    c. cause and effect

SHARPEN YOUR CRITICAL SKILLS   Answer the following questions.

1. Label the following statements *F* (fact), *O* (opinion), or *B* (both).

    a. "At some point, we all begin to question our heroes and our need

       for them." _____

b. "Most Americans seem to prefer their heroes flawless." ____

c. "Heroes are catalysts for change." ____

2. Compare paragraphs 4 and 7. Each paragraph offers a different opinion on what makes a hero. Which paragraph does a better job of arguing the author's opinion? ____

Explain the basis for your choice.

_____

_____

_____

_____

_____

3. In paragraph 9, the author tells us that the American heroic tradition has some unique features. To support that opinion, the author offers a reason: Unlike heroes of other cultures, American heroes have no connection to their communities. Do you find the author's argument convincing? Why or why not?

_____

_____

_____

4. In paragraph 10, the author tells readers that "most Americans seem to prefer their heroes flawless." How effectively does the author argue his opinion?

_____

_____

_____

5. The author suggests that Americans are making a mistake by preferring heroes that are flawless. What two reasons does he give to support this opinion?

_____

_____

_____

6. In this reading, the allusions to Billy Budd and the Lone Ranger help to make what opinion convincing?

_____

_____

_____

7. What kind of tone does the author of this essay assume?

a. friendly and informal

b. solemn and serious

c. emotionally neutral

8. In the first sentence of paragraph 9, the author tells us that the heroic tradition in America has some unique features. What word in that sentence reveals the author's attitude toward that tradi-

tion? _____

9. How would you describe the author's feelings about the American tradition of heroism?

a. The author disapproves of the American tradition.

b. The author admires the American tradition.

c. It's impossible to determine the author's personal feelings.

10. With which of the following statements do you agree?

a. The author's purpose is to tell readers about the characteristics that typically define heroes.

b. The author's purpose is to define the heroic character and celebrate the American hero in particular.

c. The author's purpose is to tell readers about the characteristics that typically define heroes and persuade them that the American ideal of a hero may be going in the wrong direction.

THINKING FOR YOURSELF

1. Do you agree with the author's description of a hero? What traits would you add? What traits would you omit?

_____

_____

_____

2. The author says that a sure test of a hero is "What are they willing to live and die for?" Is there someone or something you believe is worth living and dying for? Explain your answer.

_____

_____

_____

3. The author lists his heroes. Who are your heroes? Do they fit the author's description? Do you think you are capable of being a hero? Why or why not?

_____

_____

_____

■ **WRITING SUGGESTIONS**

1. Write a summary of "Is a Hero Really Nothing but a Sandwich?" To make sure you reduce the article to its core elements, annotate the reading before you summarize it. Remember to draw a line through any material you think you won't need.

2. Write an essay in which you describe one person whom you consider to be a hero. Begin by summarizing what you think are a hero's traits and then introduce someone who possesses the traits you describe.

Reading text

■ **READING 10**

CREATIVE ACHIEVEMENT AND THE HEROIC IDEAL

LOOKING AHEAD In this reading, the author tries to find a connection between great creators and great heroes. What do you think? Can a painter, composer, or inventor be considered heroic?

DEVELOPING A FOCUS Read the words in the section titled "Word Watch." Then read the first paragraph and the last paragraph of the selection. Based on your survey, make one or two predictions. What points do you expect the author to make?

_____

_____

In addition to making predictions, jot down one or two questions you will try to answer as you read.

_____

_____

STRATEGIES FOR IN-DEPTH LEARNING In this reading, the author argues that creativity and heroism go hand in hand. As you read, jot down the bare bones of his argument, in the margins of your book or on a separate piece of paper, reducing it to its conclusion and reasons. When you finish, ask yourself how you would rate the author's argument—sound or unsound. Then, even if you agree with the author's position, take the opposing point of view and imagine how you would counter, or challenge, his argument.

WORD WATCH Because context does not always provide enough clues, some of the more difficult words in the reading are defined below. In the reading, these words are marked with an asterisk.

archetypes: original models or types on which others are patterned

contemporary: modern

primordial: being or happening first

conceive: imagine, think up

luminaries: people who have achieved exceptional honors in their fields

paragons: models of excellence

infallible: incapable of making a mistake

conduit: conductor, connector

rubble: pieces of stone that remain after a building has been destroyed

citations: mentions, references

gaffes: ridiculous mistakes

pandemonium: noisy confusion

effigy: a crude figure or dummy

vociferous: angry, loud, outspoken

1   ONE OF THE OLDEST ARCHETYPES* IN HUMAN CULTURE IS THAT of the hero. The hero clashes with the Fates† at tremendous personal risk. This archetype is richly portrayed in the mythology of ancient Greece: the legendary exploits of Perseus, the 12 labors of Hercules, Jason's quest for the Golden Fleece, the far-reaching wanderings and adventures of Odysseus. Other cultural traditions depict the same basic ideal, whether Gilgamesh of the Sumerians, Samson of the Hebrews, Siegfried of the Germanic peoples, or Ilya Muromets of the Russians. As popular immortals, these idols have become the centerpieces of heroic literature throughout the world. Of course, the archetype remains alive and well now—only these days the classic hero shows up on the silver screen and picture tube, in contemporary* or futuristic attire. The archetype assumes the form of Indiana Jones in *Raiders of the Lost Ark* or Luke Skywalker in *Star Wars.* Many movie stars have carved out their careers as the living image of the primordial* type: Charles Bronson, Clint Eastwood, Chuck Norris, Arnold Schwarzenegger, Sylvester Stallone, and John Wayne.

2   Yet, I wish to focus on a more subtle form of heroism. The world of creative achievements is also a realm of heroic acts. These actions may spill no blood, but that does not make them less courageous. For great creators are great risk takers besides. This reality is often not fully appreciated, owing to a widely circulated myth about the creative genius: Too often, we conceive* of these luminaries* as paragons* of perfection. They supposedly conjure up magical creations with a "stroke of genius"—whether by a flash of insight or an exercise of intellectual brilliance. We too frequently see geniuses as infallible* agents, as if they had some direct conduit* to truth or beauty. This commonplace image is pure myth. Creative geniuses stumble, they trip, they make horrible mistakes. Their highest and most acclaimed successes are constructed on the low rubble* of humiliating failures.

---

†Fates: In Greek and Roman mythology, these are the three goddesses who control human destiny.

3   On the average, those periods in a creator's career when the most products ensue are the same periods that see the most masterpieces. The quality ratio of hits to total attempts neither increases nor decreases with age. Those individuals with the highest total output will, on the average, produce the most acclaimed contributions as well.

4   I know that this statement may elicit some skepticism. Aren't there "mass producers" who generate piece after piece of worthless trash? And aren't there also "perfectionists" who manage to offer the world nothing but polished gems? Yes, no doubt there are such people. Yet, they only appear every once in a while. They are the exceptions rather than the rule. For example, one study found that American Nobel laureates† published twice as many scientific papers as other scientists who were still worthy enough to make it into *American Men and Women of Science*. Other studies have determined that the number of citations* a scientist receives in the work of fellow scientists is strongly associated with the total output of publications. In fact, the total number of publications predicts the amount of citations received by a scientist's three most acclaimed works.

5   Moreover, this correspondence between quantity and quality holds over the long haul. For instance, the total length of the bibliography of a nineteenth-century scientist predicts how famous he or she is in the twentieth century. Thus, a scientist who was then in the top 10 percent of the most productive elite had a 50 percent chance of earning an entry in a 1950s edition of the *Encyclopaedia Britannica*. In contrast, their less prolific colleagues only had a 3 percent chance of earning that distinction.

6   From this principle we can make this startling inference: The most successful creators are those with the most failures. W. H. Auden put it well: "The chances are that, in the course of his lifetime, the major poet will write more bad poems than the minor." This holds for major creators in other domains. Take Albert Einstein as a case in point. In his crusade to overthrow quantum physics, he often made embarrassing gaffes.* Once, after a long exchange with Niels Bohr,† Einstein composed an elaborate argument that he thought would destroy the Copenhagen school. Bohr found a fatal flaw nonetheless: Einstein had neglected to consider the theory of relativity!‡

7   The boldness of extraordinary genius often produces more than

---

†American Nobel laureates: winners of the Nobel Prize.
†Niels Bohr: A Danish physicist who won a Nobel Prize for investigating atomic structure.
†Einstein discovered the theory of relativity.

some miscarried experiments. This trait is responsible also for some rather sensational scenes in intellectual or aesthetic history. These episodes may not be as monumental as a military hero's risking all on the battlefield, but they are dramatic nonetheless. Think, for example, of the audience at the first performance of Igor Stravinsky's *Le Sacre du Printemps* in 1913. There was such an uproar of shouting, catcalls, and feet stamping, followed soon by fistfights and spitting, that the music was soon submerged in the pandemonium.* Remember also that shortly after excerpts of James Joyce's *Ulysses* began to appear in an American literary journal in 1918, it was banned as pornography. Finally, recall the hostile response of those attending the notorious Armory Show of 1913.† Marcel Duchamp's *Nude Descending a Staircase* was denounced as "an explosion in a shingle factory." Henri Matisse and Constantin Brancusi were hanged in effigy.* Those exhibited excited the vociferous* displeasure of no less a name than ex-President Theodore Roosevelt. Yet Stravinsky, Joyce, Duchamp, and the rest were undaunted by all the ruckus. They continued to take chances in pursuing their unique visions. Hence, the willingness to take creative risks often brings with it a special knack for alienating the public. The upshot is sometimes eventful scandal and protest.

8   The need to risk failure to gain success manifests itself beyond such impractical, cultural activities. Not all of Thomas Edison's 1,093 patents protected money-making contraptions. In fact, the amount of money he lost trying to devise a new method for extracting iron ore cost him all his profits from the electric light bulb. Henry Ford, Walt Disney, and Colonel Sanders each faced bankruptcy one or more times before becoming millionaires. Elvis Presley's first performance at the Grand Ole Opry got him fired. Golf celebrity Jack Nicklaus has won only a bit more than one-quarter of the tournaments he has entered. And what about the most praised American presidents? Jefferson's first attempt to win the presidency was a failure, as was Jackson's. Franklin Roosevelt was a losing vice-presidential candidate in 1920. And before Lincoln emerged victorious in the presidential election of 1860, he had lost more campaigns than he had won. Examples like these amply illustrate the cliché "Nothing ventured, nothing gained."

9   This willingness to take the hard knocks and punches on the road to success implies a good deal more about how to achieve greatness. If you wish to do so, you obviously must exhibit a rare

---

†Armory Show: The Armory Show of 1913 exhibited most of the modern artists just beginning to make a name for themselves, and many people were appalled by the new modernist style of painting and sculpture.

self-confidence. To avoid discouragement, you need the ego strength of an Achilles or Siegfried.† In addition, you must display an awesome persistence.

10   When at first you don't succeed, you must try, try again. To use the motto of Hammer's‡ music video, you've got to be "too legit to quit."

11   By thus looking at the qualities that belong to these notable risk takers, we can view these people as heroes who echo the legendary ancients.

Dean Keith Simonton, *Greatness*.
New York: Guilford Press, 1994, pp. 255–257.

TEST YOUR
UNDERSTANDING   Circle the letter of the correct answers.

1. Which of the following accurately paraphrases the thesis statement?

    a. Creative achievements also require heroic behavior.

    b. Artists are the only true heroes.

2. According to the author, creative people are heroic because they

    a. rely solely on their own abilities.

    b. are willing to make horrible mistakes and risk failure.

    c. don't care if they ever become famous.

3. What myth about creative geniuses does the author challenge?

    a. He challenges the belief that they are cowards in the arena of physical action.

    b. He challenges the idea that their creations come about through a sudden stroke of genius.

    c. He challenges the theory that creative people never feel insecure or scared.

4. In paragraph 4, the author says that "one study found that American Nobel laureates published twice as many scientific papers as other scientists." Which main idea does this study support?

    a. The relationship between quantity and quality is usually maintained over the long haul.

    b. Many mass producers generate nothing but trash.

    c. Those who produce the most are also likely to produce the best.

---

†Hammer: formerly M. C. Hammer, the rap star.
‡Achilles or Siegfried: mythological heroes famous for their extraordinary physical strength.

5. According to the author, people in pursuit of greatness need

   a. the encouragement of their friends

   b. self-confidence and persistence

   c. financial backing

6. In paragraph 6, the allusion to Albert Einstein illustrates which main idea?

   a. Really creative people know full well the meaning of failure.

   b. Like a lot of geniuses, Einstein was not good at explaining his work to others.

7. Which statement more effectively expresses the implied main idea of paragraph 7?

   a. Too often, people with talent like to create an uproar in order to get attention for themselves and their work.

   b. Because of their intellectual daring, creative people are frequently involved in scenes that are both sensational and embarrassing.

8. In paragraph 7, which of the following is a nonessential detail?

   a. "Shortly after excerpts of James Joyce's *Ulysses* began to appear in an American literary journal in 1918, it was banned as pornography."

   b. "Those exhibited [at the Armory Show of 1913] excited the vociferous displeasure of no less a name than ex-President Theodore Roosevelt."

   check

9. According to the author, what do Elvis Presley, Thomas Edison, Walt Disney, and Colonel Sanders all have in common?

   a. They all made a great deal of money.

   b. They were all involved in embarrassing scandals.

   c. They all experienced failure.

10. Which statement do you think more effectively synthesizes the first two readings in this unit?

    a. Both readings agree on one point: A society needs to have heroes as role models.

    b. Both authors try to define the nature of heroism.

    check

SHARPEN YOUR CRITICAL SKILLS Answer the following questions.

1. Label the following statements *F* (fact), *O* (opinion), or *B* (both).

a. "We too frequently see geniuses as infallible agents." _O_

b. "Studies have determined that the number of citations a scientist receives in the work of fellow scientists is strongly associated with the total output of publications." _F_

c. "Shortly after excerpts of James Joyce's *Ulysses* began to appear in an American literary journal in 1918, it was banned as pornography." _F_

2. What opinion does the author hope readers will share after reading this selection?

   The authors hope that the reader will have a better understanding for heroes and the risk they takes. They, like others, make mistakes

3. What reason or reasons does the author give in support of his opinion?

   He give example of several sucessful peoples failures as well as the achievement.

4. As part of his argument, the author responds to an objection he thinks some readers might raise. What is that objection?

   individuals with the highest, out put will on average produce the most citation.

5. How does the author respond to that objection?

   By presenting statictic showing top 10% to the most productive scientist had a 50% chance of sucesses; less productive scientist had only a 3% of sucesses.

6. What kind of evidence does the author use in paragraph 4?

   results of Noble laureates mass produce had the most sucess.

As a critical reader, how should you respond to that evidence?

What kind of study was done? are the evidence sufficient.

7. In general, how would you describe the author's tone?

a. confident

b. solemn

c. emotionally neutral

8. With which statement do you agree?

a. The author recognizes that some people think being creative is a form of heroism, but he does not share this point of view.

b. The author personally believes that creators of all kinds deserve to be called heroic.

c. It's impossible to determine the author's personal feelings.

9. How do the author's allusions to Elvis Presley, Colonel Sanders, and Hammer affect his tone?

No effect on his confident tone mealy reinforced his opinion that success come after many failures.

10. How would you describe the author's purpose?

a. The author wants to describe the characteristics of creative people whom he considers heroic.

b. The author wants to convince readers that those who invent and create are also heroes.

THINKING FOR YOURSELF Were you convinced by the author's argument? Why or why not? Are you willing to risk failure in pursuit of future success? Why or why not?

MAKING CONNECTIONS BETWEEN READINGS At this point, you've read selections by two different authors who, to a greater or lesser degree, try to define the heroic character. On the whole, would you say the two tend to agree on the characteristics that define a hero, or do they disagree? Explain.

_____

_____

_____

WRITING SUGGESTION You probably have your own ideas about what it takes to be a hero. Write a paper in which you identify three characteristics a person must possess in order to be considered a hero. (There may be other characteristics, but you are responsible for only three.) Illustrate each characteristic by identifying some heroic person who possesses the quality or attitude you describe.

Reading text

■ READING 11

DIAN FOSSEY: LONE WOMAN IN THE MISTS

LOOKING AHEAD   To some, Dian Fossey is a hero, the woman who saved the great apes of Rwanda from certain extinction. To others, she is a villain, a madwoman who cared more about animals than people. Read this selection and make your own decision about Dian Fossey's controversial career.

DEVELOPING A FOCUS   Read the section titled "Word Watch." Then read the first and the last paragraphs of the selection. Based on that survey, make one or two predictions. What point or points do you expect the author to make?

_____

_____

In addition to making predictions, jot down one or two questions you will try to answer as you read.

_____

_____

STRATEGIES FOR IN-DEPTH LEARNING   As you read about Dian Fossey, try to determine how well she does or does not fit Ted Tollefson's description of a hero in the reading "Is a Hero Really Nothing but a Sandwich?"

WORD WATCH   Because context does not always provide enough clues, some of the more difficult words in the reading are defined below. Within the reading, these words are marked with an asterisk.

flagrantly: openly

reticent: quiet, withdrawn

advocate: to speak, plead, or argue in favor of

decimating: destroying, killing

theoretical: related more to theory than practice

zeal: enthusiasm, determination

confiscate: take, seize

parasites: organisms that grow or feed off other organisms

valid: convincing, having legal force

flora: flowers

fauna: animals

jubilant: joyous

1 ON DECEMBER 22, 1985, DIAN FOSSEY BEGAN A LETTER TO AN old friend, Rosamund Carr. She thanked Carr for some Christmas presents and spoke optimistically about the future. Granted a permit to stay in Africa for another two years, Fossey was excited and hopeful. With the visa, she could continue her work—protecting the endangered gorillas who lived high in the Virunga mountains of Rwanda. But Fossey never finished her letter. Less than a week later, she was dead. An unknown attacker had split open her skull with her own machete. The murder gave a gruesome end to Fossey's already controversial career.

2 World famous at her death, Fossey was the object of both hatred and admiration. Although some called her a hero and credited her with saving from extinction the gorillas she had studied, Fossey's methods had also been widely criticized. Stubborn, fierce, and hot-tempered, she had dedicated her life to protecting "her" gorillas. To that end, she was ready to do almost anything, and some thought she had gone too far.

3 Fossey's romance with Africa began in 1963 when she went into debt in order to go on a seven-week safari. Shortly after her arrival in Africa, she met Louis Leakey, the famous anthropologist. Leakey was deeply interested in Africa's great apes and Fossey seemed to have absorbed some of his enthusiasm. When Leakey politely told her to "keep in touch," Fossey took him seriously (Mowat, 11). Three years later, when Leakey lectured in Fossey's hometown of Louisville, Kentucky, Fossey waited in line to talk to him. Clutched in her hand were pictures and articles about her trip to Africa. Leakey was duly impressed and offered her a job.

4 On December 15, 1966, the "gorilla girl" left for Africa and made her way to Rwanda, one of Africa's smallest, poorest, and most beautiful regions. Rwanda became the site of Karisoke—the name was based on the mountains Karasimba and Visoke—Fossey's research center.

5 The center was high in the Virunga mountains and surrounded by a supposedly protected park, the Parc National des Volcans. Officially, the park was off limits to hunters and poachers; yet, in reality, park rules were persistently and flagrantly* violated. From the very beginning of her stay, Fossey was appalled by the amount of hunting and trapping that actually took place in this supposedly protected region. Determined to stop the poaching, she destroyed any snares or traps she could find: "If I can enforce the written rules of a supposedly protected park, then I must do it. And so I continued to break the bamboo, the reliable and flexible trap of the last game in Africa" (Mowat, 60).

6   Fossey's sense of mission increased as her contacts with the gorillas grew. By 1968, she had logged 466 hours of gorilla observation. No one had seen more of these normally reticent* and reclusive creatures. By 1969, she was beginning to call them by name:
"Yesterday and today afforded wonderful contacts with Group 8,
mainly Peanuts who is curious and playful" (Mowat, 79).

7   Peanuts was, indeed, a curious creature. With each passing
day he came a little nearer. Finally, on a glorious afternoon in
1970, Fossey extended her hand. To her astonishment, Peanuts
took it in one of his own. It was the first time a wild gorilla had
ever "held hands" with a human being. Dian Fossey had made
history.

8   By the early seventies, Fossey's work was becoming well
known. The *National Geographic* had published an article about
her work. Her picture had even appeared on the cover. Like it or
not, she was becoming famous.

9   The poachers, however, were not impressed. They still hunted
in the park surrounding Karisoke. In a country as poor as
Rwanda, the money and food that could be had from killing and
trapping animals was just too tempting to resist.

10   Fossey described in her journal the painful fate of a buffalo
that had wedged itself into the fork of a tree. Taking advantage of
the animal's helplessness, hunters had cut the meat off its hind
legs and left it to die a slow death. When Fossey found the animal
a few hours later, it was still alive. Feebly, the buffalo even tried
to defend itself by waving its head and snorting. Crying as she did
it, Fossey put a bullet into its brain.

11   It was after this incident that she started shooting the hunters'
cattle, crippling their hind legs. Her journal suggests she was appalled by her own behavior, but she didn't stop. From Fossey's perspective, savage methods were necessary to save "her" apes: "I am
finding myself out to avenge the cruelty of the Tutsi† by crippling
their cattle with bullets. I used to shoot above or below or near the
cattle of the Tutsi, but now I shoot them in their hind legs and have
crippled several since the buffalo was found" (Mowat, 90).

12   In general, Fossey did not try to hide her hatred of poachers.
As early as 1970, she had written the International Union for the
Conservation of Nature and suggested that poachers be shot on
sight: "I definitely advocate* giving the Conservator and qualified
Park Guards full license to kill on sight any poachers fleeing
when encountered within the interior of the park" (Hayes, 233).

13   It's not surprising, then, that when one of her assistants acci-

---

†Tutsi: an east African tribe.

dentally shot a poacher in the leg, Fossey was not unduly alarmed (Hayes, 238). Poachers were here enemies. It didn't matter if they were motivated by hunger—they were decimating* the animals she had vowed to protect. Because park officials did not seem inclined to protect park inhabitants, Fossey made herself the animals' protector.

14   But if Fossey's relationship with the natives and their government was strained and hostile, her relationship to the gorillas was not. After ten years, they had accepted her as one of their own. In particular, she had been befriended by Digit, a young silverback gorilla. The defender of his group, Digit could nevertheless be playful and affectionate, particularly if Fossey were around: "He often invited play by flopping over onto his back, waving stumpy legs in the air, and looking at me smilingly, as if to say, 'How can you resist me?'" (Mowat, 90).

15   Deeply attached to Digit, Fossey was devastated by his death in 1978. For almost a week, Digit and the other members of his group had been hounded by poachers and had finally been driven into Zaire. When the poachers closed in, Digit, in his role as protector, turned and attacked, but it was a losing battle. He was speared to death. In a final gruesome touch, they cut off his head and hands. For the poachers, these were the real trophies—tourists would pay large sums of money for these "souvenirs."

16   Fossey could barely control her fury and her grief. Initially, she channeled her emotions into writing letters to enlist support for the Digit Fund. The money she raised would be used to create and train antipoaching patrols. By this time, Fossey was thoroughly disgusted with what she called "theoretical* conservation." She wanted more than ever to engage in "active conservation": "I know what needs to be done for the protection of the gorillas—long, tiring strenuous patrols over the entirety of the Virungas" (Mowat, 175).

17   The *National Geographic* (which funded her work), conservation officials, and even some of her own research assistants were wary of such a plan. They were afraid of antagonizing the Rwandan government, whose goodwill they considered essential if research on the gorillas were to continue. But Fossey didn't see it that way. For the most part, she dismissed both park and government officials as enemies. When two more of her precious gorillas, Uncle Bert and Macho, were slaughtered, she began patrolling the mountains with even greater zeal.* As usual, her health was poor: Among other ailments she had chronic emphysema and sciatica.†

---

†sciatica: a pinched nerve in the back.

But nothing stopped her. She continued to confiscate* and destroy every trap she could find. Above all, she continued to hunt the poachers. She flatly refused to believe what the Rwandan government claimed—that the two gorillas had actually been killed as a form of retaliation for what were said to be Fossey's "tortures and humiliations" (Hayes, 304).

18   Although Fossey never acknowledged the possibility that her antipoaching activities could have endangered her gorillas, it was true that her methods had made her both feared and hated. When captured poachers were brought into camp, she circled them, screaming in a mixture of English, French, German, and Swahili. At times, she even wore a Halloween mask, set off fireworks, or ignited tear gas. Her goal was to encourage the belief that she was a witch. Determined to terrify her captives, she sometimes menaced them by holding a pair of pliers close to their genitals (Hayes, 297). When in May of 1978, Fossey was fined $600 allegedly for torturing one of Digit's suspected killers, she paid the fine without a murmur of protest (Hayes, 301).

19   By 1980, Fossey and her antipoaching patrols had effectively driven the poachers out of the area surrounding Karisoke. But she was still fighting the Rwandan government, which wanted to bring more tourists into the area. As usual, Fossey would not cooperate. She feared the effect tourists would have on her gorillas. In particular, she was afraid the gorillas would contract human parasites.* That fear was reinforced when she discovered that hookworms had played a role in the death of two gorillas (Mowat, 201).

20   However valid* her reasons for rejecting tourists, Fossey was finding herself outnumbered. The Rwandan government desperately needed the money tourism could provide. In addition, conservation agencies like the British Flora* and Fauna* Preservation Society believed that tourism could benefit the gorillas in the long run.

21   Under pressure to leave from the Rwandan government, the U.S. State Department, and even the National Geographic Society, Fossey took an extended leave of absence. She needed the time, anyway, to complete her book *Gorillas in the Mist.* She was also suffering from excruciating back pain, and an operation was in order. Cornell University had offered a teaching post, and the university seemed a good place to spread her message of active conservation.

22   But by 1983 Fossey was frantic to return to Africa. During her absence, more gorillas had been slaughtered (Hayes, 316), and she felt personally responsible for having abandoned them. To her surprise, the Rwandan newspapers welcomed her back. They published positive reports of her work, praising her for protecting the

gorillas. Her relationship with the Rwandan government seemed to be improving after all.

23   Still, not all the omens were good. In mid-October, her two pet parrots mysteriously died. Outwardly, Fossey rejected the idea that the birds had been poisoned, but she threw out their food supply (Mowat, 355). A week later, she stepped out of her cabin and found the carved image of a puff adder, a poisonous snake, lying on her doorstep. Fossey knew what the snake meant: She had been sentenced to death.

24   Nevertheless, Fossey did not let up on the poachers. By 1984, she was proudly reporting that the area she policed was free of poachers. She claimed, too, that gorillas were still being slaughtered in areas outside her control. From her perspective, her view of "active" conservation had been proven correct. Thus, she was jubilant* when she finally got her visa extended.

25   But, according to Farley Mowat, one of Fossey's biographers, that visa may have been her death warrant. The extension meant that she had two full years to interfere with any attempts to exploit the gorilla population, and many people were thoroughly sick of her interference.

26   Fossey's murderer and the reason for her murder remain unknown. Although the Rwandan government convicted research assistant Wayne McGuire after he fled the country, few people take that verdict seriously (Hayes, 321). Only one thing is clear: Had Fossey not lived, "her" gorillas might not have survived. As the famed naturalist Jane Goodall said at Fossey's funeral: "I don't think it's too much to say, if Dian hadn't been there, there might be no mountain gorillas in Rwanda today"† (Hayes, 245). Fossey, who deeply admired Goodall's landmark study of chimpanzees in the wild, would have been pleased.

Laraine Flemming

Sources
Hayes, Harold. *The Dark Romance of Dian Fossey.* New York: Simon and Schuster, 1990.
Mowat, Farley. *Woman in the Mists.* New York: Warner Books, 1988.

TEST YOUR UNDERSTANDING   Circle the letter of the correct answer.

1. What's the main idea of this selection?

---

†Rwanda has been the scene of a ferocious civil war, and it is no longer clear that the mountain gorillas will survive.

    a. Internationally famous when she died, Dian Fossey was a hero to some and a villain to others.

    b. In the end, Dian Fossey's methods brought nothing but harm to herself and to the animals she sought to protect.

2. Which paragraph introduces the thesis statement?

    a. paragraph 1

    b. paragraph 2

    c. paragraph 3

3. Which of the following details is *not* essential to developing the main idea of the entire reading?

    a. "From Fossey's perspective, savage methods were necessary to save 'her' apes."

    b. "Determined to stop the poaching, Fossey destroyed any snares or traps she could find."

    c. "Fossey never finished her letter [to Rosamund Carr]."

    d. "Fossey did not try to hide her hatred of poachers."

4. Which of the following is an essential detail?

    a. In her letter to Rosamund Carr, Fossey "spoke optimistically about the future."

    b. "Fossey's sense of mission increased as her contacts with the gorillas grew."

    c. "Fossey seemed to have absorbed some of [Louis Leakey's] enthusiasm."

5. What is the implied main idea of paragraph 7?

    a. Dian Fossey had an amazing ability to gain the trust of animals.

    b. Dian Fossey made history when Peanuts, the gorilla, reached out and held her hand.

6. In paragraph 12, which sentence is the topic sentence?

    a. sentence 1

    b. sentence 2

    c. sentence 3

7. Based on paragraphs 10 and 11, which inference is appropriate?

    a. Fossey had always wanted to shoot the Tutsi cattle; the slaughter of the buffalo provided her with an excuse.

   b. Fossey was so horrified by what the Tutsi had done to the buffalo,
     she felt justified in shooting their cattle.

8. Which of the following statements accurately paraphrases the topic
   sentence in paragraph 15?

   a. Poachers killed Digit because they knew tourists would pay large
     sums for his head and hands.

   b. The death of Digit at the hands of poachers was a horrible shock
     to Dian Fossey.

9. What inference does the author expect you to draw from the following sentence? "Outwardly, Fossey rejected the idea that the birds
   had been poisoned, but she threw out their food supply."

   a. Fossey wouldn't admit it, but she suspected the birds had been
     poisoned.

   b. Fossey couldn't bear to think about the dead birds.

10. According to the author,

   a. everyone believes Wayne McGuire murdered Fossey.

   b. no one really believes McGuire murdered Fossey.

   c. the Rwandan government is still searching for Fossey's killer.

SHARPEN YOUR CRITICAL SKILLS Answer the following questions.

1. Label the following statements *F* (fact), *O* (opinion), or *B* (both).

   a. "Rwanda became the site of Karisoke—the name was based on
     the mountains Karasimba and Visoke—Fossey's research
     center." _F_

   b. "By 1968, [Fossey] had logged 466 hours of gorilla observa-
     tion." _F_

2. In paragraph 18, the author tells us that Fossey's "methods had
   made her both feared and hated." What evidence does she use to
   argue that opinion?

She was determined to terrify
her captive, by screaming in different
launges, torturing, or ignited tear
gas, she also encourage their belief
that she was a wich.

3. In the last sentence of paragraph 18, what inference does the author expect readers to draw?

   Fossey has her retribution on the poachers, so she didnt mind paying the fine because she believe her action was justified.

4. In paragraph 15, why do you think the author puts the word *souvenirs* in quotation marks?

   To use animal body parts as Trophies is a grousome act.

5. In paragraph 20, the author says, "However valid her reasons for rejecting tourists, Fossey was finding herself outnumbered." What does the word *valid* suggest about the author's personal bias?

   a. She is inclined to agree with Fossey's view of tourism.

   b. She is inclined to disagree with Fossey's view of tourism.

6. Which statement best describes the author's attitude toward the poachers?

   a. The author is sympathetic to the poachers.

   b. The author agrees with Fossey's view of poachers.

   c. The author tries to be fair to both sides.

   Explain how you arrived at your answer.

   Although the author see Fossey reason were valid, she believe that the poacher reason were also valid.

7. In paragraph 26, the author claims that if Fossey had not lived, " 'her' gorillas might not have survived." To support her claim, she quotes writer and researcher Jane Goodall. With which statement do you agree?

   a. Goodall appears to be a qualified authority.

   b. Goodall does not appear to be a qualified authority.

Explain how you arrived at your answer.

there was enough references to support that claim.

8. In paragraph 26, the author introduces her claim about Fossey's work with the words "only one thing is clear." What effect on readers are those words meant to have?

although there maybe question about who kill fossey, it is clear that her wor protected the gorillar, had fossey not lived her gorillas might not survived.

9. How would you describe the author's tone?

a. admiring

b. angry

c. emotionally neutral

10. How would you describe the author's purpose?

a. She wants to describe the nature and scope of Fossey's work.

b. She wants to describe Fossey's work and persuade readers of its importance.

THINKING FOR YOURSELF What is your opinion of Dian Fossey? Do you think she was a hero or a villain?

I think she was a hero, Because of how she throw herself into the work to protect those animals.

MAKING CONNECTIONS BETWEEN READINGS Look again at how the author of "Is a Hero Really Nothing but a Sandwich?" defines the heroic personality, and explain why you think Dian Fossey does or does not fit his description.

■ **WRITING SUGGESTION** Having thought about how well Dian Fossey did or did not meet Ted Tollefson's criteria for a hero, you're prepared to write an essay that draws on your conclusions along with your ability to summarize and synthesize.

Begin by briefly summarizing Tollefson's criteria for heroism. Then introduce a thesis statement indicating how well Fossey does or does not meet his criteria. To argue your point, give at least three specific examples of how her life and work do or do not match Tollefson's list of heroic characteristics.

■ **READING 12**

Raoul Wallenberg: A Lost Hero

LOOKING AHEAD During World War II, the Nazis, under the leadership of Adolf Hitler, inspired terror in people, so much so that few were willing to interfere. As a result, millions of men, women, and children went to their deaths in the concentration camps of Dachau, Bergen-Belsen, and Auschwitz. Raoul Wallenberg, however, was not willing to look away from the suffering of others. Armed with nothing more than charm, intelligence, and courage, Wallenberg challenged the Nazis and frequently won.

DEVELOPING A FOCUS Read the section titled "Word Watch." Then read the first paragraph, all of the headings, and the last paragraph of the selection. Based on your survey, make one or two predictions. What points do you expect the author to make?

_____

_____

In addition to making predictions, jot down one or two questions you will try to answer as you read.

_____

_____

STRATEGIES FOR IN-DEPTH LEARNING As you read, imagine yourself in Wallenberg's place. Would you have been willing to do what he did?

WORD WATCH Because context does not always provide enough clues, some of the more difficult words in the reading are defined below. In the reading, these words are marked with an asterisk.

cultivated: refined by training and education

atrocities: acts of cruelty and violence

unorthodox: untraditional

callously: without feeling or pity

sanctuary: a place of safety

dismantled: taken apart

1 IN 1937, RAOUL WALLENBERG WAS A YOUNG MAN WHO seemed to have everything. Born into one of Sweden's richest and

most respected families, he was cultivated,* handsome, and charming. His future seemed assured. After a few years spent learning the family business, he would follow in his grandfather's footsteps and become a banker.

2   But the young Wallenberg was not content. In a letter to his grandfather, he made it clear that something was missing: "To tell the truth, I don't feel especially bankish. . . . I think it is more in my nature to work positively for something" (Lester 26).

3   Wallenberg's words were prophetic. By 1944, he was indeed working positively for something. He was risking his life to save the Jews of Budapest, Hungary. Members of the last large Jewish community in Europe, the Jews of Budapest had been targeted for extinction. Without their death, Nazi Germany could not claim that the "Final Solution," their plan to eliminate all the Jews in Europe, was a success. And, as the world now knows, the Nazis were determined to be successful.

4   Adolf Eichmann, one of the architects of Hitler's Final Solution, openly proclaimed his enthusiasm for the Hungarian "project." He personally organized the transportation of Jews to Auschwitz and insisted that the job be completed as swiftly as possible (Lester, 69). But Eichmann had reckoned without the arrival of Raoul Wallenberg. Almost single-handedly, Wallenberg saved over 100,000 Hungarian Jews. Then, in one of the great mysteries of all time, he vanished. To this day, his disappearance remains unexplained and his whereabouts, alive or dead, are unknown.

Wallenberg's American Connection

5   By late 1942, most of the world's leaders knew that the German government was determined to make all of Europe *judenrein,* or free of Jews. Although reports of atrocities* had been circulating for months, government officials had viewed them as isolated events. As 1942 drew to a close, however, both the American State Department and the British Foreign Office had to confront the terrible truth hidden behind the euphemism *Final Solution.* The Nazis were systematically killing, or, in their words "exterminating," the Jews of Europe.

6   By 1944, the American government had decided to organize the War Refugee Board. Its goal was to block "Nazi plans to exterminate all the Jews" (Lester, 61). This goal clearly required intervention in Hungarian affairs, because Hungary was the only remaining country with a large Jewish population. The country was also under German occupation.

7   As a result, Iver C. Olsen, a member of the U.S. Treasury Department, was sent to neutral Sweden. His task was to find a

Swedish representative who could enter Hungary and somehow stop deportations to the concentration camps. Within days of meeting Olsen, Raoul Wallenberg was ready to travel.

A Powerful Piece of Paper

8 Raoul Wallenberg arrived in Budapest on July 9, 1944. When he entered the Swedish embassy, he saw a long line of people wearing the yellow Star of David that proclaimed their status as Jews. Word had gotten out that the Swedes were giving travel documents or citizenship papers to Hungarian Jews who were planning to become Swedish citizens or residents. In several cases, those documents had offered protection against deportation and death.

9 One Jewish businessman had even gone to court, claiming his Swedish citizenship protected him from deportation. To everyone's surprise, he had won his case. Another man had escaped deportation to Auschwitz, the most dreaded of all concentration camps, by showing a Swedish document. The German officer in charge had simply let him go, obviously intimidated by the sight of an official document.

10 Quick to infer a valuable lesson from these incidents, Wallenberg realized immediately that the same people who could callously* inflict suffering and death could also be intimidated by a piece of paper. Inhumanity did not disturb them, but failure to follow the rules did. Inspired by that knowledge, Wallenberg designed an impressive looking document, bearing the symbol of the Swedish government. More important, it announced that anyone carrying the document was under the protection, or *Schutz*, of the Swedish government. The document was signed by Raoul Wallenberg.

11 Wallenberg's next step was to set up a small network for the distribution of the *Schutz* passes. He then visited members of the Hungarian government and showed them a letter from King Gustav of Sweden. He made it clear to all present that Sweden was committed to protecting the Jews against further aggression. Other Swedish diplomats were a bit taken aback by Wallenberg's unorthodox* efforts, citing questions of procedure and legality. But Wallenberg managed to brush all such considerations aside with one answer: "It will save lives" (Lester, 89).

12 By October of 1944, Wallenberg had been in Budapest just three short months. During that time, he had purchased a number of houses with the money provided by Olsen. Draping them with Swedish flags, Wallenberg claimed the houses were Swedish property and therefore not subject to German or Hungarian law.

In effect, they became "safe houses," places of sanctuary* for Jewish refugees.

13   When, on one occasion, Hungarian troops tried to force their way into one of Wallenberg's safe houses, he blocked their way, saying, "No one leaves this place as long as I live" (Stanglin et al., 36). The troops withdrew.

14   On October 15, 1944, Hungarian radio announced that the war was lost, and the announcer openly blamed the Germans for dragging Hungary into a losing battle. In the Jewish quarter, there was dancing in the streets. Unfortunately, the dancing was premature. Shortly after the first announcement came another more ominous broadcast. The Hungarian Nazi Party, the hated and feared *Arrow Cross*, had taken over. Along with the German Nazis still in Hungary, members of the *Arrow Cross* would continue to be loyal to Adolf Hitler. Above all, they would continue to work toward the Final Solution.

The **Arrow Cross's** *Reign of Terror*

15 The notorious Adolf Eichmann was again in Budapest, and fifteen members of the *Arrow Cross* roamed the streets hunting down and shooting Jews on sight. At one point, a small band of Jewish laborers and a handful of Communists got hold of arms, and they fought back. Immediately the German SS† and the Hungarian police were at the scene of the fighting. They rounded up hundreds of suspected sympathizers and executed them where they stood (Lester, 105). A nightmare world prior to October 15, Budapest had now become a living hell.

16   As Soviet tanks drew closer, the Nazis became more violent and more vicious. They barged into Wallenberg's "safe" houses and dragged out the "protected" Jews. They tortured their victims, shot them, and then threw their bodies into the Danube River.

17   Eichmann, however, was furious that his plans for exterminating the Hungarian Jews were being interrupted. Nazi officials had become anxious about what was going to happen when the war ended. With good reason, they were afraid of being tried as war criminals. Auschwitz was being dismantled,* and orders had been given to stop the extermination program. But Eichmann was not to be stopped; he devised yet another scheme.

18   Jews now were to be rounded up to work on the "East Wall" in Vienna. The wall would supposedly be protection against the advance of the Russians. But, more important, Eichmann knew that

---

†SS: *Schutzstaffel* (protective units), the elite guard of the Nazi party, notorious for their brutal tactics.

most of the Jews who would be marched on foot to Vienna would not survive. The cold, starvation, and hunger would do their work.

19   Wallenberg also knew that the "labor march," as it was called, was bound to be a death march. He tried to have the march postponed but succeeded only in getting exemptions for those Jews bearing *Schutz* passes. On November 9, the march began.

20   Shivering for lack of clothing and starving for food, the Jews were marched toward the Austrian border. Anyone who stumbled or fell out of line was shot. The marchers were without hope. But then Wallenberg miraculously began to turn up at points along the way. Susan Tabor, a survivor of the march, described lying on the floor of a shed so crowded she could neither stand up nor move. Suddenly she saw Wallenberg stride in, carrying a briefcase. Through a megaphone he announced that food and medical supplies would soon arrive. When he left, the marchers had new hope. As Susan Tabor was to say long after the march was over, "He made me feel human again. For the first time I had hope" (Werbell and Clarke, 91).

21   As always, true to his word, Wallenberg returned the next day with food and medicine. He also brought a stack of protective passes. Within minutes, he had created chaos by telling the marchers to assemble in various lines:

> The Jews ran helter-skelter around the brick factory. They changed lines and jostled one another to get a good place as Wallenberg backed his trucks into the yard. The *Arrow Cross* guards lost control. . . . In the confusion many Jews simply walked away or bribed individual guards to let them escape. (Werbell and Clarke, 91)

This scene was repeated many times as Wallenberg worked tirelessly to save as many Jews as he could.

The Russians Arrive

22 By January of 1945, the Russians were closing in on Budapest, and it was clear to everyone that the war was truly coming to an end. On January 13, 1945, a small group of Russian soldiers broke through the wall of a house where Wallenberg was staying. He explained who he was, and the soldiers examined his documents. But something about Wallenberg or his papers seemed to make them suspicious. A few hours later, some high-ranking Soviet officials arrived to question him, in the first of several interrogations by the Russian secret police. Nevertheless, Wallenberg was permitted to move freely through the now-liberated city of Budapest.

23   On January 17, Wallenberg dropped in on friends before leaving to visit Soviet headquarters. He was in high spirits, convinced

that the Soviets wanted his advice on postwar relief and reconstruction: "The Russians are certain to respect the suggestions of a Swedish diplomat" (Werbell and Clarke, 157).

24   Shortly after the visit, Wallenberg left Budapest under Russian escort. As he looked at the soldiers who were to accompany him, he made a cruelly prophetic joke: "I still don't know if they're coming along to protect me or guard me. Am I a guest, or a prisoner?" (Werbell and Clarke, 158).

25   Even today, no one is really sure what happened to Raoul Wallenberg after he left with his Soviet escorts. When he failed to return to Budapest as planned, the Swedish Foreign Office sent the Russians a series of messages asking for an investigation. There was no reply. After repeated refusals of requests for information, the Soviets claimed to have no knowledge of his whereabouts. Then, in 1957, Andrei Gromyko, the Soviet deputy foreign minister, claimed Wallenberg had died in 1947. According to Gromyko, Wallenberg had suffered a heart attack at the age of thirty-four. Despite Soviet claims, however, rumors persist to this day that Raoul Wallenberg is still alive.

26   Whether he is alive or dead, the file on Wallenberg needs to be opened. Wallenberg deserves to be remembered and honored. As Frederick E. Werbell and Thurston Clarke have pointed out, Wallenberg's life is an important source of inspiration: "If the Holocaust is to be taken as evidence that human nature is essentially evil, then Wallenberg's life must be considered as evidence that it is not" (p. 256).

Laraine Flemming

Sources

Lester, Elenore. *Wallenberg: The Man in the Iron Web.* Englewood Cliffs, N.J.: Prentice-Hall, 1982.

Stanglin, Douglas, Mortimer B. Zuckerman, Jeff Trimble, and David Bartal. "A Lost Prisoner of the Gulag Still Holds Moscow Hostage." *U.S. News and World Report,* June 26, 1989, pp. 34–36.

"Wallenberg Reported Shot in '47." *New York Times,* October 18, 1990, A14.

Werbell, Frederick E., and Thurston Clarke. *Lost Hero: The Mystery of Raoul Wallenberg.* New York: McGraw-Hill, 1982.

TEST YOUR UNDERSTANDING   Circle the letter of the correct answer.

1. Which of the following accurately paraphrases the thesis statement?

   a. To this day, no one knows for sure what happened to Raoul Wallenberg.

   b. After risking his life to save thousands of Hungarian Jews, Raoul Wallenberg mysteriously vanished, and, to this day, no one knows what happened to him.

2. Which of the following details is *not* essential to developing the main idea of the reading?

   a. "In 1937, Raoul Wallenberg was a young man who seemed to have everything."

   b. "Raoul Wallenberg arrived in Budapest on July 9, 1944."

   c. "Wallenberg's next step was to set up a small network for the distribution of *Schutz* passes."

3. Which statement sums up the main idea in paragraph 5?

   a. The euphemism "final solution" helped to hide a horrifying truth.

   b. By 1942, it was clear that the German government was prepared to murder all the Jews in Europe.

4. What inference did Wallenberg draw from the stories about people who had escaped deportation and death?

   a. People willing to commit murder could still be frightened by the sight of an official-looking document.

   b. The Germans really were determined to kill all the Jews in Europe.

5. According to the author, other Swedish diplomats

   a. admired Wallenberg.

   b. were taken aback by Wallenberg's unorthodox efforts.

   c. criticized Wallenberg's behavior.

6. Based on paragraph 11, which inference is appropriate?

   a. Wallenberg held other Swedish diplomats in contempt.

   b. Wallenberg was impatient with questions of procedure and legality when they concerned human lives.

7. In paragraph 13, which inference does the author expect readers to supply?

   a. The troops withdrew because they had been called back to combat.

   b. The troops withdrew because they were intimidated by Wallenberg.

8. The following sentence appears in paragraph 14: "Unfortunately, the dancing was premature." Which statement most accurately describes the function of that sentence?

   a. It helps to introduce the topic sentence.

   b. It sums up the main idea.

   c. It functions as a transition.

9. When the Russians first arrived, Wallenberg was convinced that

   a. they would kill him.

   b. they wanted his advice.

   c. they would leave him alone.

10. Which two patterns help organize the supporting details in this reading?

    a. sequence of dates and events

    b. sequence of steps

    c. comparison and contrast

    d. cause and effect

SHARPEN YOUR CRITICAL SKILLS Answer the following questions.

1. Which word or words in the following sentence suggest that it's an opinion: "In 1937, Raoul Wallenberg was a young man who seemed to have everything." _____

2. Label each of the following statements *F* (fact), *O* (opinion), or *B* (both).

   a. "By 1944, the American government had decided to organize the War Refugee Board." _____

   b. "Raoul Wallenberg arrived in Budapest on July 9, 1944." _____

   c. "Whether he is alive or dead, the file on Wallenberg needs to be opened." _____

3. In paragraph 15, what are some of the words with strong connotations the author uses to suggest for readers the horror of the situation she describes?

   _____

   _____

   _____

4. In paragraph 16, why does the author use the word *barged* rather than *entered?*

_____

_____

_____

5. During World War II, the followers of Adolf Hitler openly proclaimed their hatred and contempt for Jews. Yet, they still used a euphemism, "the final solution," to describe their plans for murdering all the Jews in Europe. What does that suggest to you?

_____

_____

_____

6. How would you describe the author's tone?

   a. angry

   b. admiring

   c. emotionally neutral

7. Many people now believe that the United States did not act quickly enough to help those being persecuted during World War II. Reread paragraphs 5, 6, and 7. Then decide which statement you think is accurate.

   a. The author leans toward the belief that the United States did not act quickly enough.

   b. The author is inclined to believe that the United States acted as quickly as possible.

   c. It's impossible to determine the author's personal feelings on this subject.

8. The author insists that the file on Wallenberg must be opened. What reasons does she give for believing that action should be taken?"

_____

_____

_____

Do you think the author's argument is convincing? Why or why not?

_____

_____

_____

_____

9. Paraphrase the quotation that ends the reading. In your own words, what does it mean?

_____

_____

_____

How do you think someone who disagrees with the point of the quotation might respond to it?

_____

_____

_____

10. How would you describe the author's purpose?

a. The author wants to tell readers about Wallenberg's exploits during World War II.

b. The author wants to tell readers about Wallenberg's exploits and convince them that the mystery of his disappearance needs to be solved.

THINKING FOR YOURSELF

1. Why do you think Raoul Wallenberg was willing to risk his life for people he did not know? What do you think motivated him? Do you think you could be capable of that kind of heroism?

_____

_____

_____

2. The reading ends with the claim that Wallenberg's memory could be a source of future inspiration. Have you been inspired by any heroes from the past? If so, which ones and why did they inspire you?

_____

_____

_____

MAKING **1.** Do you think Raoul Wallenberg has all the traits described in "Is a
CONNECTIONS Hero Really Nothing but a Sandwich?" by Ted Tollefson? Does he
BETWEEN have additional traits not mentioned by Tollefson?
READINGS

_____

_____

_____

2. What points of comparison can you find between Raoul Wallenberg and Dian Fossey? What points of contrast?

_____

_____

_____

■ **WRITING** Write a paper arguing for or against the importance of heroes as role
SUGGESTION models. Do you think we do or do not need heroic figures from the
past to guide our present day actions?

Remembering World War II

 For some historians, World War II was a crucial turning point in U.S. history, forever changing the face of American society. Viewed from this perspective, America's battle with Hitler and his allies made the country more aware of both its strengths and its weaknesses.

The Road to War

Introducing Rosie the Riveter

World War II: The Fight Against Racism

The Tragedy of Japanese Internment

■ **READING 13**

THE ROAD TO WAR

LOOKING AHEAD   In this reading, the authors of a history textbook describe some of the events that led up to World War II.

DEVELOPING A FOCUS   Read the section titled "Word Watch." Then read the first and last paragraphs, along with all the words printed in boldface. Based on your survey, make one or two predictions. What points do you expect the authors to make?

_____

_____

_____

In addition to making predictions, jot down one or two questions you will try to answer as you read.

_____

_____

_____

STRATEGIES FOR IN-DEPTH LEARNING   In this reading, the authors introduce several terms essential to understanding the events that led up to World War II. In the margins or on a separate sheet of paper, list the sequence of dates and events leading up to the war.

WORD WATCH   Because context does not always provide enough clues, some of the more difficult words in the reading are defined below. In the reading, these words are marked with an asterisk.

annexation: the taking of land or territory in order to incorporate it into some larger state or country

concede: give in

harassment: the act of irritating or tormenting

cede: give over, agree

buckling: bending or crumpling

émigrés: people who leave a country (often for political reasons)

1 WORLD PEACE WAS CRUMBLING FAST AS 1938 STARTED. THE fighting in China and Spain raged on with increased intensity. From Berlin, Hitler pronounced his intentions to unify all German-speaking lands and create a new German empire, or *Reich.* Austria, Hitler's homeland, was the first target and, in an **Anschluss,** was merged with Germany. Hearing only mild protests from other nations, Hitler confidently moved to incorporate other questionably German-speaking areas into the Reich. He turned next to the German population of the Sudeten region of western Czechoslovakia, demanding its annexation* to Germany. With a respectable military force and defense treaties with France and the Soviet Union, the Czechoslovakian government was prepared to resist.

2 War loomed in September 1938, as German troops massed along the Sudeten border and as the Czechs appealed for help to defend their nation. Neither France nor the Soviet Union nor Britain, however, wanted a confrontation with Hitler. And when Hitler claimed he wanted only what was Germany's by right and vowed that he would seek a territory beyond the Sudetenland, they were willing to compromise. On September 30, Britain's prime minister **Neville Chamberlain** met with Hitler in Munich and accepted Germany's annexation of the Sudetenland (see Map). Without British and French support, the Czechs had no option but to concede* the loss of territory. Chamberlain returned smiling to England promising "peace in our time." Roosevelt wired his congratulations to the prime minister.

3 The policy of **appeasement** did not end Hitler's aggressive policies, however. Within Germany, Hitler stepped up the persecution of the country's Jewish population. Germany was home to nearly half a million Jews, who since Hitler's rise to power had suffered increasing discrimination and harassment.* In 1938, Hitler launched government-sponsored violence against the German-Jewish population. Synagogues and Jewish businesses and homes were looted and destroyed. Detention centers—concentration camps—at Dachau and Buchenwald soon confined over fifty thousand Jews. Thousands of German and Austrian Jews fled to other countries.

4 Many applied to enter the United States, but most were turned away. American anti-Semitism was strong, and the State Department, citing immigration requirements that no one be admitted to the country who would become "a public charge," routinely denied entry to German Jews whose property and assets had been seized by the German government. Despite thousands of applications between 1933 and 1939, the State Department implemented

Anschluss Political union, especially the one absorbing Austria into Nazi Germany in 1938.

Neville Chamberlain British prime minister who pursued a policy of appeasement toward the fascist regimes of Europe before World War II.

appeasement Policy of granting concessions to potential enemies to maintain peace.

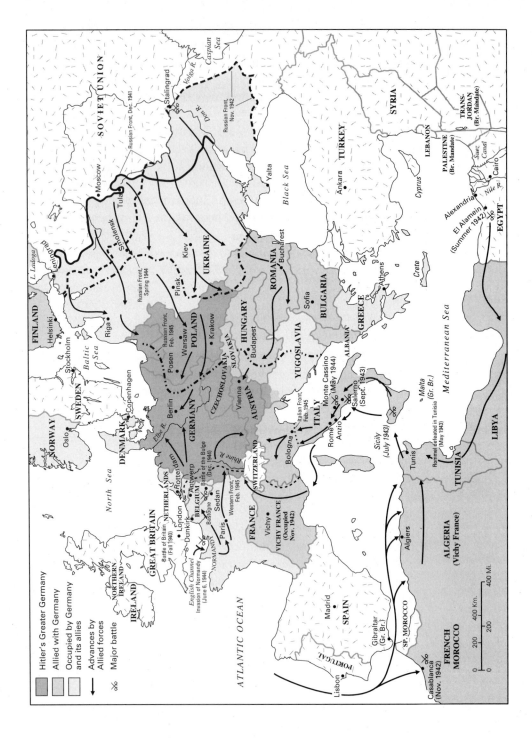

The European Theater By the end of 1942, the Axis nations of Italy and Germany, through conquest and annexation, had occupied nearly all of Europe. This map shows the alignment of Europe and the area controlled by Germany and its allies.

the immigration laws so strictly that nearly three-fourths of the 27,400-person quota for Germany and Austria went unfilled. Roosevelt regretted this rebuff of Jewish immigrants, but with little public interest in changing immigration rules, he did nothing more than offer sympathetic words to those wanting to allow more Jewish émigrés* to enter America.

5   Not only was Hitler persecuting German Jews, but he was also pressuring Poland to cede territory to Germany that contained large German populations. Convinced that Hitler was a threat to humanity, Roosevelt sounded a dire warning to Americans in his 1939 State of the Union address. "Events abroad have made it increasingly clear to the American people that the dangers within are less to be feared than dangers without," he warned. "This generation will nobly save or meanly lose the last best hope of earth." Quickly, events seemed to verify Roosevelt's prediction of danger. Hitler ominously concluded a military alliance with Italy, "the pact of steel," invaded and seized what remained of Czechoslovakia, and demanded that Poland turn over to Germany the **Danzig corridor** that connected Poland to the Baltic Sea. British and French officials, unwilling to appease Hitler any longer, pledged to protect Poland.

6   Meanwhile, unable to conclude an agreement with the British and the French, the Soviet Union had reached a secret, last-minute agreement with Germany—the **Ribbentrop-Molotov Nonaggression Pact** of August 23, 1939—which divided Poland between them. No longer worried about a Soviet attack, Hitler invaded Poland on September 1, 1939. Two days later, Britain and France declared war on Germany. Buckling* under new **blitzkrieg** tactics that emphasized movement and maneuver, Polish forces collapsed. Within a matter of days, German troops had overrun nearly all of Poland. On September 17, Soviet forces seized the eastern parts of Poland as agreed on in the Soviet-German nonaggression pact. World War II had begun.

Carol Berkin, Christopher L. Miller,
Robert W. Cherny, and James L. Gormly.
Making America: A History of the United States.
Boston: Houghton Mifflin, 1995, pp. 801–803.

Danzig corridor
Territory adjoining the city of Danzig, which connected Poland with the Baltic Sea and which Germany demanded from Poland in 1939.

Ribbentrop-Molotov Nonaggression Pact
Secret 1939 agreement in which Germany and the Soviet Union pledged not to fight one another and arranged to divide Poland after the invasion.

blitzkrieg Sudden, swift military offensive that allowed Germany to defeat Poland in a matter of days.

TEST YOUR UNDERSTANDING   Circle the letter of the correct answer.

1. Which statement more effectively sums up the implied main idea of the reading?

   a. Adolf Hitler was determined to dominate all of Europe, and he was willing to do or say anything to achieve his goal.

b. In dealing with Adolf Hitler, the policy of appeasement advocated by Neville Chamberlain was a spectacular failure.

2. According to the reading, Hitler's first target was

   a. Austria

   b. France

   c. Czechoslovakia

3. Neville Chamberlain promised England

   a. to fight until the very end.

   b. to win glory for Britain.

   c. peace in our time.

4. Chamberlain hoped to keep his promise by means of

   a. the Ribbentrop-Molotov Nonaggression Pact.

   b. the policy of appeasement.

   c. *blitzkrieg* tactics.

5. Which sentence paraphrases the topic sentence in paragraph 3?

   a. Because of Hitler's government-sponsored violence against Jews, thousands of Jews fled to other countries.

   b. Hitler's violence against Jews continued despite the policy of appeasement.

6. Which sentence best expresses the main idea of paragraph 4?

   a. During World War II, anti-Semitism in America reached its peak.

   b. Most of the Jews who tried to escape to the United States were turned away.

7. In paragraph 2, which statement is *not* an essential detail?

   a. "On September 30, Britain's prime minister Neville Chamberlain met with Hitler in Munich and accepted Germany's annexation of the Sudetenland."

   b. "Without British and French support, the Czechs had no option but to concede the loss of territory."

   c. "Roosevelt wired his congratulations to the prime minister."

8. In paragraph 4, the authors say, "American anti-Semitism was strong, and the State Department . . . routinely denied entry to German Jews whose property and assets had been seized by the German government." What inference do the authors expect readers to draw?

    a. The State Department was wrong to deny entry to any German Jews likely to suffer persecution.

    b. Anti-Semitism was the reason behind the State Department's refusal to grant entry to any German Jews seeking to escape persecution.

9. What pattern of organization do you recognize in paragraph 3?

    a. comparison and contrast

    b. cause and effect

    c. sequence of dates and events

10. Which two patterns of organization underlie the entire reading?

    a. comparison and contrast

    b. cause and effect

    c. sequence of dates and events

    d. classification

SHARPEN YOUR CRITICAL SKILLS Answer the following questions.

1. Is the following statement a fact (*F*), an opinion (*O*), or a blend of both (*B*)? "World peace was crumbling fast as 1938 started." _____ Explain your answer.

_____

_____

_____

2. In paragraph 1, the authors tell us that fighting in China and Spain "raged on with increased intensity." Why do you think the authors chose to use the word *raged* rather than *continued?*

_____

_____

_____

3. In paragraph 1, the authors tell us that "Hitler confidently moved to incorporate other questionably German-speaking areas into the Reich." What word in that sentence do the authors use to challenge Hitler's argument for annexation? _____

4. Is the following statement a fact (*F*), an opinion (*O*), or a blend of both (*B*)? "With respectable military force and defense treaties with France and the Soviet Union, the Czechoslovakian government was

prepared to resist." _____
Explain your answer.

_____

_____

_____

5. In paragraph 4, the authors describe attempts by German Jews to enter the United States. They tell us, however, that "American anti-Semitism was strong." What evidence do they offer for that

claim? _____
How might critical readers respond to their claim?

_____

_____

_____

6. In paragraph 4, the authors tell us that "Roosevelt regretted this rebuff of Jewish immigrants, but . . . he did nothing more than offer sympathetic words." How do you think the authors personally viewed Roosevelt's position on Jewish immigration?

_____

_____

_____

Explain your answer.

_____

_____

_____

7. In paragraph 4, the authors imply a reason for Roosevelt's reluctance to increase Jewish immigration. What reason do they suggest?

_____

_____

_____

What does the reason suggest about the authors' view of Roosevelt's presidency?

_____

_____

_____

8. Over the years, the policy of appeasement adopted by Britain and France has been harshly criticized. How do you think the authors personally view this policy?

   a. The authors think the policy of appeasement was a mistake.

   b. They think that the policy of appeasement has been unfairly criticized.

   c. It's impossible to determine the authors' personal feelings.

9. How would you describe the authors' tone?

   a. sad

   b. angry

   c. emotionally neutral

10. Which of the following statements more effectively describes the authors' purpose?

   a. The authors want to inform readers about the events leading up to World War II and describe America's immigration policy during that period of time.

   b. The authors want to inform readers about the events leading up to World War II and suggest that the policy of appeasement and America's immigration policies were both mistakes.

THINKING FOR YOURSELF Neville Chamberlain's policies have been widely criticized. However, at the time, many people thought appeasing Hitler would work, and they supported Chamberlain's policies. What mistaken belief about Adolf Hitler did supporters of appeasement hold?

_____

_____

_____

■

WRITING During World War II, movies were an important propaganda tool.
SUGGESTION With the help of the reference librarian in your school or local library, do some research on propaganda films made during World War II. Write a paper describing how World War II affected or shaped the kinds of films Hollywood produced. The following sources will help get you started in your research:

Dick, Bernard F. *The Star Spangled Screen.* Louisville: University of Kentucky Press, 1985.

Koppes, Clayton R., and Gregory D. Black. *Hollywood Goes to War: How Politics, Profits and Propaganda Shaped World War II.* Los Angeles: University of California Press, 1987.

Shindler, Colin. *Hollywood Goes to War: Films and American Society 1939–1952.* Boston: Routledge and Kegan Paul, 1979.

■ **READING 14**

INTRODUCING ROSIE THE RIVETER

LOOKING AHEAD In the following selection, the authors focus on how World War II affected the lives of women. As you'll see, the war had a profound effect even on those women who stayed at home.

DEVELOPING A FOCUS Read the section titled "Word Watch." Then read the first and last paragraphs of the selection and look at the accompanying illustration. Based on your survey, make one or two predictions. What points do you expect the authors to make?

_____

_____

In addition to making predictions, jot down one or two questions you will try to answer while you read.

_____

_____

STRATEGIES FOR IN-DEPTH LEARNING As you read, annotate the selection by jotting key statistics in the margins and listing the effects of the war on women's lives.

WORD WATCH Because context does not always provide enough clues, some of the more difficult words in the reading are defined below. In the reading, these words are marked with an asterisk.

census: an official counting of the population

hoopla: commotion, excitement

inducement: something that brings about an action

structural: having to do with the way parts are arranged

inflation: a persistent increase in the level of consumer prices

demographic: related to the study of human populations; their size, growth, and density

1   CENSUS* DATA AND OTHER GOVERNMENTAL RECORDS SHOW that many women entered higher-paying and more skilled jobs as early as World War I. But those gains were short-lived. With the

return of peace, women faced layoffs, renewed wage discrimination, and segregation into female-only jobs, such as secretarial and clerical work. They made little headway over the next decade, despite the hoopla* about the emancipated "new woman"† of the twenties. Behind the stereotype of the smart-talking flapper with her cigarette, bobbed hair, and boyish clothes, traditional ideas about women and their proper roles prevailed in the labor marketplace.

2   In 1920, 23 percent of women worked; by 1930, the figure was only 24 percent. Access to the professions, while increased, remained heavily restricted. For example, women earned over 30 percent of all graduate degrees but accounted for only 4 percent of full professors on college faculties. Most women workers toiled at unskilled jobs; most were young, single, and without children. Between 1920 and 1930, the percentage of women in manufacturing fell from 22.6 (the same as 1910) to 17.5, while percentages of women in both domestic service and clerical work—the lowest-paying jobs—rose.

3   Real gains for women came during World War II. A rapidly expanding war economy absorbed most of the reserve labor force of under- or unemployed male workers. The military alone siphoned off some 15 million men and women. That left married women as the single largest untapped labor reserve. Suddenly, the propaganda machinery that had once discouraged women from competing with men for jobs urged them to enlist in the work force. The patriotic appeal had the desired effect. What faithful wife could sit at home when the media warned that her husband in the service might die from the lack of ammunition? "Commando Mary" and "Rosie the Riveter" became symbols of women who heeded their country's call.

4   Patriotism by itself did not explain the willingness of married women to take jobs. Many found higher war wages an attractive inducement.* Indeed, with so many husbands earning low military pay, families needed additional income to survive. Absent husbands also meant a lower birthrate and fewer demands for household services. That left women more time and opportunity for work outside the home. And wartime restrictions on leisure activities made jobs a more attractive outlet for women's energies. Whether stated as raw numbers or percentages, the statistical gains for women were impressive. From 1940 to 1945, some 6.5 million women entered the work force, over half of them for

---

†"New woman": term applied to women who had supposedly rejected the restrictions applied to women in the nineteenth century.

In the midst of the war, photographs of women who resembled Rosie the Riveter, the "cover girl" for the Saturday Evening Post, *inspired other women to join the war effort.*

the first time. Women accounted for just 25 percent of workers in 1940 but 36 percent in 1945.

5   Perhaps more significant were the kinds of women who now found employment outside the home. Young, single women no longer dominated. By 1950, married women were a majority of the female work force, compared with only a third in 1940. Similarly, older women between ages fifty-five and sixty-four became a major group, rising from 17 percent in 1940 to 35 percent by 1960. It was not only the numbers of working women that soared but also the quality of their jobs. Women had an opportunity to work in skilled areas of manufacturing and to earn much higher wages. Black women in particular, who had been concentrated in low-paying farm and domestic jobs, rushed to the factories that offered higher pay and better hours. Women on the assembly lines—shaping sheet metal, building airplanes, and performing a host of skilled tasks—shattered many stereotypes about traditional male and female roles.

---

†Charles Atlas: a famous bodybuilder.

6   Yet, for all these undeniable gains, the situation brought about by a world at war was a special case, and most Americans perceived it that way. The men returning home intended to pick up their jobs, while most assumed that women would return to their traditional household duties. As a result, the war led to few structural* changes affecting women's economic roles. For example, working mothers needed some form of day care for their young children. The government was slow to provide it and, even where it existed, many mothers were reluctant to use it. They or other family members continued to have primary responsibility for children. One result was a much higher absentee rate for working mothers. In addition, those mothers worked shorter hours. For them, the responsibilities of the job were secondary to those of the home.

7   Most professions continued to maintain barriers against women. Although female workers flooded government bureaucracies and factories, few received managerial status. And many employers found ways to avoid government regulations requiring equal pay for men and women. General Motors, for example, simply changed its job classifications from overtly segregated male-female categories to "heavy-light," thus leaving women in the "light," lower-paying categories. Fearful that rapidly rising wages would spur inflation,* the government was slow to enforce its own rules protecting women from discrimination.

8   Certain social trends seemed to underscore the traditional resistance to working mothers. Statistics indicated that wartime stresses threatened to undermine the family. Alcohol abuse, divorce, and juvenile delinquency all increased, and some observers blamed those problems on working mothers. In fact, there was no clear evidence that the families of those women had any disadvantage over those whose mothers stayed home. Extraordinary wartime mobility, not the fact that the mothers worked, seems to have accounted for many of those problems. The sudden rush of workers, both male and female, to industrial centers overtaxed all manner of public services, including housing and schools, which were of particular importance to families with young children. The war disrupted families whether mothers worked or not.

9   What is striking is that by 1945, despite all the gains women had made, most attitudes about women and work had not changed substantially. Surveys showed that Americans, whether male or female, continued to believe that child rearing was a woman's primary job. Thus, the marked demographic* shift of women into the work force was revolutionary in import, but it brought no revolution in cultural attitudes toward sex roles. As historian Wil-

liam Chafe commented, "The events of the war years suggested that most Americans would accept a significant shift in women's economic activities as long as the shift was viewed as 'temporary' and did not entail a conscious commitment to approve the goals of a sexual revolution."

10   Despite the general expectation that women would return to the home after the war, female laborers did not simply drop their wrenches and pick up frying pans. Many continued to work outside the home, although mostly to support their families, not to find career alternatives. As peace came in 1945, polls indicated that over 75 percent of all working women wanted to continue at their jobs. About 88 percent of high school girls surveyed said they hoped for a career as well as the role of homemaker. Though employment for women did shrink slightly, a significantly higher percentage of women were working in 1950 than in 1940 (28 percent versus 24). Even more striking, that figure continued to rise, reaching 36 percent by 1960. Those numbers included older women, married women with children, and women of all social classes.

James West Davidson and Mark Hamilton Lytle,
After the Fact. New York: Alfred A. Knopf,
1986, pp. 369–372.

TEST YOUR UNDERSTANDING   Circle the letter of the correct answer.

1. Which statement more effectively sums up the implied main idea of the reading?

   a. Although World War II enormously increased opportunities for women, those opportunities tended to diminish once the war was over.

   b. Discrimination against women in the workplace has a very long history, and the treatment of women during World War II is a perfect example of this.

2. According to the authors, in World War I, women

   a. did not experience any gains in the workplace.

   b. experienced gains in the workplace that carried over into World War II.

   c. experienced gains in the workplace that quickly vanished once the war was over.

3. Which sentence more effectively sums up the implied main idea of paragraph 3?

a. During World War II, married women went to work alongside single women.

b. World War II created employment opportunities for women.

4. In paragraph 3, which of the following is *not* an essential detail?

a. "A rapidly expanding war economy absorbed most of the reserve labor force of under- or unemployed male workers."

b. "The military alone siphoned off some fifteen million men and women."

c. "What faithful wife could sit at home when the media warned that her husband in the service might die from the lack of ammunition?"

5. Which statement more effectively sums up the implied main idea of paragraph 4?

a. During World War II, most women entered the work force because their men were gone, and they badly needed money.

b. During World War II, women entered the work force for a variety of reasons.

6. Paragraph 4 relies on which pattern of organization?

a. comparison and contrast

b. cause and effect

c. sequence of dates and events

7. According to the reading, during World War II,

a. all obstacles to women in the work force vanished.

b. most professions maintained barriers against women.

c. women did not apply for managerial jobs.

8. Which statement more effectively sums up the implied main idea of paragraph 5?

a. World War II gave older women a chance to enter the work force and perform skilled labor.

b. Because of World War II, women from all walks of life entered the work force and were allowed to work in highly skilled areas.

9. According to the authors, women on the assembly line

a. destroyed a good many myths about male and female roles.

b. proved incapable of handling the pressure.

c. outperformed the men who had previously done the same work.

10. According to the authors, when the war ended,

    a. women were encouraged to stay on in their jobs.

    b. women were anxious to leave the work force and get back to being housewives.

    c. men returned home expecting to take back their old jobs.

SHARPEN YOUR CRITICAL SKILLS Answer the following questions.

1. In paragraph 1, the authors tell readers that women made little economic headway in the decade following World War I. What evidence do they give to support their opinion?

_____

_____

_____

_____

2. In paragraph 3, the authors tell readers that real gains for women came during World War II. What evidence do the authors give to argue their opinion?

_____

_____

_____

3. What opinion is the main idea of paragraph 7?

_____

_____

_____

4. What evidence do the authors use to argue the opinion in paragraph 7?

_____

_____

_____

_____

Do you think the authors do a good job of arguing their opinion? Why or why not?

_____

_____

_____

5. In paragraph 9, the authors claim that "despite all the gains women had made, most attitudes about women and work had not changed substantially." To support their opinion, the authors cite evidence drawn from surveys. What questions about those surveys do you think critical readers might pose?

_____

_____

_____

6. In addition to surveys, what other type of evidence do the authors use in paragraph 9?

_____

_____

_____

7. How would you describe the author's tone?
   a. funny
   b. solemn
   c. emotionally neutral

8. Because alcohol abuse, divorce, and juvenile delinquency increased at the same time mothers went to work, some people argued that working mothers were to blame. What type of faulty reasoning can you detect in this argument?
   a. circular argument
   b. questionable cause and effect
   c. irrelevant facts

9. In paragraph 9, the authors tell readers that "despite all the gains women had made, most attitudes about women and work had not

changed substantially." Based on the paragraph, what would you say about the authors' personal bias?

a. The authors are inclined to believe that women were badly treated after the war was over.

b. The authors are inclined to believe that women should not have expected long-lasting changes in their economic roles.

c. It's impossible to determine the authors' personal feelings.

10. Which statement more effectively describes the author's purpose?

a. The authors want to describe for readers how World War II expanded the economic opportunities of women.

b. The authors want to persuade readers that the experience of women workers during World War II is an excellent example of discrimination on the basis of sex.

THINKING FOR YOURSELF Do you think it was or was not fair that women were expected to give up their jobs when men returned home from the war? Explain your answer.

_____

_____

_____

MAKING CONNECTIONS BETWEEN READINGS Write a synthesis statement that combines ideas from "Introducing Rosie the Riveter" with the earlier reading "Women in Management."

_____

_____

_____

■ **WRITING SUGGESTIONS** During World War II, images in newspapers and magazines of Commando Mary and Rosie the Riveter helped pave the way for a change in women's status. Write a paper describing how some current image or images of women—in the news, on television, or in movies—have affected the way women think, look, or behave. If you wish, focus on males instead of females and describe how some image or images of men have had an influential effect.

■ **READING 15**

WORLD WAR II: THE FIGHT AGAINST RACISM

LOOKING AHEAD In this reading, historian Sean Dennis Cashman outlines the effect World War II had on the lives of African-Americans.

DEVELOPING A FOCUS Read the section titled "Word Watch." Then read the first paragraph, the illustration, and the last paragraph of the selection. Based on your survey, make one or two predictions. What points do you expect the author to make?

_____

_____

In addition to making predictions, jot down at least two questions you will try to answer as you read.

_____

_____

STRATEGIES FOR IN-DEPTH LEARNING Formulate two or three essay questions you think might appear on an exam. When you finish the reading, write out the questions. Then mentally or on paper see how well you can answer your own questions.

WORD WATCH Because context does not always provide enough clues, some of the more difficult words in the reading are defined below. In the reading, these words are marked with an asterisk.

segregated: separated on the basis of race

rationalized: gave reasons that were really excuses

sophistry: argument based on faulty logic

abridged: condensed, abbreviated

integration: the process of opening an institution to all races on an equal basis

exacerbated: worsened

smoldering: burning

disenfranchised: denied the right to vote

doctrines: body of principles or rules that organize a group

obsolete: outmoded, no longer of any use

plasticity: ability to be shaped or molded

1 DURING WORLD WAR II (1939–1945), 1.15 MILLION AFRICAN-Americans entered the armed services and many fought overseas. However, the armed forces were totally segregated* and the African-American press continued to emphasize similarities between fascist persecution of the Jews in Europe and racial segregation in the United States. Throughout the war, the Red Cross kept "white blood" and "black blood" in separate containers.

2 Although chiefs of staff would have preferred to think that the armed services were immune from racial conflict, they came under increasing pressure to abandon their ironclad segregation code of 1941. By the terms of this code, African-Americans could not enlist in the Marine or Air Corps. In the navy, they could serve only in menial tasks. The army did admit African-Americans but maintained segregated training facilities and units and retained African-American troops primarily in a supportive capacity rather than in combat. African-American officers were assigned to so-called Negro units and had to serve under white superiors. No African-American officer could ever become superior to a white in the same unit.

3 The army rationalized* this policy, partly on the sophistry* that African-Americans were poor fighters, partly on the grounds that the army was not a suitable laboratory for social experiments, and partly in the belief that integration would destroy the morale of white soldiers. The War Department insisted that it could not "ignore the social relationships between negroes and whites which have been established by the American people through custom and habit." However, as the numbers of African-American soldiers increased sevenfold, from one hundred thousand in 1941 to seven hundred thousand in 1944, so did their dissatisfaction with military segregation.

4 African-American recruits came primarily from the North because those from the South were usually neither sufficiently healthy nor well enough educated to pass induction tests. African-Americans from the North were less likely to accept Jim Crow.† One African-American leader, Edgar Brown, advised Roosevelt in a letter of May 20, 1942, how "many of these young people have lived all their lives in New York, Detroit, Philadelphia, Chicago and other metropolitan areas where their civil rights have never before been abridged."* Thus, gradually (and reluctantly) chiefs of staff came to accept that military segregation was wasteful of manpower, that it was exposing the armed services to liberal criticisms, and that it was depressing the morale of an ever

---

†Jim Crow: policies of strict separation on the basis of race.

larger section of the army. Somewhat shamefaced, the army began to use African-Americans in combat and the navy introduced a program of cautious integration.* Nevertheless, the army remained totally segregated. The agitation for integration led Army Chief of Staff George C. Marshall to declare, "My God! My God! . . . I don't know what to do about this race question in the army. I tell you frankly, it is the worst thing that we have to deal with. . . . We are getting a situation on our hands that may explode right in our faces."

5   Thus, the war exacerbated* racial difference. As Richard Polenberg says in *One Nation Divisible* (1980), "From the black perspective, the lowering of some barriers made those remaining seem more intolerable. To many whites, however, the remaining barriers seemed even more desirable than before." A student quoted by Mary F. Berry and John W. Blassingame in *Long Memory: The Black Experience in America* (1982) expressed smoldering* resentment among African-Americans: "The Army Jim Crows us. The Navy lets us serve only as mess men. The Red Cross refuses our blood. We are disenfranchised,* Jim Crowed, spat upon. What more could Hitler do than that?" However, in contrast to their position in World War I, groups of African-Americans and their political leaders were now a political force to be reckoned with.

6   Nazi emphasis on racism helped discredit racial doctrines* in the United States. For several decades, progressive anthropologists such as Franz Boas and Otto Kleinberg had challenged the idea that some races were superior to others. During the war, their successors argued these points for a mass audience. Ruth Benedict in *Race: Science and Politics* (1940), Gunnar Dahlberg in *Race, Reason and Rubbish* (1942), and Ashley Montagu in *Man's Most Dangerous Myth: The Fallacy of Race* (1942), all emphasized how much all human beings have in common; that individual differences are more important than racial averages; that so-called racial traits are really determined by culture and environment; and that the notion of racial purity was, at best, obsolete,* especially given increasing migration and intermarriage.

7   In short, such authors argued for the plasticity* rather than the permanence of human nature. Thus, Ashley Montagu in *Man's Most Dangerous Myth* declared how the rise of fascism "shows us today where we end up if we think the shape of the nose or the color of the skin has anything to do with human values and culture."

Sean Dennis Cashman, *African-Americans and the Quest for Civil Rights, 1900–1990.* New York: New York University Press, 1991, pp. 74, 75, 79.

TEST YOUR UNDERSTANDING Circle the letter of the correct answer.

1. Which implied main idea more effectively sums up the main idea of the reading?

   a. World War II revealed a harsh fact about life in America: Even the military was not immune to racism.

   b. Despite the military's policy of racial segregation, World War II actually helped strike a blow against racism in America.

2. Prior to World War II, the Joint Chiefs of Staff liked to think that

   a. the armed services were in the forefront of the fight against racism.

   b. the armed services were immune to racial conflict.

   c. racism in the military had been eliminated during World War I.

3. Which of the following was *not* one of the terms of the military's segregation code in 1941?

   a. African-Americans were not permitted to enlist in either the Marine or Air Corps.

   b. African-Americans were barred from enlisting in the U.S. Army.

   c. African-American officers could not be ranked higher than white officers in the same unit.

   d. African-Americans in the Navy were restricted to serving in menial positions.

4. Based on what the author says about the Red Cross, which inference is more appropriate?

   a. Like the military, the Red Cross helped to enforce Jim Crow.

   b. The Red Cross openly challenged the military's Jim Crow laws.

5. Which statement paraphrases the topic sentence of paragraph 5?

   a. World War II tended to increase racial tension in America.

   b. The military's treatment of African-Americans during World War II created racial solidarity.

6. Who was worried that the racial tensions in the army were about to explode?

   a. Harry Truman

   b. Dwight D. Eisenhower

   c. George C. Marshall

7. For decades before the war, anthropologists like Franz Boas and Otto Kleinberg argued

   a. that some races were superior to others.

   b. against the idea that some races were superior to others.

   c. that anthropologists should have no opinions on racial relations.

8. Choose the better paraphrase of the following statement: "During World War II, authors like Ruth Benedict, Gunnar Dahlberg, and Ashley Montagu argued for the plasticity rather than the permanence of human nature."

   a. During the war, some intellectuals set forth their theories about human nature: For people like Ruth Benedict, Gunnar Dahlberg, and Ashley Montagu, the human race was constantly improving.

   b. During World War II, writers like Ruth Benedict, Gunnar Dahlberg, and Ashley Montagu argued that human nature was not rigidly fixed but subject to growth and change.

9. In books like *Race: Science and Politics, Race, Reason and Rubbish,* and *Man's Most Dangerous Myth: The Fallacy of Race,* the authors argued which of the following points?

   a. Racism will one day simply disappear.

   b. Fascism and racism had nothing in common.

   c. The notion of racial purity was out of date.

10. According to the author, Nazi emphasis on the importance of racial purity

   a. helped to encourage racism in America.

   b. helped to discredit racism in America.

   c. had no effect on racism in America.

SHARPEN YOUR CRITICAL SKILLS Answer the following questions.

1. Label the following statements *F* (fact), *O* (opinion), or *B* (both).

   a. "During World War II (1939–1945), 1.15 million African-Americans entered the armed services." _____

   b. "Although chiefs of staff would have preferred to think that the armed services were immune from racial conflict, they came under increasing pressure to abandon their ironclad segregation code of 1941." _____

2. What reasons did the army put forth in support of segregation?

_____

_____

_____

3. Do you think the author considers the Army's argument in favor of

segregation to be solidly grounded in logic and reason? _____
Explain your answer.

_____

_____

_____

4. In paragraph 2, the author refers to the "ironclad segregation code
of 1941." Why does the author use the word _ironclad?_ What effect
does he want to have on his readers?

_____

_____

_____

5. In paragraph 4, the author points out that the chiefs of staff "reluctantly" came to accept that military segregation was wasteful of
manpower. Why does the author include the word _reluctantly?_ What
does he want to imply?

_____

_____

_____

6. How would you describe the author's tone?

    a. angry

    b. casual

    c. emotionally neutral

7. Overall, which of the following statements best describes the author's personal bias?

a. The author thinks the military's position was understandable for that time and should not be judged too harshly.

b. The author considers the military's position to be an embarrassing error in judgment that cannot be defended.

c. The author does not reveal how he feels about the military's policy of segregation.

8. How did the anthropologists who criticized the notion of racial superiority support their claims? What four reasons did they give to convince their audience?

_____

_____

_____

_____

_____

_____

_____

_____

9. How is it possible that the Nazi emphasis on racism helped discredit racial doctrines in the United States?

_____

_____

_____

10. What do you think is the author's primary purpose in writing?

a. The author wants to inform readers about the effect World War II had on racism in the military.

b. The author wants to persuade readers that the military's segregationist policies toward African-Americans undermined the war effort.

THINKING FOR YOURSELF Were you surprised to find out that the American military had once practiced segregationist policies or did you already know about it? If you already knew, what was the source of your information?

_____

_____

_____

MAKING CONNECTIONS BETWEEN READINGS   Create a synthesis statement that brings together what you've learned from this reading and from "Introducing Rosie the Riveter." What connection can you make between the two?

_____

_____

_____

WRITING SUGGESTIONS

1. At present, women are forbidden to take part in combat operations during wartime. Write a paper in which you argue for or against women taking part in combat. As an introduction to your opinion, summarize the early military policies on African-Americans and point out how that military policy changed under pressure. Then introduce your opinion and give at least two reasons why, in the case of women, military policy should or should not change.

2. Currently, admitted homosexuals are not allowed to serve in the armed forces. Using the same pattern described above, argue that homosexuals should, or should not, be accepted into the military.

■ **READING 16**

THE TRAGEDY OF JAPANESE INTERNMENT

LOOKING AHEAD In 1942, Franklin Delano Roosevelt, despite the protests of his wife, Eleanor, signed *Executive Order 9066*. The reading that follows describes the misery and suffering that *Executive Order 9066* caused Japanese-Americans.

DEVELOPING A FOCUS Read the section titled "Word Watch." Then read the headings along with the first and the last paragraphs of the selection. Based on your survey, make one or two predictions. What points do you expect the authors to make?

_____

_____

_____

In addition to making predictions, jot down questions you will try to answer as you read.

_____

_____

_____

STRATEGIES FOR IN-DEPTH LEARNING Beside each heading, write a brief statement that sums up the key point of each section.

WORD WATCH Because context does not always provide enough clues, some of the more difficult words in the reading are defined below. In the reading, these words are marked with an asterisk.

refuge: place of safety

unscrupulous: lacking any moral or ethical sense

affiliation: connection

foremost: most important

fervor: intense emotional feelings

dereliction: neglect, abandonment

reticent: shy, withdrawn

rebuff: rejection

unsubstantiated: unproven, lacking in evidence

reparation: repayment for injury

1 ON THE MORNING OF DECEMBER 7, 1941, JAPANESE SUB-marines and carrier planes launched an attack on the U.S. Pacific Fleet at Pearl Harbor. Two hundred American aircraft were destroyed, eight battleships were sunk, and approximately eight thousand naval and military personnel were killed or wounded. This savage attack and its horrifying consequences propelled the United States into World War II.

2 For people of Japanese descent living in the United States—both the American born *Nissei* and the Japanese born *Issei*—the attack on Pearl Harbor was doubly catastrophic. It was tragic enough that their adopted country was going to war with the land of their ancestors. But the attack on Pearl Harbor also unleashed a storm of fury and outrage against America's Japanese citizens. The result was *Executive Order 9066* issued in February 1942. Signed by the president of the United States, Franklin Delano Roosevelt, the order condemned 120,000 Japanese-Americans—two-thirds of them native born—to be evacuated from their homes and interned in camps for the duration of the war. Even some Japanese-Americans who had volunteered to fight for the United States were viewed as potential spies. They were stripped of their uniforms and sent to relocation camps because they were considered too dangerous to go free.

The Reality of the Camps

3 In discussing the camps, government administrators favored euphemisms. The camps were temporary "resettlement communities"—"havens of refuge"* designed to protect the Japanese-Americans from those who did not trust them (Weglyn, 89). Comforted by words like *community* and *refuge,* few Americans were confronted by the reality of camp life. If they had been, there probably would have been a ground swell of public outrage.

4 Erected at breakneck speed, the camps were crude and flimsy. The "family apartments," as they were called, were tarpaper shacks surrounded by barbed wire. They usually measured twenty by twenty-four feet and housed anywhere from five to eight people. Furniture, except for that brought by residents, was almost nonexistent. The apartments contained cots, blankets, mattresses, and a light fixture—nothing more.

5 Because the buildings were shoddy, the weather created hardships. In the summer, residents of the Manazar Camp in California sweltered. The sun beating down on tarpaper roofs turned rooms into ovens. Occasionally, the asphalt floors melted (Weglyn, 80). Those living in colder climates like the Gila Relocation Center in Arizona or the Granada Center in Colorado fared little

better. They were exposed to freezing temperatures that turned their "homes" into iceboxes.

6   There were other hardships as well. Because walls would have added to building expenses, there were few of them. Camp residents had almost no privacy. They ate and showered together. Even the toilet facilities were communal, and there was no way to be alone.

Economic Losses

7   Japanese-Americans also suffered terrible economic losses. Forced by the government to settle their affairs in a matter of days, they fell victim to unscrupulous* people who bought their property at the lowest possible prices. The property and possessions they couldn't sell were stored, but no one seemed concerned with protecting what the Japanese-Americans left behind. Much of it was stolen or vandalized (Conrat, 22). In the end, the Japanese who were interned lost property valued at more than $500 million; they lost as well their leading position in the truck-garden, floral, and fishing industries.

Psychological Loss

8   But the tragedy of relocation was not limited to physical hardship and economic loss. For Japanese-Americans, the worst hardship was psychological. They had lost face in their adopted country. They had suffered the embarrassment and humiliation of being herded together and forced to live in poverty. For a proud people, it was a spiritual death sentence (Girdner and Loftis, 238). Their family life was disrupted, and they felt themselves powerless. Although the young were able to bear up under such indignity, some of the old could not. One elderly man committed suicide and was found holding an Honorary Citizenship Certificate in his hand (Weglyn, 78).

No Evidence of Espionage

9   Although many people seemed convinced that only a network of Japanese-American spies could account for the success of Japan's attack on Pearl Harbor, there was no evidence of such spying. On the contrary, there was a great deal of evidence affirming the loyalty of America's Japanese residents.

10   Two months prior to the attack on Pearl Harbor, Curtis B. Munson, a special representative of the U.S. State Department, conducted a study of Japanese-Americans. His objective was to find the degree of their loyalty to America. The results of Munson's re-

search suggested that Japanese-Americans were deeply loyal to their adopted country. Their deepest affiliation* was to America rather than to the land of their birth. From Munson's perspective, they showed a "patriotic eagerness" to be Americans. There was, in fact, no Japanese-American threat: "There is no Japanese problem on the coast. There will be no armed uprising of Japanese" (Weglyn, 47).

11   Unfortunately, the Munson report became one of the war's best-kept secrets. As Eugene Rostow, one of America's foremost* authorities on constitutional law expressed it, "One hundred thousand persons were sent to concentration camps on a record which wouldn't support a conviction for stealing a dog" (Weglyn, 53).

How Could It Happen Here?

12   Given the lack of evidence against Japanese-Americans, given the suffering they endured, the question must be raised: How could it happen? How could a country famous for its democratic fervor* allow loyal citizens to be imprisoned?

13   *The Humiliation of Pearl Harbor.*   Japan's attack on Pearl Harbor was extraordinarily swift and successful. Later investigations laid most of the blame at the feet of the two men in charge of the area, Rear Admiral Husband E. Kimmel and General Walter C. Short.† They were found guilty of errors in judgment and dereliction* of duty. Initially, however, Americans found it hard to blame their own military commanders. It was much easier to believe rumors about a network of Japanese-American spies operating on the West Coast of the United States.

14   *A History of Prejudice.*   Then, too, as historians Donald Pike and Roger Olmstead point out, "a century of anti-Orientalism stood back of the relocation order" (Conrat, 16). Prejudice against Asians had first been ignited when the Chinese arrived during the gold rush of the 1850s. As the number of gold seekers increased, it was clear that there simply wasn't enough gold to go around. American miners retaliated by demanding restrictions on Chinese miners, who were seen as intruders on American soil. When the Japanese began arriving in the 1890s, they inherited the anger and distrust originally directed at the Chinese.

---

†The subject of who was to blame for Japan's success is still being debated today. Some historians believe Kimmel and Short were forced to take all the blame even though others were at fault as well.

15   Throughout the beginning of the twentieth century, anti-Japanese sentiment tended to swell and ebb with the economy. In times of economic expansion, evidence of prejudice diminished. But in times of recession, the Japanese were singled out for restriction and ostracism. Prevented by labor unions from working in the city, they moved to agricultural areas, where they became successful farmers. Their thrift and industry made them significant competitors, able to purchase several hundred thousand acres of land. But their success backfired when California passed the Alien Land Law preventing Japanese from purchasing land or leasing it for more than three years.

16   Japan's entry into World War I on the side of the United States temporarily curbed anti-Japanese sentiment in America. But it flared up again following the war, when Japan invaded Manchuria and China, withdrew from the League of Nations, and refused to limit naval arms. A threat to her neighbors, Japan was also perceived as a threat to America. As a result, the United States passed the Japanese Exclusion Act of 1924, which specifically limited Japanese immigration. By the time Pearl Harbor exploded, the country was psychologically prepared to mistrust Japanese-Americans.

17   *Fear of the Unknown.*   Following their internment, Japanese-Americans tended to take the blame for their misfortunes. They blamed themselves for being too clannish, for trying to preserve Japanese customs, for being reticent* and reclusive when they should have been forward and open. Tragically, they had a point. "Because little was known about the minority which had long kept itself withdrawn from the larger community in fear of rebuff,* it was possible to make the public believe anything" (Weglyn, 36). Fed on vicious stereotypes about Oriental cunning and largely ignorant of Japanese customs, far too many Americans found it easy to believe the myth of Japanese conspiracy and sabotage.

18   *Government Secrecy.*   The decision to relocate the Japanese-Americans was hardly a public one. It was made by a few government officials who justified their actions in various ways. When General John L. DeWitt was questioned about evidence of Japanese-American treachery, he offered this logic: "The very fact that no sabotage has taken place to date is a disturbing and confirming indication that such action will take place" (Weglyn, 39). According to this argument, Japanese-Americans had to be imprisoned because they hadn't *yet* done anything wrong. From De-

Witt's perspective, their failure to engage in any spying activities was proof that they would do so any day. Viewed this way, internment was a form of preventive medicine.

19   When members of humanitarian, religious, and civil liberties groups protested the internment, they were given another explanation. They were told that the camps were nothing more than "protective custody." The government allegedly needed to protect its Japanese-American citizens because Pearl Harbor had aroused so much anti-Japanese sentiment.

20   If friends and neighbors of Japanese-American citizens protested the relocation policy, yet another reason was proposed. Military officials insisted that Japanese-Americans were in possession of evidence that made internment a necessity. What this evidence was, however, had to be kept top secret—government security was involved.

The Final Verdict

21 Initially, the U.S. Supreme Court upheld the government's internment policy. In 1943, the Court claimed that "residents having ethnic affiliations with an invading enemy may be a greater source of danger than those of different ancestry" (Norton et al., 801). Similarly, in the 1944 Korematsu case, the Court approved the removal of Japanese-Americans from the West Coast. However, Justice Frank Murphy called the decision the "legalization of racism." In his anger, he echoed Circuit Court Judge William Denman, who had compared Japanese-American internment to the policies of the Nazis: "The identity of this doctrine with that of the Hitler generals . . . justifying the gas chambers of Dachau is unmistakable" (Norton et al., 802).

22   Thirty-eight years after these Supreme Court decisions, the government formed a special Commission on Wartime Relocation and Internment of Civilians. Not surprisingly, that commission did not share the earlier view of the Supreme Court justices. On the contrary, it recommended that victims of the internment policy be compensated for their suffering. In the view of the commission, they had been victimized by "race prejudice, war hysteria, and a failure of political leadership" (Norton et al., 802).

23   A year later, in 1983, the Korematsu case was overturned in a federal district court. The court ruled that Fred Korematsu had been the victim of "unsubstantiated* facts, distortions, and misrepresentations" (Norton et al., 802). In clearing Fred Korematsu, the court also implicitly cleared the other men, women, and children who had shared his fate.

24   Currently, reparations* are being paid to Japanese-Americans who suffered from the policy of internment. Although money can never make up for the humiliation and hardship they suffered, the reparations are a much needed form of public apology.

Laraine Flemming

Sources

Conrat, Maisie, and Richard Conrat. *Executive Order 9066.* California: Historical Society, 1972.

Girdner, Audrie, and Anne Loftis. *The Great Betrayal.* London: Collier-Macmillan, 1969.

Norton, Mary Beth, et al. *A People and a Nation.* Boston: Houghton Mifflin, 1986, pp. 801–802.

Weglyn, Michi. *Years of Infamy.* New York: William Morrow, 1976.

TEST YOUR UNDERSTANDING   Circle the letter of the correct answer.

1. Which of the following more accurately paraphrases the thesis statement?

   a. The attack on Pearl Harbor shocked the United States and ended any indecision about the country's entry into World War II.

   b. The attack on Pearl Harbor caused a storm of outrage against people of Japanese descent living in the United States.

2. In discussing the camps, government administrators

   a. were not ashamed to describe them.

   b. refused to discuss them.

   c. favored euphemisms.

3. For Japanese-Americans, the worst hardship was

   a. physical.

   b. economic.

   c. psychological.

4. According to the reading, there was a good deal of evidence indicating that

   a. America's Japanese residents supported Japan.

   b. America's Japanese residents were loyal to the United States.

   c. America's Japanese residents engaged in espionage.

5. Following their internment, Japanese-Americans

   a. tended to be resentful of their treatment.

b. tended to blame themselves.

c. refused to talk about their suffering.

6. Which sentence paraphrases the topic sentence in paragraph 5?

a. During the summer months, residents of the camps in California suffered terribly from the heat.

b. Because the buildings in the camps were cheaply built, the weather added to the suffering of the camp's residents.

7. In paragraph 7, which sentence is the topic sentence?

a. sentence 1

b. sentence 2

c. sentence 3

8. What's the implied main idea of paragraph 13?

a. Because Americans were reluctant to blame the bombing of Pearl Harbor on their own commanders, they found it easier to believe rumors about a Japanese-American spy ring.

b. Even today, no one really knows for sure how the Japanese were able to launch their surprise attack on Pearl Harbor.

9. What's the implied main idea of paragraph 21?

a. Most Americans believed that the U.S. Supreme Court's decision to uphold the policy of internment was unjust.

b. Although initially the U.S. Supreme Court upheld the policy of internment, there were those who strongly criticized the judges' decision.

10. Paragraphs 14 through 16 rely on which two patterns of organization?

a. classification

b. cause and effect

c. sequence of steps

d. sequence of dates and events

SHARPEN YOUR CRITICAL SKILLS Answer the following questions.

1. The title of the reading suggests that the author's purpose is

a. to inform readers about the internment of Japanese-Americans.

b. to persuade readers that Japanese-Americans were badly treated during their years of internment.

2. In paragraph 3, the author describes some of the euphemisms government administrators used to describe the camps. Why do you think the administrators favored euphemisms?

_____

_____

_____

3. The author says that words like *community* and *refuge* "comforted" Americans. Given what they represented, how could those words provide comfort?

_____

_____

_____

4. Label each of the following statements fact (*F*), opinion (*O*), or a blend of both (*B*).

a. *Executive Order 9066* "condemned 120,000 Japanese-Americans . . . to be evacuated from their homes." _____

b. If Americans had been "confronted by the reality of camp life, . . . there probably would have been a ground swell of public outrage." _____

c. "Although money can never make up for the humiliation and hardship [Japanese-Americans] suffered, the reparations are a much needed form of public apology." _____

5. Outline the argument offered by General John L. DeWitt.

Conclusion: _____

_____

Reason: _____

_____

6. Do you think General DeWitt had a convincing reason for his conclusion? _____ Explain your answer.

_____

_____

_____

7. In paragraph 16, the author says that anti-Japanese sentiment flared up again following World War I. What evidence does the author offer for this conclusion?

_____

_____

_____

8. In paragraph 17, the author describes the stereotypes that fed anti-Japanese sentiment. How do you think the author views those stereotypes?

_____

_____

_____

What word reveals her personal bias?

_____

9. How would you describe the author's tone?
   a. serious
   b. outraged
   c. emotionally neutral

10. In paragraph 24, what personal point of view does the author reveal?

_____

_____

_____

_____

THINKING FOR YOURSELF Do you think it's important for Americans to know about shameful incidents in their history like the internment of Japanese-Americans? Why or why not?

_____

_____

_____

MAKING CONNECTIONS BETWEEN READINGS Create a synthesis statement that combines the main ideas of readings 14 (Introducing Rosie the Riveter), 15 (World War II: The Fight Against Racism), and 16 (The Tragedy of Japanese Internment).

_____

_____

_____

■ **WRITING SUGGESTION** Write a paper in which you describe at least two different ways that schools can help discourage the kind of prejudice that contributed to tragedies like the Holocaust and the internment of Japanese-Americans. Be sure to give specific examples of how your suggestions could be put into practice.

GLOSSARY OF TERMS
for *Reading for Thinking*

Allusions   Allusions are the references to people, places, and events authors use to create both tone and meaning. In the following sentence, the author alludes to the character of Hamlet to make her point: "His Hamlet-like indecision was beginning to irritate her."

Annotating   When readers annotate a text, they jot notes in the margins. The notes can include lists of key points, questions, comments, ideas for papers, and potential test questions.

Appropriate inferences   Appropriate inferences are the conclusions a reader draws about ideas in a text that are implied but not directly stated. Although appropriate inferences are, to a degree, based on the reader's personal knowledge, they must be firmly grounded in, or based on, the author's actual words.

Bias   Bias in writing reveals the author's personal inclination to support or criticize a particular idea or event.

Cause and effect pattern   Writers using a cause and effect pattern of development describe how one event or series of events (the cause or causes) lead to another event or series of events (the effect or effects).

Classification pattern   Readings relying on the classification pattern describe how some larger group can be broken down into subgroups, each with its own set of specific characteristics.

Comparison and contrast pattern   Readings that rely on the comparison and contrast pattern of development highlight the similarities or differences between two topics. Sometimes authors who use this pattern do both; they point out the similarities and the differences between two topics.

Context   The context of a word is the sentence or passage in which the word appears.

Cornell system of notetaking   A system for taking notes that divides a page into three parts. One column is for notes, and the other is for recall cues. The space at the bottom of the page is for summarizing and synthesizing.

Facts   Statements of fact describe without evaluating or interpreting. They are not influenced by an author's personal experience or background and their accuracy can be checked or verified.

Generalizations   Generalizations sum up or draw conclusions about a number of different but in some way related people, places, or events.

Implied main idea   The implied main idea of a reading is suggested but not directly stated.

Inappropriate inferences Inappropriate inferences are conclusions based more on the reader's personal experience than on the author's words.

Inferences Inferences are the conclusions a reader draws about ideas that are implied in a text but not directly stated.

Informative writing Informative writing describes events or ideas without including personal judgments by the author.

Main idea The main idea is the central point or message of a passage or reading.

Opinions Statements of opinion reflect the author's point of view. Unlike statements of fact, they are shaped by an author's personal experience, training, and background, and they cannot be checked for accuracy.

Paraphrase A paraphrase translates an author's ideas into someone else's words without altering or changing the original meaning.

Persuasive writing Persuasive writing expresses an opinion that the writer wants readers to share or at least to consider.

Purpose An author's purpose is his or her intention in writing. Although there are many reasons why authors write—to criticize, describe, celebrate, amuse, and so on—most of them fall into two general categories: writing meant to inform and writing meant to persuade.

Recall cues Recall cues are words or phrases that readers use to help themselves remember a cluster of related ideas.

Sequence of dates and events In this pattern of organization, the author lists a series of dates and events according to the order in which they occurred.

Sequence of steps When a sequence of steps is used to organize a reading, the supporting details trace the individual steps or stages that make up some larger process or activity.

 Specialized vocabulary Specialized vocabulary consists of the words and terms essential to understanding a particular subject.

SQ3R SQ3R is a study technique for reading and understanding textbooks. The letters stand for survey, question, read, recite, review.

Summaries Summaries reduce a reading to about one-third or one-quarter of its original length. A good summary includes the main idea of a reading and only the most essential details.

Supporting details Supporting details are the examples, reasons, studies, and statistics that develop, explain, or prove an author's point.

Synthesizing In the process of synthesizing, readers combine ideas or information from separate sources.

Thesis statement Thesis statements sum up main ideas in longer readings. Like topic sentences, thesis statements give written form to an author's central point or main idea.

Tone Like tone of voice, tone in writing is the author's way of expressing his or her attitude toward a particular subject. Depending on audience and subject matter, a writer's tone can range widely. It can be angry and sarcastic in one context and humorous or lighthearted in another.

Topic The topic of a paragraph is the subject the author chooses to discuss or explore. It's the person, place, or event most frequently mentioned or referred to in a passage or selection.

Topic sentence The topic sentence expresses in writing the main idea of a paragraph.

INDEX

ACKNOWLEDGMENTS

Simon Adams and Lesley Riley, eds., reprinted by permission from *Reader's Digest Fact & Fallacies.* Copyright © 1988 The Reader's Digest Association, Inc.

Jane E. Brody. Copyright © 1993 by The New York Times Company. Reprinted by permission.

Carol Berkin, Christopher L. Miller, Robert W. Cherny, and James Gormly, from *Making America.* Copyright © 1995 by Houghton Mifflin Company. Used by permission.

Roy Berko, Andrew Wolvin, and Karlyn Wolvin, from *Communicating.* Copyright © 1992 by Houghton Mifflin Company. Used by permission.

Sean Dennis Cashman, from *African-Americans and the Quest for Civil Rights, 1900–1990.* Copyright © 1991. Reprinted by permission of New York University Press.

Dennis Coon. Reprinted by permission from pp. 139, 222, 256, 330, 419 of *Essentials of Psychology: Exploration and Application,* 6/e, by Dennis Coon. Copyright © 1994 by West Publishing Company. All rights reserved.

Dennis Coon. Reprinted by permission from pp. 143–144, 524 of *Introduction to Psychology,* 5/e by Dennis Coon. Copyright © 1994 by West Publishing Company. All rights reserved.

James West Davidson and Mark Hamilton Lytle, from *After the Fact* by James West Davidson and Mark Hamilton Lytle. Copyright © 1986, 1982 by Alfred A. Knopf Inc. Reprinted by permission of the publisher.

Andrew DuBrin, from *Leadership.* Copyright © 1995 by Houghton Mifflin Company. Used by permission.

Michael Elliot, from *Newsweek,* July 17, 1995, © 1995, Newsweek, Inc. All rights reserved. Reprinted by permission.

Barbara Engler, from *Personality Theories.* Copyright © 1995 by Houghton Mifflin Company. Used by permission.

William C. Frederick, James E. Post, Keith Davis, from *Business and Society.* Copyright © 1992. Reproduced with permission of the publisher, The McGraw-Hill Companies.

E. D. Hirsch, from "Restoring Cultural Literacy in the Early Grades," *Educational Leadership,* vol. 45, no. 4, December 1987/January 1988, p. 10. Reprinted by permission of the author.

Kenneth Janda, Jeffrey M. Berry, and Jerry Goldman, from *The Challenge of Democracy.* Copyright © 1995 by Houghton Mifflin Company. Used by permission.

Saul Kassin, from *Psychology.* Copyright © 1995 by Houghton Mifflin Company. Used by permission.

Donald G. Kaufman and Cecilia Franz, from *Biosphere 2000,* adaptation of pp. 155 and 306, and tables on pp. 179 and 233. Copyright © 1996. Used with permission of Kendall/Hunt Publishing Company.

William M. Kephart and Davor Jedlicka, from *The Family, Society, and* *the Individual* by William M. Kephart and Davor Jedlicka. Copyright © 1991. Reprinted by permission of HarperCollins College Publishers.

Ron Kline, from "A Scientist: I Am the Enemy." Originally published in *Newsweek,* December 18, 1991. Reprinted by permission of Ronald M. Kline, M.D., Director of Pediatric Bone Marrow Transplant Program, University of Louisville Health Sciences Center.

Charles J. Krebs, excerpts from *The Message of Ecology* by Charles J. Krebs. Copyright © 1988 by Charles J. Krebs. Reprinted by permission of HarperCollins Publishers, Inc.

David Knox, reprinted by permission from pp. 160–161, 230–234 of *Choices in Relationships: An Introduction to Marriage and the Family* by David Knox. Copyright © 1985 by West Publishing Company. All rights reserved.

Michael D. Lemonick, © 1995 Time Inc. Reprinted by permission.

Sy Montgomery, from *Nature's Everyday Mysteries.* Copyright © 1993. Reprinted by permission of the author.

Noble et al., from *Western Civilization.* Copyright © 1994 by Houghton Mifflin Company. Used by permission.

Mary Beth Norton, et al., from *A People and a Nation.* Copyright © 1986, 1993, 1994 by Houghton Mifflin Company. Used by permission.

Charles Panati, excerpt from *Panati's Browser's Book of Beginnings* by Charles Panati. Copyright © 1984 by Charles Carroll Hudson. Reprinted by permission of Houghton Mifflin Company. All rights reserved.

William Pride and O. C. Ferrell, from *Marketing.* Copyright © 1993 by Houghton Mifflin Company. Used by permission.

Pride, Hughes, and Kapoor, from *Business.* Copyright © 1993 by Houghton Mifflin Company. Used by permission.

Barry L. Reece and Rhonda Brandt, from *Effective Human Relations.* Copyright © 1993 by Houghton Mifflin Company. Used by permission.

Andrew L. Revkin, copyright © 1985 by The New York Times Company. Reprinted by permission.

Zick Rubin, Letita Anne Peplau, and Peter Salovey, from *Psychology.* Copyright © 1993, 1990 by Houghton Mifflin Company. Used by permission.

John W. Santrock, from *Life-Span Development,* 5th ed. Copyright © 1995 by William C. Brown Communications, Inc. Reprinted by permission of Times Mirror Higher Education Group, Inc., Dubuque, Iowa. All rights reserved.

Michael Schaller, Virginia Scharf, and Robert Schulzinger, from *Present Tense.* Copyright © 1992 by Houghton Mifflin Company. Used by permission.

Kevin Seifert and Robert Hoffnung, from *Child and Adolescent Development.* Copyright © 1994 by Houghton Mifflin Company. Used by permission.

Kevin Seifert, from *Educational Psychology.* Copyright © 1991 by Houghton Mifflin Company. Used by permission.

Dean Keith Simonton, from *Greatness.* Copyright © 1994. Reprinted by permission of The Guilford Press.

David Stout, copyright © 1995 by The New York Times Company. Reprinted by permission.

Deborah Tannen, text of pp. 81–85 from *You Just Don't Understand* by

Deborah Tannen, Ph.D. Copyright © 1990 by Deborah Tannen, Ph.D. By permission of William Morrow & Co., Inc.

Alex Thio, from *Sociology* by Alex Thio. Copyright © 1992. Reprinted by permission of HarperCollins College Publishers.

Ted Tollefson, from "Is a Hero Really Nothing but a Sandwich?," *Utne Reader,* May/June 1993. Reprinted by permission of the author. Ted Tollefson, a Unitarian Universalist Minister, is co-founder of Mytaos Institute in Minnesota.

David Van Fleet and Tim Peterson, from *Contemporary Management.* Copyright © 1994 by Houghton Mifflin Company. Used by permission.

Robert L. Williams and James D. Long, from *Manage Your Life.* Copyright © 1991 by Houghton Mifflin Company. Used by permission.